D0866931

Gary L. Hill
Dennis S. Sears
Lovisa Lyman
Editors

Teaching Legal Research and Providing Access to Electronic Resources

Teaching Legal Research and Providing Access to Electronic Resources has been co-published simultaneously as *Legal Reference Services Quarterly,* Volume 19, Numbers 3/4 2001.

Pre-publication
REVIEWS,
COMMENTARIES,
EVALUATIONS . . .

"**A** unique mixture of historical, theoretical, and practical approaches to legal research instruction in one convenient location. VISIONARY ARTICLES SUCH AS THESE ARE ESSENTIAL TO FORGING THE VIBRANT, RESPONSIVE APPROACHES TO LEGAL RESEARCH INSTRUCTION that will be expected by new generations of inquisitive legal researchers."

Gail A. Partin, MSLS, JD
Associate Law Librarian
Sheely-Lee Law Library
The Dickinson School of Law
of the Pennsylvania State University

More pre-publication
REVIEWS, COMMENTARIES, EVALUATIONS . . .

The Haworth Information Press
An Imprint of The Haworth Press, Inc.

Teaching Legal Research and Providing Access to Electronic Resources

Teaching Legal Research and Providing Access to Electronic Resources has been co-published simultaneously as *Legal Reference Services Quarterly,* Volume 19, Numbers 3/4 2001.

The *Legal Reference Services Quarterly* Monographic "Separates"

Below is a list of "separates," which in serials librarianship means a special issue simultaneously published as a special journal issue or double-issue *and* as a "separate" hardbound monograph. (This is a format which we also call a "DocuSerial.")

"Separates" are published because specialized libraries or professionals may wish to purchase a specific thematic issue by itself in a format which can be separately cataloged and shelved, as opposed to purchasing the journal on an on-going basis. Faculty members may also more easily consider a "separate" for classroom adoption.

"Separates" are carefully classified separately with the major book jobbers so that the journal tie-in can be noted on new book order slips to avoid duplicate purchasing.

You may wish to visit Haworth's website at . . .

http://www.HaworthPress.com

. . . to search our online catalog for complete tables of contents of these separates and related publications.

You may also call 1-800-HAWORTH (outside US/Canada: 607-722-5857), or Fax
1-800-895-0582 (outside US/Canada: 607-771-0012), or e-mail at:

getinfo@haworthpressinc.com

Teaching Legal Research and Providing Access to Electronic Resources, edited by Gary L. Hill, JD, MLL, BA, Dennis S. Sears, JD, MA, MLIS, MBA, and Lovisa Lyman, MA, MLIS, BA (Vol. 19, No. 3/4, 2001). *"A unique mixture of historical, theoretical, and practical approaches to legal research instruction in one convenient location." (Gail A. Partin, MSLS, JD, Associate Law Librarian, Sheely-Lee Library, The Dickinson School of Law of the Pennsylvania State University)*

Emerging Solutions in Reference Services: Implications for Libraries in the New Millennium, edited by John D. Edwards, JD, MALS (Vol. 19, No. 1/2, 2001). *"The authors provide practical advice on how to cope with everything from tight budgets to training needs to knife wielding patrons. I highly recommend that law school reference librarians purchase and read this outstanding work." (Bill Draper, BA, MS, JD, Reference Librarian and Lecturer, Biddle Law Library, University of Pennsylvania, Philadelphia)*

Law Librarians Abroad, edited by Janet Sinder, AB, JD, MS (Vol. 18, No. 3, 2000). *"A pure pleasure! Law librarians seeking information on how to find professional work abroad and useful advice on how to survive in a foreign land will be amply rewarded. Delightful." (Peter C. Schanck, JD, MLS, Law Library Director and Professor of Law, Marquette University Law Library, Milwaukee, Wisconsin)*

The Political Economy of Legal Information: The New Landscape, edited by Samuel E. Trosow (Vol. 17, No. 1/2, 1999). *Through this informative book you will gain new insights into such important issues as how industry consolidation will affect small legal publishers and the possibility that the law that governs public access to judicial opinions mandates citation reform.*

Symposium of Law Publishers, edited by Thomas A. Woxland, MLS, JD (Vol. 11, No. 3/4, 1991). *"Librarians involved in collection development would find the symposium useful as it provides an insider's view of the legal publishing industry." (Canadian Law Libraries)*

The Legal Bibliography: Tradition, Transitions, and Trends, edited by Scott B. Pagel, JD, MLS (Vol. 9, No. 1/2, 1989). *"An excellent introduction to major bibliographic titles and future concerns for the novice law librarian or student of legal librarianship. . . . A useful addition to the reference shelf of the private law or acquisitions librarian." (Legal Information Alert)*

Practical Approaches to Legal Research, edited by Kent C. Olson, JD, MLS, and Robert C. Berring, JD, MLS (Supp. #01, 1988). *"A long overdue book–a legal research manual for librarians. . . . A readable and entertaining text on locating and using law books. . . . Almost everything a law librarian needs to know about legal research is covered in this book." (Legal Information Alert)*

Teaching Legal Research and Providing Access to Electronic Resources

Gary L. Hill
Dennis S. Sears
Lovisa Lyman
Editors

Teaching Legal Research and Providing Access to Electronic Resources has been co-published simultaneously as *Legal Reference Services Quarterly,* Volume 19, Numbers 3/4 2001.

The Haworth Information Press
An Imprint of
The Haworth Press, Inc.
New York • London • Oxford

Published by

The Haworth Information Press®, 10 Alice Street, Binghamton, NY 13904-1580

The Haworth Information Press®, is an imprint of The Haworth Press, Inc., 10 Alice Street, Binghamton, NY 13904-1580 USA.

Teaching Legal Research and Providing Access to Electronic Resources has been co-published simultaneously as *Legal Reference Services Quarterly*™, Volume 19, Numbers 3/4 2001.

The development, preparation, and publication of this work has been undertaken with great care. However, the publisher, employees, editors, and agents of The Haworth Press and all imprints of The Haworth Press, Inc., including The Haworth Medical Press® and Pharmaceutical Products Press®, are not responsible for any errors contained herein or for consequences that may ensue from use of materials or information contained in this work. Opinions expressed by the author(s) are not necessarily those of The Haworth Press, Inc.

Cover design by Thomas J. Mayshock Jr.

Library of Congress Cataloging-in-Publication Data

Teaching legal research and providing access to electronic resources / Gary L. Hill, Dennis S. Sears, Lovisa Lyman, editors.
 p. cm.
 "Co-published simultaneously as Legal reference services quarterly, v. 19, no. 3/4 2001.
 Includes bibliographical references and index.
 ISBN 0-7890-1369-X (alk. paper)–ISBN 0-7890-1370-3 (alk. paper)
 1. Legal research–Study and teaching–United States. 2. Information storage and retrieval systems–Law–Study and teaching–United States. I. Hill, Gary L. II. Sears, Dennis S. III. Lyman, Lovisa. IV. Legal reference services quarterly.
 KF240 .T4 2001
 340'.07'2073–dc21   2001039153

Indexing, Abstracting & Website/Internet Coverage

This section provides you with a list of major indexing & abstracting services. That is to say, each service began covering this periodical during the year noted in the right column. Most Websites which are listed below have indicated that they will either post, disseminate, compile, archive, cite or alert their own Website users with research-based content from this work. (This list is as current as the copyright date of this publication.)

(continued)

(continued)

Special Bibliographic Notes related to special journal issues
(separates) and indexing/abstracting:

- indexing/abstracting services in this list will also cover material in any "separate" that is co-published simultaneously with Haworth's special thematic journal issue or DocuSerial. Indexing/abstracting usually covers material at the article/chapter level.
- monographic co-editions are intended for either non-subscribers or libraries which intend to purchase a second copy for their circulating collections.
- monographic co-editions are reported to all jobbers/wholesalers/approval plans. The source journal is listed as the "series" to assist the prevention of duplicate purchasing in the same manner utilized for books-in-series.
- to facilitate user/access services all indexing/abstracting services are encouraged to utilize the co-indexing entry note indicated at the bottom of the first page of each article/chapter/contribution.
- this is intended to assist a library user of any reference tool (whether print, electronic, online, or CD-ROM) to locate the monographic version if the library has purchased this version but not a subscription to the source journal.
- individual articles/chapters in any Haworth publication are also available through the Haworth Document Delivery Service (HDDS).

Teaching Legal Research and Providing Access to Electronic Resources

CONTENTS

ABOUT THE EDITORS

Gary L. Hill, JD, MLL, BA, is Deputy Law Librarian at Brigham Young University Howard W. Hunter Law Library at J. Reuben Clark Law School. He received his BA from BYU, his MLL from the University of Denver and his JD from Samford University. In addition to his administrative duties, he teaches courses in beginning and advanced legal research and works at the reference desk. Prior to coming to BYU in 1983, Mr. Hill practiced law and worked as a lawyer-librarian at the Tarlton Law Library at the University of Texas at Austin. Mr. Hill has authored a number of articles as well as the monograph *Survey on Legal Research Instruction* (Rothman, 1998) for the AALL Publication Series.

Dennis S. Sears, JD, MA, MLIS, MBA, is a Senior Law Librarian currently responsible for reference and legal research at Howard W. Hunter Law Library at Brigham Young University's J. Reuben Clark Law School. He teaches legal research to first-year law students as part of the Introduction to Advocacy course and advanced legal research seminars on non-legal databases, federal taxation, and foreign and international law. He has served in a number of professional organizations, most recently as President of WesPac and Co-Chair of the Education Committee for the FCIL SIS of AALL. He has published in *Legal Reference Services Quarterly, Law Library Journal,* and *Spectrum*. After graduation with his JD/MBA in 1985 from Brigham Young University, he clerked in the Fourth Judicial District Court for the Honorable Boyd L. Park. After his clerkship, he worked for the Salt Lake Tax Administration before returning to academia. He received his MLIS in 1993.

Lovisa Lyman, MA, MLIS, BA, from BYU, is Collection Development Librarian at Brigham Young University Hunter Law Library, where she has been a professional faculty member since 1981. In addition to her collection development duties, she works at the reference desk and teaches legal writing to LLM foreign law students. From 1997 to 1999 she participated in proposing, planning, and teaching lawyering skills (legal research and writing) courses at Brigham Young University J. Reuben Clark Law School. She edited two titles in the AALL Publication Series (*Law Librarianship: A Handbook* (Rothman, 1983) and *Law Librarianship: A Handbook for the Electronic Age* (Rothman, 1995)) and has published articles in *Law Library Journal* and *Spectrum*. From 1995 to 1998, she served on the AALL Committee on Relations with Information Vendors (CRIV) and as CRIV Co-Chair from 1997 to 1998.

Introduction:
Reference Services–
Teaching Legal Research
and Providing Access
to Electronic Resources

The old saw, "Those who can, do; and those who can't, teach" is redis-covered every semester by some disgruntled law student somewhere. Though it may apply to the occasional law professor, it does not apply to law librari-ans who teach legal research because teacher/librarians actively research and teach at the same time. They are the ones called upon to find the elusive case neither the partner nor his entourage of clerks can locate as well as the correct citation for a professor's law review article on women's rights in Argentina. Their students range from grandparents being instructed in the stacks about how to obtain visitation rights to opulent boardrooms full of attorneys learn-ing about the latest electronic resources. But though they "do" and "teach" to the full satisfaction of most of their students/patrons, they are typically eager to do even better. The intent of this volume is to address that need.

The first six articles deal with teaching legal research both generally and specifically. Dennis Sears' launching article offers exhaustive research on the evolution of legal research instruction–two competing methodologies in par-ticular. To this he adds his own research on a successful program that blends the best of both approaches. The next three articles treat teaching in academ-ic, government, and law firm settings. Herbert Cihak explains how research is taught in his library and how the staff stretches to handle a wide variety of teaching functions, including directing the legal writing program. Judy

[Haworth co-indexing entry note]: "Introduction: Reference Services–Teaching Legal Research and Providing Access to Electronic Resources." Hill, Gary L., Dennis S. Sears, and Lovisa Lyman. Co-published simultaneously in *Legal Reference Services Quarterly* (The Haworth Information Press, an imprint of The Haworth Press, Inc.) Vol. 19, No. 3/4, 2001, pp. 1-3; and: *Teaching Legal Research and Providing Access to Electronic Resources* (ed: Gary L. Hill, Dennis S. Sears, and Lovisa Lyman) The Haworth Information Press, an imprint of The Haworth Press, Inc., 2001, pp. 1-3. Single or multiple copies of this article are available for a fee from The Haworth Document Delivery Service [1-800-342-9678, 9:00 a.m. - 5:00 p.m. (EST). E-mail address: getinfo@haworthpressinc.com].

Meadows, Lisa Mecklenberg, and Stephen Jordan illustrate the value of point-of-need training for judges, the local bar, and the multitude of *pro se* patrons who frequent government law libraries. In addition, they show how they extend their services to rural areas of the state via electronic media, including videotape and distance learning. Amy Eaton shares her expertise on formal and informal instruction in a large firm. Her creative approaches include paper and electronic publications designed to draw in the attorney who has no time for formal presentations.

Jean Davis, Victoria Szymczak, Katherine Topulos, and Stefanie Weigmann cover the territory of foreign, comparative, and international legal research instruction. Beginning with the mandate that this research is best taught by librarians, they move to a discussion of the various teaching models, resources helpful to starting a program, and enlivening the classroom with a variety of activities.

This article leads smoothly into Kristin Gerdy's scholarly discussion of teaching styles and how recognizing learning preferences among adult students can result in long-lasting learning.

The next eight articles cover electronic tools that can be employed in both teaching research and performing research.

Suzanne Miner begins the set with hints on dealing with the computer-phobic patron and brief clues on how to moderate the over-exuberant computer user. Her article harks back to Gerdy's article on learning styles since learning preferences apply to computer instruction as well.

Susan Lewis-Somers and Kristin Gerdy, doing double duty, discuss lower-cost and free electronic resources in informative detail. They conclude that the big dealers in the media market are not the only recourse for either librarians or patrons.

Marci Hoffman and Janice Hyde present two home-grown legal research databases–one, the largest collection of international human rights documents on the web and the other a mammoth Law Library of Congress effort to provide electronic access to legal information from around the world. The human rights database ably responds to a burgeoning need for a broadly-accessible collection of core human rights materials. Hyde, a librarian at the Law Library of Congress, describes both the vision and the reality of the GLIN database, which offers ever-broadening access to foreign legal jurisdictions.

Once databases are established, the next questions for most librarians are how the databases can be used by patrons and how electronic information can be delivered. Anne Klinefelter addresses the first question in her discussion of copyright and electronic resources. She deals particularly with proposed uniform law that could further restrict current usage rights. James Duggan gives insight into present and future methods for document delivery paying particular attention to how these changes will affect patron/librarian interaction.

This section ends with a think piece by David Armond. Armond reviews the historic mission of access services and then provides a convincing defense for expanding access services' role to provide back up for the reference department in managing patron access to digital collections.

The articles in this collection cover a spectrum of law library teaching, state-of-the-art electronic access, and probable directions law library teaching and research will take in the near future. We thank the authors who have been generous in sharing their expertise. Each has unique insight and experience that will be of value to the reader. We also thank our colleague David Armond who, in addition to writing an article, has worked tirelessly to mesh the various idiosyncracies of all the contributors' computers to provide excellent copy for the publisher.

Gary L. Hill
Dennis S. Sears
Lovisa Lyman

The Teaching
of First-Year Legal Research Revisited:
A Review and Synthesis of Methodologies

Dennis S. Sears

SUMMARY. The evolution of reference and legal research instruction at BYU Hunter Law Library clearly illustrates the continuum along which many law school libraries have moved in refining and expanding reference services. The end result–better prepared law student researchers–has been pursued and obtained through a hybrid of the bibliographic approach and the newer emphasis on practical advocacy. An extensive review of the literature supports BYU's approach. *[Article copies available for a fee from The Haworth Document Delivery Service: 1-800-342-9678. E-mail address: <getinfo@haworthpressinc.com> Website: <http://www.HaworthPress.com> © 2001 by The Haworth Press, Inc. All rights reserved.]*

Dennis S. Sears is a Senior Law Librarian currently responsible for reference and legal research at Howard W. Hunter Law Library at Brigham Young University's J. Reuben Clark Law School. He teaches legal research to first-year law students as part of the Introduction to Advocacy course and advanced legal research seminars on non-legal databases, federal taxation, and foreign and international law. He has served in a number of professional organizations, most recently as President of WestPac and Co-Chair of the Education Committee for the FCIL SIS of AALL. He has published in *Legal Reference Services Quarterly, Law Library Journal,* and *Spectrum.* After graduation with his JD/MBA in 1985 from Brigham Young University, he clerked in the Fourth Judicial District Court for the Honorable Boyd L. Park. After his clerkship, he worked for the Salt Lake Tax Administration before returning to academia. He received his MLIS in 1993.

[Haworth co-indexing entry note]: "The Teaching of First-Year Legal Research Revisited: A Review and Synthesis of Methodologies." Sears, Dennis S. Co-published simultaneously in *Legal Reference Services Quarterly* (The Haworth Information Press, an imprint of The Haworth Press, Inc.) Vol. 19, No. 3/4, 2001, pp. 5-26; and: *Teaching Legal Research and Providing Access to Electronic Resources* (ed: Gary L. Hill, Dennis S. Sears, and Lovisa Lyman) The Haworth Information Press, an imprint of The Haworth Press, Inc., 2001, pp. 5-26. Single or multiple copies of this article are available for a fee from The Haworth Document Delivery Service [1-800-342-9678, 9:00 a.m. - 5:00 p.m. (EST). E-mail address: getinfo@haworthpressinc.com].

Reference and legal research instruction in the academic setting lie along a continuum of service that provides assistance to patrons, usually law students, in mastering legal materials to a needed level. At Howard W. Hunter Law Library, serving Brigham Young University's J. Reuben Clark Law School, reference and legal research instruction have been viewed as part and parcel of the same function, the main differences being the forum, the formality of the training, and the depth of the training involved. In this context, reference services have evolved substantially over the past decade. The impetus for this evolution has been a parallel evolution in the first-year legal research program during the same period of time.

A SELF-PACED FIRST-YEAR LEGAL RESEARCH PROGRAM

Legal Research

In the late 70s, a first-year legal research program was developed at BYU as a self-paced program through which students worked on their own. *The Legal Research Manual*[1] focused on the very basics of legal research. It was divided into chapters, each dedicated to a specific type of legal material, i.e., cases, statutes, regulations, citators, law reviews, etc. Each chapter provided a very brief description of specific legal materials, an example of how to use the materials, and an exercise at the conclusion of the chapter. After the chapter was completed students were required to take a quiz[2] on the materials presented in the chapter.

Each chapter, although self-contained, was organized to build on the student's experience with legal materials presented previously in the chapter. In addition, the examples, exercises, and quizzes paralleled each other but provided less information at each step in the process so that students proceeding through the learning process developed an ability to use the materials more and more independently of the explanations in the *Manual*.

Examples were placed throughout the chapter to provide immediate hands-on experience with and reinforcement of information preceding the example. The examples began with a legal research question. The students were then provided a step-by-step explanation of how to find the answer.

At the end of each chapter, an exercise consisting of the same number of questions as examples in the chapter was included. The questions in these exercises had no accompanying explanation. However, the exercises were open-book, so students could review the research process if necessary. Correct answers were provided at the end of the *Manual* so that students could check the accuracy of their own answers. The purpose of these exercises was to further reinforce the newly acquired research skills presented in the chapter.

Finally, upon the completion of each chapter, a quiz tested the skills of the students to use the materials presented. Even so, the quizzes were "open book" so that students could review the explanations and examples given in the *Manual* if needed. The whole purpose of this process was to develop and continually reinforce the basic legal research skills of students.

Reference

In the early days of the *Manual,* the law library had only one reference librarian, although librarians from the administrative and technical service areas assisted with coverage of the reference desk. The role of the reference librarian during this time was limited to overseeing the updating of the *Manual* each summer, including its examples, exercises, and quizzes. Based on staffing constraints, the role of those at the reference desk was to provide basic assistance to law students with regards to the materials with which any particular student was working at the time. The "teaching" of first-year legal research was limited to fielding basic legal research questions at the reference desk while students worked through the *Legal Research Manual* on their own.

INSTITUTING FORMAL TEACHING

The First-Year Legal Research Program

Reorganization of the library staff and funding to hire an additional reference person opened the way for formal teaching of legal research to first-year students. Among the factors contributing to this decision was the amount of one-on-one time spent with many first-year students explaining legal materials and clarifying the research principles, often over and over again. This time increased substantially with the tendency of some students to try to "short-circuit" the prescribed learning process when the pressures of substantive law courses competed for their time and their efforts.

Naturally, the role of the reference staff had to move a good way along the reference/legal research continuum as its focus shifted from reference desk assistance to formal classroom instruction. Reacting to requests for assistance by law students was replaced, in part, by a proactive role in the classroom. Even with this change, *The Legal Research Manual* remained the text for the course. Classes were topically oriented, focusing on the characteristics and use of legal materials.

Revamping the Legal Writing Program

While the library was using the *Manual* to teach legal research, the basics of legal writing, such as identifying issues, legal reasoning, etc., were taught in a class comprised of the entire first-year class. The actual reading and grading of a non-research memorandum and a research memorandum were assigned to first-year small section substantive law faculty. In fact, these faculty members drafted the fact situations for the memoranda and provided the cases for the non-research memoranda, usually in the area of first-year substantive law that they taught.

In 1997, the law school decided to address a need increasingly voiced by practicing attorneys to prepare law graduates with better developed practical skills. The legal research program had long since provided law students with practical legal research skills, but the legal writing program had been limited to the drafting of a non-research memorandum, a research memorandum, and a moot court brief, usually on unrelated topics. The result was a "lawyering skills" program later renamed Introduction to Advocacy.

In the lawyering skills program, classes were team-taught by a part-time legal writing faculty and the reference staff. The legal research program, as it had developed over the years, was wholly integrated into the lawyering skills program. In order to reinforce the seamless nature of the course, legal writing and legal research were scheduled and taught during the same time in the same classroom. The only apparent difference to the students was who walked into the class to teach on a given day.

The basis of the lawyering skills program was a legal problem for each class that was written so that law students could be taken through the entire legal process–from intake memorandum to appellate brief–during the course of the year.

Despite these substantial innovations in the legal writing portion of the lawyering skills program, those teaching legal research continued to teach in much the same way they had before. The decision to continue as they had in the past was based on the perception that the essentials of legal research must be taught and mastered, to some degree, before law students could be expected to use legal materials creatively. The reference staff was, however, involved in the grading of the legal research portion of each of the major writing assignments, giving them an opportunity to evaluate how well research skills had been translated into practice. In class, they addressed specific legal research issues related to the problems only if they were raised by law students or requested by the legal writing instructors.

One significant innovation on the part of the reference staff with regards to teaching was increased in-library familiarization with legal materials. This change was the product of student feedback on teacher evaluations where a recurrent complaint was the lack of in-library experience. In fact, this comment occurred in an average of 31.7% of course evaluations over the past few years. Frustrated teachers addressed the complaints as well as they could short of taking thirty or more students to the library at once. They used overheads exemplifying particular research characteristics of a title, i.e., tables of cases, tables of statutes, cross references, etc. They rolled book trucks loaded with volumes into the classroom and passed the samples among the students. Unfortunately, given the size of each class, only a few students were able to benefit from actually having the volume in their hands. Usually the lecture moved on to another title while the volume from the previous discussion was still circulating. At that point, students had the option of spending a few minutes to familiarize themselves with that title and missing the ongoing lecture or following the lecture and simply passing the volume to the next student.

Technology has provided a partial solution. PowerPoint presentations are now utilized to scan and label sample pages. Pictures of many of the titles discussed can likewise be imported into presentations. This innovation has eliminated the need for the cart of library books that never made the rounds of the class.

The second solution has been more in-library exposure to materials, which has evolved from general tours, to topic-specific tours, to short lectures, to short in-library "exercises" in conjunction with the classroom lectures. It should be noted that these in-library exercises did not take the place of the legal research exercises or the quizzes that were associated with the *Legal Research Manual*. These exercises were developed simply to orient the law students to the location of the materials and to give them some basic exposure to the characteristics of the materials they had been introduced to in class. The exercises are passed out to preassigned groups of two or three so that students will have the benefit of working together. Their joint efforts serve to reinforce what they have learned in class and correct any misconceptions they may have formed. The teacher's role is to act as a resource, moving from group to group, answering questions and, when necessary, reviewing and clarifying concepts covered in class.

This approach, first instituted in fall of 1999, has contributed greatly to the ability of students to better grasp the concepts taught to them in class. One indication of this trend is the number of first-time failures on legal research quizzes. In the Fall of 1998, 8.7% of first-year law students failed a quiz on their first try. This percentage dropped to 6.0% in the Fall of 1999.

Although evidence indicates that BYU students respond positively to the increased focus on practical advocacy skills, a careful review of the literature with regards to teaching legal research also appears to bear out the primarily bibliographical direction the Howard W. Hunter Law Library has taken in teaching legal research.

TEACHING METHODOLOGIES FOR LEGAL RESEARCH:
A REVIEW OF THE LITERATURE

A large number of published articles discuss the various methodologies for teaching legal research. Conclusions about these methodologies range from the "view . . . that the various 'skills' . . . are best learned in the practice of law,"[3] to the attitude "that . . . special attention should not be given to the particular skills [of legal writing and research] in special classes–that exercises in legal writing and research should be worked into the ordinary substantive law courses because it is impossible to separate fullness of understanding from the skills of discovery and expression,"[4] to the conviction that "[a] purely mechanical exercise . . . [is] the best introduction to the books, . . . acting as a guide to the discovery of [the material's] nature."[5]

Out of this debate, two major positions have arisen: those who advocate the bibliographic approach[6] to teaching legal research– "acquainting new law students with . . . the use of law books"[7] by using "library exercise problems,"[8] and those who are process oriented[9] or for whom problem-solving[10] is preeminent. The goal of both is to create a learning experience that engenders a genuine appreciation of the professional significance of legal research and develops the necessary skills to survive in practice.[11]

The criticisms leveled at the bibliographic approach to teaching legal research have focused on three major issues: unnecessary bibliographic detail, lack of educational validity, and the concern that students will mistakenly develop the attitude that all legal problems have "one right answer."

Bibliographic Detail

Many of those involved with teaching legal research, especially in the problem-solving[12] camp, have criticized the bibliographic method for its "verbal descriptions of the books"[13]– "lectur[es] . . . on the bibliographical minutiae of a series of apparently unrelated books"[14]–and "the inclusion of a plethora of mechanical details in the suggested processes for use of the books described,"[15] such as "a course emphasizing legal history and the development of law books,"[16] "an abstract library reference course, composed of idle and singular questions, that do not build toward a realistic end"[17] but instead "introduce research tools one by one without linking them to each other"[18]–in sum, "boring commentaries on books."[19] These critics conclude that "[t]his descriptive, or bibliographic, approach virtually ignores the legal research process itself–that is, the process through which researchers decide how and when to draw on law books in developing comprehensive strategies for researching legal problems."[20]

In emphasizing sources instead of research strategies, the teacher tends to lose sight of the fact that those being taught are law students, not library science students.[21] This criticism has merit because in teaching legal research as in any other type of teaching, audience is the first consideration. Interestingly, some of those who advocate the bibliographic approach recognize the limited value of extensive bibliographic detail,[22] "emphasi[zing] . . . the mysteries and intricacies of legal bibliography."[23] They have discarded "[t]he old method of the instructor wheeling in the truck load of books and describing the content of volume by volume–the so called 'laundry list' approach– . . . [as] 'foolish and misplaced.'"[24] They have come to stress the need for "basic sessions"[25] focusing on "the indexing and organizational systems used by legal research tools."[26]

True, "[t]he use of research publications requires knowledge of various use methods and update techniques."[27] In fact, summer clerks and first-year associates have been criticized if they "are not familiar with the contents or mechanics of basic legal research tools [and] they cannot identify the circumstances or the sequence in which they should consult various sources."[28] On the other hand, "[t]he researcher must be free to think about the facts and law of his problem as he pursues his research–free from the disquiet and the distractions of thinking about what tools to use or how to use them."[29]

Although less descriptive in their characterizations, those advocating the "bibliographic method" have criticized the process orientation referring to "canned situations,"[30] "learning research 'on the fly,'"[31] the "learn-by-doing method,"[32] "simulations,"[33] the "sink or swim" method,[34] and "a trial-by-ordeal"[35] which result in

> tunnel vision [wherein students] learn only the narrowed, and often most ineffective, paths to solving their research questions because they have no idea what the larger picture of legal research looks like.
> As a result, students learn to do only "A" to "B" research in which they solve a research problem using tool "A" to find answer "B." Because they do not learn how the tools work together or why certain types of information are found in certain types of research tools students come to assume that tool "A" can only be used in one particular way, for one particular purpose, to reach part "B."[36]

Bibliographic approach advocates view learning legal research absent a regime that compels students to "examine [the] . . . basic research tools and learn how to use them"[37] largely serendipitous. Absent a regime, a student will gravitate to "one research tool . . . which appears to give good results. Satisfied, he hitches his wagon to this method and never fully explores other research systems."[38]

Meanwhile, many of those in the problem-solving camp have not entirely abandoned the idea of bibliographic detail[39] but tend to concede the necessity of some bibliographic instruction,[40] either express[41] or implied,[42] in describing their teaching experience.[43] They often provide at least a basic orientation to legal materials[44] before moving to "hands-on" instruction.[45] This orientation will be general and brief[46] and may take the form of "an introductory contextual and functional bibliographic lecture. . . ."[47] or a "[g]uided experience for the student . . . [that] will teach the types of literature, its contents, a method of research. . . ."[48] The subsequent "'hands-on' experience"[49] is designed to expose students "to the variety of sources of legal authority."[50] Those advocating the process approach are evidently as cognizant as those advocating the bibliographic approach that simply allowing a student to submit an answer to a given problem, without somehow insuring an exposure to as many appropriate titles as possible, will cause the student to return to the same title repeatedly because of familiarity with the title and previously experienced success.

Another way to provide students with the needed orientation[51] may be required reading assignments in a textbook covering "detailed bibliographic information."[52] This approach simply shifts the forum in which bibliographic detail is addressed from the classroom to the textbook and allows the lecturer to "elucidate and emphasize information in the text, highlight the differences among various legal resources, and explain when it would be appropriate to use each source and what one would expect to find when it is used."[53]

Despite their grudging admission of some sort of bibliographic introduction, proponents of the process approach seem to share an underlying conviction that "the mental processes necessary for the understanding of legal bibliography are uncomplicated and untaxing."[54] Their objective is to "lend reality to the tedious study of books, authorities and research authorities, allowing the student to relate these materials to the formulation of a complete legal action."[55]

In support of those advocating the bibliographic approach as well as those advocating the process approach who concede the necessity of some bibliographic instruction, is the conclusion of a foremost educator: "The fundamental on which all higher levels of cognition rest . . . is the factual basis of a given subject. No higher cognitive task, such as analysis or synthesis of the subject matter, can take place without the acquisition of knowledge, the basic facts, of the first level."[56]

> Another authority applies this principle to legal research:
> [B]efore this level can be reached [the ability to formulate legal research strategies], the basic "building block" skills must be taught and learned well. . . .
> [N]o substantial legal research endeavor, no strategy, no creative approach, may seriously be considered without a firm knowledge of the first level of cognition in the subject area, that is, the learning of the

sources of primary and secondary law, how the laws are categorized and classified, and what finding aids are available.

The first objective of a legal research course, then, is that students become knowledgeable, skilled, and facile in the use of the "nuts and bolts" of legal research.[57]

Critical of putting the proverbial horse before the cart, i.e., legal research strategy before legal research skill, she further argues:

> Developing a strategy and approach to legal research calls for a different level of instruction, building as it does on basic research skills. . . . [I]f such a theme [legal research strategy] is introduced at the same time that the student is still learning the basics, its usefulness and applicability may be questionable.[58]

Educational Value

The second criticism of the bibliographic approach is that it is "of limited educational value."[59] Although addressed to some extent in the preceding discussion of bibliographic detail, the focus of this criticism is on legal research exercises themselves. The exercises or problems usually associated with these courses have been often derogatorily characterized as "canned exercises,"[60] "closed universe exercises,"[61] "expeditions,"[62] "'finger' exercises,"[63] "law-related scavenger hunt[s],"[64] "make-work,"[65] "mechanical operations,"[66] "'search and destroy' assignments,"[67] and "treasure hunts."[68] Milder characterizations of the exercises such as "abstract research questions,"[69] "drill exercises,"[70] "disassociated questions,"[71] "[d]iscrete and tedious follow-up research exercises,"[72] "'fill-in-the-blank' exercises,"[73] "individual assignments,"[74] "library exercises,"[75] "memorization and drill,"[76] "pattern-drill exercise[s],"[77] "practical exercises,"[78] "problem program,"[79] "short answer assignments,"[80] "short problems,"[81] "tiresome, academic exercises,"[82] "written exercises,"[83] "worksheet exercises"[84] have criticized the "artificiality"[85] of this approach where "each source is presented in a vacuum [and] relationships between different types of material are never made clear to students."[86] They also criticize focusing on "the minute intricacies of the assignments"[87] and "a series of unrelated drill exercises,"[88] the result of which is "a somewhat kaleidoscopic knowledge of basic research materials. . . . "[89] Even those who concede the necessity of "research exercises"[90] claim "[t]hese exercises get too bad of a reputation in the first-year course. . . . "[91]

Additional concerns raised by this approach include that the "treasure hunt" method is "time-consuming;"[92] "frustrating;"[93] and "create[s] resentment and promote[s] violations of the honor code."[94]

Advocates of the problem-solving method claim superiority for this method because it requires students to explain their answers rather than "blindly copy out an answer," although some admit that "learning how to use most research tools is a fairly mechanical process"[95] of simply "getting to grips with the law."[96]

On the other hand, while recognizing the drudgery of the bibliographic method, authorities also recognize the value of the method: "In the past, legal research technique has been taught by short 'fill-in-the-blank' exercises. These exercises were preceded by illustrated lectures and expository reading assignments. Although these methods are *effective,* they are dull."[97] This criticism is countered, in part, by the observation and suggestion that "legal bibliography could be taught the first semester when the student is relatively less sophisticated and more apt to accept the *necessary* drudgery." Drudgery or not, "[m]any students find the 'treasure hunt' aspects of a well-designed legal writing problem to be more interesting and creative than simply studying cases."[98]

One-Right-Answer

This criticism, "one-answer, right-answer, checklist solutions to most legal research problems,"[99] focuses on the concern that the "treasure hunt" method engenders an "erroneous" belief "that a legal question has only one right answer."[100] Say critics, "Instead of training law students to explore the research materials for the various kinds of information contained in them, law schools teach them to view legal research as a hunt for identifiable prey,"[101] all calculated to find "the 'answer.'"[102]

Yet, even those who profess allegiance to the "process" of legal research because a one-right-answer approach may be unrealistic and somewhat misleading to students recognize that "research problem[s] . . . should not be tricky or complicated but straightforward and reasonably solvable."[103]

Further, in actual practice, new attorneys may be trained with one-right-answer questions. One law firm librarian who puts a practical spin on this issue argues that "[l]aw librarians see the *process* of research as the point of the exercise; the students, on the other hand, are interested almost exclusively in the *results* of the process–short-range 'answers,' or at least the basic legal propositions that they can use to manufacture into an answer to a discrete legal question."[104] This focus on a discrete answer not only reflects the mentality of students and new attorneys but, to at least some extent, reflects reality. The above firm librarian's in-house training program includes "a short list of research exercises, drawn from the *actual issues* in [a] transaction." These exercises are reviewed at the end of a week of training by the firm's chief librarian who indicates "not only the *ultimate* answers, but the various means of reaching those answers, explaining which were the most efficient methods."[105]

CONCLUSION

The first criticism leveled at the bibliographic approach, needless bibliographic instruction, has some validity. Much bibliographic detail is of value only to librarians. But, by its nature, the law and its practice is research-based, more so than other professions. Most legal titles have a number of research aids–tables of cases, tables of statutes, etc. This characteristic is not typical of the publications of other disciplines. Instruction focused on these access points is necessary if the full research potential of any given title is to be recognized by law students.

The second criticism, questionable educational value, also has some validity. Conducted in a vacuum without relevance to any anticipated practical application, either in law school or in legal practice, even excellent instruction has little educational value. Classroom instruction should be followed by hands-on assignments and hands-on assignments should become the foundation for more extensive, coordinated research efforts, all as quickly as possible. Immersing students in the research process without having taught the basics of legal research, however, may well leave students just as disoriented and frustrated as teaching them bibliographic detail without providing them perspective on the relevance of that detail.

The final criticism, that students mistakenly develop the attitude from the bibliographic approach that all legal problems have one right answer, is not necessarily a predetermined outcome. Research problems can be written that allow for more than one right answer. However, early in the teaching of legal research, the focus should be on the acquisition and development of basic research skills, not on the fact that most legal problems do not have a single right answer.

Thus, though a review of the literature is informative, the lack of accord between advocates of the bibliographical approach and advocates of the problem-oriented approach persists. However, as mentioned above, several innovations at BYU have enhanced our essentially bibliographic approach in the eyes of students and resulted in the statistically significant improvement in their performance on quizzes. It seems safe to conclude that the legal research program at the Howard W. Hunter has evolved in the right direction.

The approach that we have taken is three pronged. The first prong is to introduce law students to legal materials. This is accomplished by both in-class lectures and in-library exercises. Although in-class lectures have come under severe criticism, simply walking into a law library and beginning to research without some foundation is also unrealistic. The best approach is a combination of the two. After an initial exposure to the materials, the law students meet in the law library for a short orientation on the physical location of the materials that were discussed in class and a hands-on exercise. Legal research teams of two to three students work through the exercises designed to physically expose teams to the materials that were discussed in class and to reinforce the characteristics presented in the lecture.

The second prong of this approach is the use of an in-house produced *Legal Research Manual* that focuses on the essentials of legal research. This *Manual* helps law students further develop a basic facility in working with legal materials through examples, exercises, and quizzes directly based on the text of the manual and written in a parallel format to reinforce the skills presented in each chapter. This prong of the approach culminates in a comprehensive concept-based final. Preparation for this final forces students to review the entire course of instruction and provides them an opportunity to integrate the various lecture topics into a more holistic approach to research.

The third prong of this approach integrates legal research skills into a legal writing program that is problem-based. An extensive fact situation forces students to draw on many of the resources they have reviewed in the *Manual* and handled in the library. The resulting legal documents attest to the value of the program.

NOTES

1. *The Legal Research Manual* is an in-house produced manual written by law librarians at Brigham Young University to introduce law students to the essentials of legal research. Although a number of excellent legal research texts were and are available on the market, most contain historical materials and detailed descriptions that are valuable but beyond the immediate needs of first-year law students. The *Manual,* reworked each year to insure currency, has evolved over the years to reflect the increase in online legal research services as well as the requirements of advanced legal research.

2. Quizzes were intended to test the student's familiarity with and ability to use basic legal materials. A standard of 80% was designated as a pass/fail point. Those students with a score that fell below 80% on a particular quiz had the opportunity to review the quiz with the reference librarian and then to either retake another version of the quiz or to correct the errors made on the quiz so that the final score would be above the 80% mark. The decision to have a student retake another version of the quiz or to correct the errors on the quiz already taken was at the discretion of the reference librarian, depending on the type and extent of mistakes made by the student.

3. Roy Moreland, *Legal Writing and Research in the Smaller Law Schools,* 7 J. Legal Educ. 49, 49 (1954); *see also* Thomas A. Woxland, *Why Can't Johnny Research? or It All Started with Christopher Columbus Langdell,* 81 L. Libr. J. 451, 461 (1989) (The attitude of law schools that de-emphasize legal writing and research courses "is that legal research is a fairly easy skill to learn and that if the skill is not

learned osmotically during law school, it will be learned incidentally during the long practice apprenticeship that many of their graduates undergo.").

4. Moreland, *supra* note 3.

5. William R. Roalfe & William P Higman, *Legal Writing and Research at Northwestern University,* 9 J. Legal Educ. 81, 83 (1956).

6. *See* Robert N. Cook, *Teaching Legal Writing Effectively in Separate Courses,* 2 J. Legal Educ. 87, 88 (1949) ("[A] first-semester course . . . includes basic research of the type usually taught in Legal Bibliography. . . . During the first part of the course the emphasis is on thorough, accurate, and fast law-research."); G. Robert Ellegaard, *Proceedings of the Forty-First Annual Meeting of the American Association of Law Libraries Held at Pennsylvania Hotel, New York City on June 21 to 24, 1948,* 41 L. Libr. J. 182, 182 (1948) ("study of the organization and content of legal literature"); Mortimer Schwartz, *Legal Method at Montana,* 6 J. Legal Educ.102 (1953); Ruth Fleet Thurman, *Blueprint for a Legal Research and Writing Course,* 31 J. Legal Educ.134 (1981).

7. *The Teaching of Legal Writing and Legal Research: A Panel,* 52 L. Libr. J. 350, 364 (1959); *see also* Rhonda Carlson et al., *Innovations in Legal Bibliography Instruction,* 74 L. Libr. J. 615, 615 (1981) ("The basic objective is to familiarize the students with the organization and function of legal research tools."); James Huffmann, *Is the Law Graduate Prepared to Do Legal Research,* 26 J. Legal Educ. 520 (1974); Margit Livingston, *Legal Writing and Research at De Paul University: A Program in Transition,* 44 Alb. L. Rev. 344, 346 (1980) ("[T]he law librarians . . . seek to explain the functions of the various legal research tools, methods for using these tools, and ways to coordinate them into an effective research strategy."); Schwartz, *supra* note 6, at 106 ("Class sessions are devoted to supplementary lectures on the features of specific law books, discussions of assigned problems to be distributed, and answering questions of students. . . . [The assignments consist of] a series of problems which require the students to become acquainted with the types and forms of law books, by working out rather mechanical solutions to questions."); Helene S. Shapo, *The Frontiers of Legal Writing: Challenges for Teaching Research,* 78 L. Libr. J. 719, 725 (1986) ("a . . . comprehensive study of the types of research materials available in the law school library").

8. Christine A. Brock, *The Legal Research Problem,* 24 De Paul L. Rev. 827, 832 (1975); *see also* Carlson, *supra* note 7, at 616 ("Assignments include general short answer questions, integrated questions designed to show students the relationship between kinds and classes of legal materials and some standard 'treasure hunt' type of questions."); Robin K. Mills, *Legal Research Instruction in Law Schools, The State of the Art or, Why Law School Graduates Do Not Know How to Find the Law,* 70 L. Libr. J. 343, 345 (1977) ("library problems requiring short answers"); Schwartz, *supra* note 6, at 103 ("an . . . assignment consisting of a three-page-question-and-short-answer exercise designed to familiarize the neophytes with the law library's resources . . . and what procedures must be observed in using them").

9. *See* Patricia J. Harris & J. William Draper, *Teaching Legal Research: Picking the Pearls and Avoiding the Barnacles,* 2 Integrated Legal Res. 16, 17 (1990); Kathleen M. Carrick, *A Case Study Approach to Legal Research: The Kent State Case,* 73 L. Libr. J. 66 (1980); Livingston, *supra* note 7, at 344; Thomas Michael

McDonnell, *Joining Hands and Smarts: Teaching Manual Legal Research Through Collaborative Learning Groups,* 40 J. Legal Educ. 363 (1990); Betsy McKenzie, *Teaching Legal Research Basics to Graduate Students,* 2 Integrated Legal Res. 12 (1990); William R. Roalfe, *Some Observations on Teaching Legal Bibliography and the Use of Law Books,* 1 J. Legal Educ. 361, 365, 371 (1949); Roalfe, *Legal Writing and Research at Northwestern University, supra* note 5; Marjorie Dick Rombauer, *First-Year Legal Research and Writing: Then and Now,* 25 J. Legal Educ. 538 (1973); Marjorie Dick Rombauer, *Regular Faculty Staffing for an Expanded First-Year Research and Writing Course: A Post Mortem,* 44 Alb. L. Rev. 392, 394 (1980) ("Teaching research and analysis together requires a functional teaching approach (introducing legal materials and their features in the order in which they are used) rather than a bibliographic teaching approach (introducing books and their features as isolated units)."); Kurt M. Saunders, *Thinking About Research; Research About Thinking, in Expert Views on Improving the Quality of Legal Research Education in the United States* 85, 86 (1991); Jerome J. Shestack, *Legal Research and Writing: The Northwestern University Program,* 3 J. Legal Educ.126 (1950); Michael J. Slinger, *Legal Research Instruction at Notre Dame,* 2 Integrated Legal Res. 8, 11 (1990); Fritz Snyder, *Improving Law Student Research Skills, in Expert Views on Improving the Quality of Legal Research Education in the United States* 99 (1991); Christopher G. Wren & Jill Robinson Wren, *The Teaching of Legal Research,* 80 L. Libr. J. 7, 8 (1988) ("legal research as a process for seeking solutions to legal problems").

10. Education Commentary, *Class Assignments in Legal Research,* 1 Legal Res. J. Issue, 3, 8, 9 (1976):

> Professor Rombauer decided, after many years, that the best way of teaching legal research was a "functional approach." Mechanical "fill-in-the-blank" exercises proved to be dull, as they did not force the students to use a full research sequence. On the other hand, complex formal memorandum assignments tended to obscure research difficulties. Therefore, a middle ground was necessary.
>
> This intermediate technique is the "functional approach." It requires the students to learn research skills while actually solving problems.

See also Jack Achtenberg, *Legal Writing and Research: The Neglected Orphan of the First Year,* 29 U. Miami L. Rev. 218, 244-45 (1975); Robert Batey, *Legal Research and Writing From First Year to Law Review,* 12 Stetson L. Rev. 735, 736 (1983) ("The first-year course in research and writing typically involves an introduction to the reference materials available in a law library, followed by a series of problems that the student must research and then analyze in written form."); William D. Hawkland, *Report On an Experiment in Teaching Legal Bibliography,* 8 J. Legal Educ. 511 (1956); Frederick C. Hicks, *The Teaching of Legal Bibliography,* 11 L. Libr. J. 1, 5-6 (1918) ("There are at least three divisions of the subject which we have spoken of as legal bibliography. They are, first, legal bibliography proper, which deals with the repositories of the law; second, methods of finding this law, which is an art to be acquired; and third, brief-making, which has to do with the orderly presentation of arguments based on authorities, and in conformity with the rules of the court to which they are addrest (sic)."); Donald Kepner, *The Rutgers Legal Method Program,* 5 J. Legal Educ. 99, 99 (1952) ("[W]e have preferred to use problems which require comprehensive treatment of some subject which the student normally would not study in the regular curriculum."); Anita L. Morse, *Research, Writing, and Advocacy in the Law School Curriculum*, 75 L. Libr. J. 232, 256 (1982).

11. Albert Brecht, *Accelerated Legal Research at U.S.C. Law Center*, 75 L. Libr. J. 167, 168 (1982) ("[L]egal research is a necessary element for effective legal scholarship. . . . ").

12. Rombauer, *First-Year Legal Research and Writing: Then and Now, supra* note 9, at 540. While accepting, in principle, Rombauer's thesis, Sadow and Beede maintain that "if the course that Rombauer proposed will still include a basic introduction to legal bibliography, the library staff should be responsible for that facet." Sandra Sadow & Benjamin R. Beede, *Library Instruction in American Law Schools*, 68 L. Libr. J. 27, 29 (1975).

13. Richard I. Aaron, *Legal Writing at Utah–A Reaction to the Student View*, 25 J. Legal Educ. 566, 569 (1973); *see also* Richard A. Danner, *From the Editor: Teaching Legal Research*, 78 L. Libr. J. 599, 599 (1986) ("classroom show-and-tell lectures"); Hicks, *The Teaching of Legal Bibliography, supra* note 10, at 6 ("Legal bibliography proper is not merely a description of books."); Marjorie Dick Rombauer, *Regular Faculty Staffing for An Expanded First-Year Research and Writing Course: A Post Mortem, supra* note 9 ("description of features and functions of legal materials"); Sadow, *supra* note 12, at 28 ("show-and-tell"); Wren, *The Teaching of Legal Research, supra* note 9, at 8 ("[T]raditional legal research instruction has focused exclusively or almost exclusively on describing law books."), 20 ("surveys law books").

14. Gregory E. Koster, *Teaching Legal Research: The View from Utopia, in Expert Views on Improving the Quality of Legal Research Education in the United States* 53, 54 (1991); *see also* Danner, *supra* note 13, at 601 ("bibliographic detail"); Wren, *The Teaching of Legal Research, supra* note 9, at 9 ("book focused" and "bibliographic characteristics of law books"), 15 ("inventorying the characteristics of law books"), *see also* 45.

15. C. A. Peairs, Jr., 39 L. Libr. J. 262 (1946) (reviewing Hobart Coffey, *Legal Materials and Their Use in the Preparation of a Case* (1946)); *see also* Hawkland, *supra* note 10, at 513 ("use-of-books course"); Wren, *The Teaching of Legal Research, supra* note 9, at 10 ("At most, a bibliographically oriented explanation covers the mechanics of moving around within a discrete law book or within related sets of law books."), 29, 32 ("mechanical use"), *see also* 53; Christopher G. Wren & Jill Robinson Wren, *Reviving Legal Research: A Reply to Berring and Vanden Heuvel*, 82 L. Libr. J. 463, 466 (1990) ("[T]he bibliographic method of instruction . . . [focuses] on the characteristics of law books and on a narrow, mechanistic conception of how to use law books.").

16. Roalfe, *Some Observations on Teaching Legal Bibliography and the Use of Law Books, supra* note 9, at 376; *see also* Frederick C. Hicks, *Instruction in Legal Bibliography at Columbia University Law School*, 9 L. Libr. J. 121, 121 (1916) ("The lectures dealt with legal bibliography in general rather than methods of using law books, and attempted to trace the development of the various classes of Anglo-American law books from their beginnings in England to their present-day descen-

dants in the United States.''); Wren, *The Teaching of Legal Research, supra* note 9, at 31, 32; Wren, *Reviving Legal Research, supra* note 15, at 468.

17. Wesley Gilmer Jr., *Teaching Legal Research and Legal Writing in American Law Schools,* 25 J. Legal Educ. 571, 572 (1973).

18. Jane Rolnick and Jonathan Gordon, *Legal Research and Writing as an Integrated Process,* 3 Integrated Legal Res. 21 (1990).

19. David Lloyd, *A Student View of the Legal Research and Legal Bibliography Course at Utah and Elsewhere–A Proposed System,* 25 J. Legal Educ. 553, 564 (1973); *see also* Wren, *The Teaching of Legal Research, supra* note 9, at 20, 21.

20. Wren, *The Teaching of Legal Research, supra* note 9, at 8.

21. "Because we are teaching law, not library science, students, our students receive only the information necessary for them to use the material correctly." Joyce Manna Janto & Lucinda D. Harrison-Cox, *Teaching Legal Research: Past and Present,* 84 L. Libr. J. 281, 290 (1992); *see also* Ellegaard, *supra* note 6 ("bibliographer"); Wren, *The Teaching of Legal Research, supra* note 9, at 10 ("[I]f acquiring bibliographic knowledge were a productive way to learn how to do legal research, law students could attend library science schools for this aspect of their education."), 31, 52, 60; Wren, *Reviving Legal Research, supra* note 15, at 472.

22. Ellegaard, *supra* note 6 ("overwhelm the law student who is plunged into a welter of bibliographic detail . . . tend to burden the student with tedious detail. . . . ").

23. Albert P. Blaustein, *On Examinations in Legal Bibliography,* 23 J. Legal Educ. 452, 452 (1971).

24. Julius J. Marke, *How Legal Research Should Be Taught,* 202 N.Y.L.J. 4 (Oct. 17, 1989) at 4; *see also* Robert C. Berring & Kathleen Vanden Heuvel, *Legal Research: Should Students Learn It or Wing It,* 81 L. Libr. J. 431, 437 (1989).

25. Marke, *supra* note 24:

The basic pedagogical techniques in research training are these:

One–demonstration of search methods by the instructor accompanied by a running commentary of exposition.

Two–imitative practice of the demonstrated method by the student under the immediate supervision and guide of the instructor[;]

see also Ellegaard, *supra* note 6, at 183; Hicks, *Instruction in Legal Bibliography at Columbia University Law School, supra* note 16, at 123:

The seminars were chiefly practice work, but each was introduced by a description of the legal aids involved. . . . The subject for discussion was stated in two forms, first, as a problem to be solved, and second, in terms of the legal aids which must be used to solve the problem. . . . [E]ach student was given a problem, and all were asked to go into the law library, work out the answers, and return to the seminar bringing with them the books which had been used. Each student having a different problem, it was helpful then to go over the results together, taking up first those cases in which some difficulty had been experienced.

26. Marke, *supra* note 24, at 6; *see also* Ellegaard, *supra* note 6, at 183.

27. Legal [Research] Institute, *Model Research Examination,* 4 Legal Res. J. Issue 3 7, 8 (1980); *see also* Blaustein, *supra* note 23, at 453 ("For is it vital to acquire

knowledge about the materials of legal research before putting them to use."); Brecht, *supra* note 11 ("[I]t is important that students acquire a firm grasp of bibliography skills.").

28. Joan S. Howland & Nancy J. Lewis, *The Effectiveness of Law School Legal Research Training Programs,* 40 J. Legal Educ. 381, 390 (1990).

29. Blaustein, *supra* note 23, at 453; *see also* Berring *supra* note 24, at 442 ("Students cannot learn to perform complicated research tasks without understanding the nature of the tools involved. . . . ").

30. Lloyd, *supra* note 19, at 560.

31. Berring, *supra* note 24, at 440.

32. *Law School Libraries: A Panel,* 58 L. Libr. J. 387, 405 (1965); *see also* Berring, *supra* note 24, at 440.

33. Shapo, *supra* note 7, at 726.

34. *Law School Libraries: A Panel, supra* note 32, at 403; *see also* Schwartz, *supra* note 6, at 107.

35. Berring, *supra* note 24, at 442.

36. Marke, *supra* note 24; *see also* Berring, *supra* note 24, at 439.

37. Blaustein, *supra* note 23, at 453; *see also* Shestack, *supra* note 9, at 127 ("a working knowledge of all of the tools of legal research"); Brecht, *supra* note 11 ("[A] student performs exercises requiring the student to work with the particular tools in an area. . . . ").

38. Shestack, *supra* note 9, at 127; *see also* Roalfe, *Legal Writing and Research at Northwestern University, supra* note 5, at 90 ("[T]he student [who] has at least been exposed to many of the initial approaches to the law, and a knowledge of these alternatives . . . should be far more competent than the student who has worked out one or two methods on his own and is ignorant of the others.").

39. Janto, *supra* note 21 ("We lay the foundation; bibliographic information can be given to students after they have grasped the basics.").

40. Even without . . . time constraints, we would not change the level of bibliographic information given to the students. We intentionally omit as much bibliographic detail as possible. Because we are teaching law, not library science, students, our students receive only the information necessary for them to use the material correctly.

Janto, *supra* note 21; *see also* Wren, *The Teaching of Legal Research, supra* note 9, at 9 ("Process-oriented instruction, by presenting information about law books as part of a comprehensive explanation of the research process . . . only gives students as much bibliographic information as they need."), 18, 45; Wren, *Reviving Legal Research, supra* note 15, at 472, 476.

41. *The Teaching of Legal Writing and Legal Research: A Panel, supra* note 7, at 359-60.

We need to drill, drill in the use of law books–have the student pick up an individual volume, examine it, handle it, etc. Without this automatic use of books and without this drill which instills automatic utilization of books, a student's mind is not free to think about the legal problem. . . . A student's mind is free for analysis only if his use of the tools is automatic. To accomplish this it requires drill, drill, drill which is dull, dull, dull.

... We must give lectures on how to use law books. We must show students what law books look like. . . . We must assign drill problems requiring the student to pick up a Shepards and answer certain questions using this material.

See also Kathy Garmer, *Research Refresher at Southern Illinois University*, 2 Integrated Legal Res. 14 (1990) ("laboratory sessions in the library"); Roalfe, *Some Observations on Teaching Legal Bibliography and the Use of Law Books, supra* note 9, *at 366-68 (library problems); Rolnick, supra* note 18, at 22 ("[T]he research component should be limited initially to an introduction to legal research methods and resources [including] . . . use . . . strengths . . . relationships . . . characteristics."); Slinger, *supra* note 9, at 9 ("exercises almost every week"); Wren, *The Teaching of Legal Research, supra* note 9, at 18.

42. McKenzie, *supra* note 9, at 13 ("work sheet"); *see also* Snyder, *supra* note 9. In his article, Snyder states that "Teaching assistants or adjunct instructors will help familiarize students with the basic sources. . . . One of the exercises, perhaps number four, should be a case-finding exercise. . . . " Snyder further states with regards to this exercise that "[w]e are interested in the *process* here. . . . " Apparently, implied in the description of this first year course is a bibliographic familiarization of the basic sources in lessons 1-3. Snyder, *supra* note 9, at 100.

43. Snyder, *supra* note 9, at 100.

44. "Professor Rombauer states that research cannot be separated from problem analysis. . . . She tells the students to analyze the problem. Then they are given a brief description of the books and are sent to the library to do preliminary research." *See also* Achtenberg, *supra* note 10, at 231-32; Hawkland, *supra* note 10, at 513 ("[P]rior to their first research efforts, the students were given . . . a short expository lecture on the use of law books."); Janto, *supra* note 21 ("We intentionally omit as much bibliographic detail as possible. . . . [O]ur students receive only the information necessary for them to use the material correctly."); Kepner, *supra* note 10 ("material on legal bibliography with emphasis on the problem of using law books in an expeditious manner.").

45. John D. Edwards, *Teaching Legal Research: Evaluating Options, in Expert Views on Improving the Quality of Legal Research Education in the United States* 30, 33 (1991); *see also* Carrick, *supra* note 9, at 68 (quoting Committee on Curriculum, Harvard Law School, *Report of the Committee on Curriculum* 63 (Warren A. Seavey, Chairman, June 15, 1936)) ("The use of law books is best learned by using law books for a purpose, not listening to lectures on how to use them."); McDonnell, *supra* note 9 ("The following three-step method was employed: (1) the students read about the tool; (2) the instructor discussed the tool in class; and (3) immediately following the discussion, students went to the library to work in groups in the presence of the instructor.").

46. McDonnell, *supra* note 9, at 365; *see also* Carrick, *supra* note 9 at 68 (quoting Committee on Curriculum, Harvard Law School, *Report of the Committee on Curriculum* 63 (Warren A. Seavey, Chairman, June 15, 1936) ("Some formal preliminary instruction is necessary, but that is all.")); Hawkland, *supra* note 10 ("We tell the students the names of all the books, generally what the books contain, how they can be used in research, etc., and then we send them to the library and ask them to solve a problem. . . . "); Morse, *supra* note 10, at 255, 256 ("That a law student

should know how to look up a case, statute, periodical, or treatise cited in a case book is not questioned: some sort of introductory instruction, preferably before classes begin, can be given in how to use basic tools."); Roalfe, *Legal Writing and Research at Northwestern University, supra* note 5, at 83, 84 ("A purely mechanical exercise was felt to be the best introduction to the books . . . acting as a guide to the discovery of [the material's] nature. . . . [and providing a] general exposure to the collection as background. . . . "); Wren, *The Teaching of Legal Research, supra* note 9, at 53 ("introducing students to a given bibliographic feature of a law book in the course of explaining the step in the legal research process at which the feature becomes useful to researchers").

47. Koster, *supra* note 14, at 59; *see also* Legal [Research] Institute, *supra* note 27 ("Book Use Procedures"); Wren, *The Teaching of Legal Research, supra* note 9, at 10 ("[b]ibliographic information requires context to make it meaningful for a legal researcher"), 36.

48. Gilmer, *supra* note 17, at 571; *see also* Legal [Research] Institute, *supra* note 27 ("Problem Analysis Procedure"); Wren, *The Teaching of Legal Research, supra* note 9, at 48, 56.

49. Davalene Cooper, *Adopting the "Stepchild" into the Legal Academic Community: Creating a Program for Learning Legal Research Skills, in Expert Views on Improving the Quality of Legal Research Education in the United States* 11, 15 (1991); *see also* Danner, *supra* note 13 ("hands-on library instruction").

50. Danner, *supra* note 13, at 601.

51. Hawkland, *supra* note 10, at 513 ("Regular classroom work in Legal Bibliography . . . was conducted throughout the semester.").

52. Janto, *supra* note 21, at 292; *see also* W. L. Matthews, Jr., *First Year Legal Writing and Legal Method in a Smaller Law School,* 8 J. Legal Educ. 201, 203 (1955).

53. Janto, *supra* note 21, at 292.

54. *Law School Libraries: A Panel, supra* note 32, at 403.

55. Carrick, *supra* note 9, at 71, accepts the tedium associated with learning and mastering legal research skills, advocating not that it be eliminated but rather that it be imbued with reality.

56. Benjamin S. Bloom, *quoted in* Susan S. Katcher, *Reflections on Teaching Legal Research, in Expert Views on Improving the Quality of Legal Research Education in the United States* 45, 46 (1991).

57. *Id.* at 46-47.

58. *Id.* at 45.

59. Janto, *supra* note 21, at 291; *see also* Education Commentary, *supra* note 10, at 9 ("Precise utilization methods are quickly forgotten. What the student should retain are the basic parameters of problem-solving through the systematic use of legal materials."); *Law School Libraries: A Panel," supra* note 32, at 406 ("[N]ot only is the retention of information poor because motivation is lacking, but they are in a way an insult to the intelligence of law students."). *But see* Thurman, *supra* note 6 ("Having completed legal bibliography, students progress more rapidly, with less trauma, and better results [in the research and writing course].").

60. Danner, *supra* note 13, at 602; Donald J. Dunn, *Why Legal Research Skills Declined, or When Two Rights Make a Wrong, in Expert Views on Improving the Quality of Legal Research Education in the United States* 19, 22 (1991); Lloyd, *supra* note 19, at 554-55.

61. Dunn, *supra* note 60, at 25.

62. Shapo, *supra* note 7.

63. Livingston, *supra* note 7, at 358.

64. Kathleen G. Sumner, *An Alternative to Traditional Legal Research, Legal Writing, Legal Drafting and Appellate Advocacy Programs, in Expert Views on Improving the Quality of Legal Research Education in the United States* 111, 116 (1991).

65. *The Teaching of Legal Writing and Legal Research: A Panel, supra* note 7, at 365.

66. Roalfe, *Some Observations on Teaching Legal Bibliography and the Use of Law Books, supra* note 9, at 365.

67. Edwards, *supra* note 45, at 31; Wren, *The Teaching of Legal Research, supra* note 9, at 11.

68. Danner, *supra* note 13, at 601, 602; Achtenberg, *supra* note 10, at 225; Carlson, *supra* note 7, at 618; Cooper, *supra* note 49, at 12; Dunn, *supra* note 60, at 25; Edwards, *supra* note 45, at 31; Carol L. Golden, *Teaching Legal Research as an Integral Step in Legal Problem Solving, in Expert Views on Improving the Quality of Legal Research Education in the United States* 37, 41 (1991); Janto, *supra* note 21, at 291; McKenzie, *supra* note 9; Shapo, *supra* note 7, at 726; Wren, *The Teaching of Legal Research, supra* note 9, at 11, 46, 56.

69. Carrick, *supra* note 9, at 71.

70. Danner, *supra* note 13, at 602; Mills, *supra* note 8, at 343 ("essentially drills in the use of various legal research tools"); Morse, *supra* note 10, at 247 ("lecture and drill exercises").

71. Berring, *supra* note 24, at 443.

72. Rolnick, *supra* note 18.

73. Achtenberg, *supra* note 10, at 231.

74. Lloyd, *supra* note 19, at 557.

75. Woxland, *supra* note 3, at 453.

76. *Id.*

77. Morse, *supra* note 10, at 255.

78. Lloyd, *supra* note 19, at 554, 556.

79. Lloyd, *supra* note 19, at 563.

80. Lloyd, *supra* note 19, at 563; Danner, *supra* note 13; Shapo, *supra* note 7 ("short answer exercises").

81. Woxland, *supra* note 3, at 453.

82. Mersky, Roy M., *Institute on the Teaching of Legal Research: Opening Remarks,* 3 Integrated Legal Res. 1, 1 (1990).

83. Lloyd, *supra* note 19, at 564-65.

84. Lloyd, *supra* note 19, at 560.

85. Danner, *supra* note 13, at 599-601 ("artificial research situation").

86. Janto, *supra* note 21, at 291.

87. Sumner, *supra* note 64, at 112.

88. Danner, *supra* note 13, at 599, 602.

89. *The Teaching of Legal Writing and Legal Research: A Panel, supra* note 7, at 355.

90. Woxland, *supra* note 3, at 454.

91. Snyder, *supra* note 9, at 101.

92. Janto, *supra* note 21, at 291; *see also* Education Commentary, *supra* note 10 ("needlessly repetitious and boring"); *Law School Libraries: A Panel, supra* note 32, at 406 ("How can you apply the adage 'by not doing your own work you hurt only yourself' to work that merely wastes your time?")

93. Janto, *supra* note 21, at 291.

94. *Law School Libraries: A Panel, supra* note 32, at 406.

95. Mills, *supra* note 8, at 343; *see also* Hicks, *The Teaching of Legal Bibliography, supra* note 10, at 6:

> It is a mistake to speak of any of the processes of finding the law as mechanical processes, for one has not truly found the law until one understands it, and this requires a knowledge of substantive law which comes only with the passage of time and much experience. Nevertheless, there is a species of manual training in the use of law books and libraries which should be learned before or coincidently with the substance of law itself. This has been defined as the art of finding known cases and statutes, and includes the use of catalogs, the arrangement of libraries, the interpretation of citations, their translation from one form to another, the location of cases when only their titles are known, the tracing of the legislative and judicial history of statutes and the judicial history of cases[;]

Hicks, "The Teaching of Legal Bibliography," *supra* note 10, at 6 ("legal research and its mechanical processes"); Huffmann, *supra* note 7 ("Legal research . . . is in the first instance a clerical, mechanical task of compilation. . . . It is the learning of a mechanical skill which has as its purpose the determination of what is there."); Louis C. James, *Legal Writing at Stetson,* 7 J. Legal Educ. 413, 415 (1955) ("The students there are acquainted with the 'mechanical tools' of the profession, and are given special problems as library assignments. . . . Legal Bibliography [gives] the students adequate familiarity with the 'mechanical tools' of the profession."); Roalfe, *Legal Writing and Research at Northwestern University, supra* note 5 ("A purely mechanical exercise was felt to be the best introduction to the books . . . acting as a guide to the discovery of [the material's] nature."); Schwartz, *supra* note 6, at 106 ("a series of problems which require the students to become acquainted with the types and forms of law books, by working out rather mechanical solutions to questions."); John H. Wigmore, *The Job Analysis Method of Teaching the Use of Law Sources,* 16 Ill. L. Rev. 499 (1922) ("[T]he law-sources are the tools of the trade."). *But see* Brecht, *supra* note 11, at 169 ("[L]egal research is not a simplistic or a purely mechanical endeavor.").

96. Roalfe, *Legal Writing and Research at Northwestern University, supra* note 5.

97. Achtenberg, *supra* note 10, at 231 (emphasis added).

98. Achtenberg, *supra* note 10, at 225 (emphasis added).

99. Katcher, *supra* note 56, at 49.

100. The students, thus pressed for the "right answer," look for it, and when it is known, they believe they have learned, regardless of the method or methods employed in arriving at the solution. . . .

Our program was predicated on the belief that useful information concerning law books can be acquired only by using law books in a useful, professional way. Using law books to answer legal bibliography questions, we felt, would not be a useful employment of the books, because the answers to these problems, standing alone, have no value to the students except as answers to legal bibliography problems. We wanted the students to seek the answers not for the value of seeking, but because the search would result in useful information.

Hawkland, *supra* note 10, at 511-12; *see also* Wren, *The Teaching of Legal Research, supra* note 9, at 46.

101. Kathleen Vanden Heuvel, *Editorial,* 9 Legal Reference Services Q. 1, 3 (1989).

102. Golden, *supra* note 68, at 41.

103. McDonnell, *supra* note 9, at 367.

104. Timothy P. Terrell, *What Does and Does Not Happen in Law School to Prepare Students to Practice Law: A View From Both Sides of the Academic/Practice Dichotomy,* 83 L. Libr. J. 493, 499 (1991).

105. *Id.* at 501.

Teaching Legal Research:
A Proactive Approach

Herbert E. Cihak

SUMMARY. Questions about the importance and viability of legal research and writing as a part of the law school curriculum are not novel. Confronting these questions head-on, however, is a responsibility that should be handled by law librarians. This article addresses the issue of teaching legal research in an academic law library setting. The reasons why the author has pursued an aggressive approach when dealing with legal research instruction are explored. The methods employed to carry out that legal research instruction mandate are examined. *[Article copies available for a fee from The Haworth Document Delivery Service: 1-800-342-9678. E-mail address: <getinfo@haworthpressinc.com> Website: <http://www.HaworthPress.com> © 2001 by The Haworth Press, Inc. All rights reserved.]*

INTRODUCTION

According to surveys done by the ABA and the Legal Writing Institute, the number of academic law librarians who teach legal research has de-

Herbert E. Cihak is Director of the Law Library and Professor of Law at the University of Kentucky College of Law. As such, he has been involved with a wide spectrum of legal research instructional activities. For the past three years, he has served as Director of Legal Research and Writing for the College of Law. In this capacity, he teaches legal research to all first-year law students and supervises twelve adjunct legal writing instructors. In addition, he teaches an advanced legal research course to third-year law students. In his role as Chief Information Officer for the College of Law, he is heavily involved in information technology issues and with integration of technology into the classroom. His written and oral presentations often focus on legal research skills, tools, and instruction. He earned his JD at the University of Nebraska and his MLS at Brigham Young University (E-mail: hcihak@pop.uky.edu).

[Haworth co-indexing entry note]: "Teaching Legal Research: A Proactive Approach." Cihak, Herbert E. Co-published simultaneously in *Legal Reference Services Quarterly* (The Haworth Information Press, an imprint of The Haworth Press, Inc.) Vol. 19, No. 3/4, 2001, pp. 27-40; and: *Teaching Legal Research and Providing Access to Electronic Resources* (ed: Gary L. Hill, Dennis S. Sears, and Lovisa Lyman) The Haworth Information Press, an imprint of The Haworth Press, Inc., 2001, pp. 27-40. Single or multiple copies of this article are available for a fee from The Haworth Document Delivery Service [1-800-342-9678, 9:00 a.m. - 5:00 p.m. (EST). E-mail address: getinfo@haworthpressinc.com].

creased as legal research and writing are more and more frequently combined and taught by writing faculty.[1] At the same time, the research skills of law students are on a downward spiral. Howland and Lewis document this plunge in an informative survey.[2] Law librarian Donald Dunn substantiates this decline and attributes it, in part, to "the increased emphasis in law schools on legal writing,"[3] in consequence of which, while "legal writing entered the expressway; legal research took the off-ramp."[4] Further, law librarians and legal research have even been pummeled by one of America's most popular authors.[5] In this environment, it may seem unwise to continue to advance the argument that academic law librarians should teach legal research. Notwithstanding the obstacles that face such instruction, law librarians have an obligation to press forward in this important work.[6] Legal writing instructors have not demonstrated that they have the expertise to provide this instruction.[7] Likewise, law faculty have demonstrated that they do not have the interest in tackling the task.[8] Say two authorities on the subject: "Regular faculty members generally do not teach a research course, and when they do decide to teach one, the results are invariably disastrous. Most law faculty members cannot teach legal research because they do not understand it themselves. If compelled to teach the course, they rebel."[9] Perhaps it is time for law schools to cede the stewardship for legal research instruction to those information professionals who have been trained and are qualified to teach legal research instruction–law librarians.[10] And it is time for any reticent law librarians to accept the obligation to take a more proactive approach toward teaching legal research.[11]

TO TEACH OR NOT TO TEACH LEGAL RESEARCH– DOES IT REALLY MATTER?

Unless we are unaware of the course that legal education has charted, librarians understand the importance placed on lawyering skills. The MacCrate Report identified ten fundamental lawyering skills,[12] and legal research was included in the enumeration.[13] In order to conduct effective legal research, MacCrate emphasized that lawyers should possess a working knowledge of "the nature of legal rules and legal institutions, the fundamental tools of legal research, and the process of devising and implementing a coherent and effective research design."[14] While it is not difficult for librarians to assist future lawyers in gaining these skills, some have suggested that if academic law librarians do not do so, then they will have paved the way for an educational malpractice suit.[15]

ABA Standards also highlight the need to help law students gain legal research proficiency. Standard 302(a) reads in part: "A law school shall offer to all students in its J.D. program: (1) instruction in the substantive law, values and skills (including legal analysis and reasoning, legal research, problem solving and oral and written communication) generally regarded as necessary to effective and responsible participation in the legal profession. . . . "[16] Under the ABA rules for approval of law schools, an evaluation of programs must be undertaken every seven years.[17]

Teaching legal research classes provides an opportunity to showcase an institution's talented law librarians. A flattened organizational structure and a liberation leadership model have allowed us more time to focus on teaching.[18] A part of our University of Kentucky College of Law Library Mission Statement includes: " . . . to support the College of Law's academic programs. . . ."[19] Providing classroom instruction in legal research, by librarians whose reputations and stature are enlarged,[20] is identified as the first goal and objective in our strategic action plan. Our librarians consider teaching legal research skills one of their most important functions. Seizing these teaching opportunities lays the groundwork for the development of a network of lifelong law library supporters.

A proactive approach toward teaching legal research provides the opportunity for a law library organization to cope with the information explosion and thrive in the new millennium. Management guru Peter Drucker has taught that "leadership is vision."[21] Law library leaders need to exert their influence to encompass legal research instruction as a part of their vision. Hockey great Wayne Gretzy remarked, "You miss 100 percent of the shots you don't take."[22] Law librarians need to continue to take their best shots at teaching legal research, for we cannot shrink our way to greatness.[23] Teaching legal research really does matter!

PROMOTING LEGAL RESEARCH BY EMBRACING A "BIG TENT" PHILOSOPHY

Recently I prepared a short article for a law school alumni publication dealing with the changing scope or focus of legal research.[24] Not only have the traditional legal research tools changed, but research topics now include a broader emphasis on administrative law, inter-disciplinary study, and international and foreign law. Librarians must adapt to this change in teaching legal research as well. Proactive librarians will make sure that they are prepared for their roles as information experts. In addition to expertise, law librarians must be visible by marketing their services. This can be accomplished by using a big tent philosophy when teaching legal research. Librarians should teach legal research and related topics to their customers anytime and anywhere. Let me describe how law librarians meet this challenge at the University of Kentucky.

First-Year Legal Research and Writing Program–A Joint Effort

The obstacles facing legal research and writing instruction are familiar–lack of sufficient credit hours, student inattention, deficiencies in the skills of instructors, and lack of law school support.[25] One legal educator has stated that teaching some of the intricacies of legal research to first-year law students is akin to "teaching a pig to sing–the pig doesn't do it very well and certainly doesn't appreciate the lesson."[26] While I cannot minimize the substantial problems that legal research and writing instructors encounter, I believe that these hurdles are surmountable.

Who teaches legal research? As director of a three-credit legal research and writing program, I have tried to bring order and stability to our two-semester program. I am not advocating that law library directors supervise a joint legal research and writing program–in fact I suggest that a full-time faculty member be hired to oversee the writing and oral advocacy program[27]–but I am of the opinion that law librarians need to collaborate with legal writing instructors to ensure that legal research and writing assignments mesh. This past year, I used the voluntary assistance of five other law librarians to aid me with first-year legal research instruction, although I have taught all of the classes myself. When legal research and writing programs are separate, it is imperative that legal research be taught by skilled law librarians.

When is first-year legal research taught? There are certainly valid reasons for teaching legal research later than sooner in a law student's career.[28] Since most legal research programs work in tandem with legal writing instruction, however, basic legal research tools must be introduced early in the first semester in order to provide students with sufficient knowledge to conduct memorandum research. At Kentucky, legal research instruction begins the first week that classes meet. We make a concerted effort to teach particular research topics before these topics are needed for legal writing assignments.

What material should be taught to first-year legal research students? This question generated a passionate debate over a decade ago among Christopher and Jill Wren and Robert Berring and Kathleen Vanden Heuvel when the issue of the role that bibliographic instruction and research process plays in the teaching of legal research was aired in the pages of *Law Library Journal.*[29] I have attempted to blend bibliographic instruction with research process. In following this method, I have used several required textbooks.[30] Each year my pattern of instruction includes case law, digests, citators, statutes, legislative history, administrative law and secondary sources. I have determined that what works best for my classes is to introduce secondary materials at the beginning of the course. Most years, ALR and the Restatements of law are presented. For the future, I have considered removing federal administrative law and legislative history from the first-year legal research curriculum. It seems to me that fine-tuning our legal research classes is a plus, even though this effort requires a substantial investment in time and resources.

How is legal research instruction taught? The methods of legal research instruction in place at law schools around the country run the gamut from large class lectures to board games.[31] I have utilized large class instruction, but turned to Microsoft PowerPoint presentations for small group legal research sections during the past five years.[32] We divide the first-year students into small group sections of twelve-to-eighteen students. These eight-to-ten small group sections meet once a week for fifty minutes in the law library. A twenty minute lecture[33] is followed by thirty minutes of in-class "hands-on" assignment work. Out-of-class assignments and an exam are also part of our two-month program. Although there is some debate about the timing of Westlaw and LEXIS instruction,[34] we have delayed this instruction until early in the second semester of the first year. University of Kentucky law librarians are actively involved in teaching and promoting CALR instruction.

Advanced Legal Research Class–Seizing the Momentum

Advanced legal research courses have been featured in law school course offerings since the early 1970s.[35] This course is the ideal vehicle for librarians to utilize to promote the teaching of legal research. An advanced research course for second- or third-year law students brings together students who want to learn and materials that need to be taught.

One dilemma that I have encountered in teaching advanced legal research is how to accommodate the student demand. I favor teaching in a seminar-type setting–with about fifteen students maximum. When I limited the class to fifteen students, a waiting list developed. To handle this problem, I restricted the class to third-year students. The next year, when the demand for spaces in the class escalated, I opened the class to thirty students. In order to accommodate these extra students, I met with all thirty students for the first hour of class instruction and then met with groups of fifteen students in the next two hours for in-class assignment work. Next semester, I will teach forty-five students in a lecture format for one hour. In the three hours that follow my lecture presentation, I will meet with groups of fifteen students for an hour of "hands-on" in-the-library lab work.[36]

The topics covered in my advanced legal research course differ significantly from the first-year legal research offering. A review of basic research fundamentals and tools, including digests and citators, is presented. CALR tools are given more emphasis, and Westlaw and LEXIS representatives are encouraged to come and discuss services such as Dialog and NEXIS. Every year, this two-credit course is substantially revised, although the following topics have been included: international, foreign and transnational law; securities law; environmental law; criminal law; banking law; labor law; family law; and employment law. Looseleaf services, trial practice materials, and ALR are also covered. A review of statutory law, legislative history, and administrative law research is also presented. *Legal Research in a Nutshell* is used as the text for this course.

The format for the advanced legal research course allows some flexibility. I have attempted to assist those students who are interested in pursuing research on topics not included in the law school curriculum or who are interested in developing research skills in areas of future practice. I assign a graded research "process" memo with no page limit but with research guidelines that must be addressed. Students can choose from topics in the areas of environmental, property, tax, patent, immigration, employment, or religious liberty law to research. A mid-semester exam is given that focuses on a review of fundamental legal research concepts and tools. This exam is usually a combination of multiple choice, short answer, and exhibit questions. A take-home final exam is also given. This exam requires students to prepare a legal research memo that emphasizes substance over process. Students can choose to take a products liability, family law, or criminal law version. They have one week to work on the exam.

The advanced legal research class is ideally suited for PowerPoint instruction. Slides can easily be updated. Students are given copies of the presentations in the slide note format. One popular feature of this class has been the handouts that are distributed. For each research topic presented, I prepare an annually revised bibliography. These bibliographies include titles, call numbers, and locations of sources housed in our library. Bibliographies highlight cases, decisions, rulings, and opinions, as well as looseleaf services, periodicals, texts, and Internet resources. I am able to keep these bibliographies up-to-date by using the monthly acquisitions list that our library staff prepares. Former students often ask for revised topic bibliographies. Evaluations for my advanced legal research course have been complimentary.

Teaching with Technology–What and When or How Much Is Enough?

Librarians are in the business of technology management. I agree with Joan Howland who suggests that librarians should "aggressively exploit the opportunities presented by technological advancements."[37] Whether we bear the title of Associate Dean for Information Technology, Chief Information Officer for the College of Law, or Director of the Law Library, there are a number of ways that librarians can use technology to teach legal research.[38]

The biggest obstacle to overcome before technology can be integrated into classroom instruction is law faculty phobia. A first step is convincing faculty that teaching law with computers can help achieve important pedagogical goals.[39] Once faculty members understand that computer technology can actually enhance classroom instruction, then resistance to technological change will disappear. Librarians stand as mediators between faculty and technology.

There are a number of technology issues impacting law schools today. Law librarians, as technology issue experts, should remember that while these issues may have merit, almost all technology acquired will provide greater access to legal research resources. First, the cost of new technology continues to escalate. There are yearly updates to hardware and presentation software that must be budgeted.[40] One caveat: librarians must be careful not to be left holding the price tag for the whole college of law computing budget. Librarians are familiar with stretching tight budgets, so they stand in a unique position where they can weigh the value of purchasing legal research materials in various formats. Judging the quality of software purchases may be a more difficult matter.

Second, the battle between building computer labs and requiring laptop ownership is cranking up. In my legal research and advanced legal research courses, we must have access to our computer lab for some class instruction. Mandating laptop computer ownership for all students and doing away with these expensive computer labs might seem reasonable. This option cannot be implemented at Kentucky, however, because we do not yet have enough computer instruction integrated into our classroom instruction to merit that policy switch. As students continue to pressure law faculty to teach with technology, this issue may well become a moot point.

Third, the need for smart classrooms will increase. A decade ago Chicago-Kent constructed a smart building in order to assist with the integration of computers into legal technology.[41] Our law school courtroom was recently renovated. Modern voice-activated cameras, state-of-the-art videotaping equipment, and upgraded window treatments were installed. New LCD projectors were also acquired.[42] The law school courtroom renovation has allowed me to increase the number of students who can be taught legal research via PowerPoint instruction. One drawback is that I still must utilize a technology cart containing my computer and LCD projector. Stationary equipment would be a real boon.

Fourth, some technology may only be transitional. For the past few years I have been involved in marketing our electronic library research tools and services.[43] I am not sure which electronic formats will endure, although some have suggested that CD-ROM technology is already on the way out.[44] A market will probably exist for a number of legal research tools in CD-ROM or DVD format in the foreseeable future, but librarians need to keep a close watch on these ever-changing products. Law Librarians have been presented with the exciting opportunity to push legal research instruction onto the Internet[45] and over distance learning channels.[46] We cannot wait until the new technology frontiers are defined before we embark on teaching legal research.

Finally, the issue of who controls law school web sites is tied to information technology and libraries. Even if librarians are not responsible for their college's web site, they must be at the forefront of web development. One prominent and important feature of our current law school web site is our library link to legal research starting points. Demands by admissions, career services, faculty, and our development office for increased web presence must be addressed, but providing links to legal research information is critical to our law library mission. While some significant challenges do exist when seeking to utilize technology to teach legal research, the benefits to be gained surely outweigh the costs involved.

Individual and Group Instruction–Leading a Horse to Water

Law librarians are provided with limitless opportunities to instruct law faculty and students on the finer points of legal research methodology and tools. A few law schools have implemented aggressive faculty service programs.[47] We have determined that our law faculty can benefit from CALR instruction, assistance with Internet searches, and individualized training on the use of presentation software. Even though first-year legal research classes may not be uniformly appreciated, our law students have always expressed an interest in participating in additional research workshops where specific research topics can be addressed. This past year, we also implemented instructional workshops dealing with the basics of computer technology for incoming students and a review of basic instruction for returning students. Providing ways to access basic research sources is always a part of any instruction that is provided. For the past several years our librarians have taken part in the spring National Legal Research Teach-Ins. This event is an occasion when meaningful legal research teaching occurs and when individual research assignments can be evaluated. The bottom line is that most law faculty and students will have to be persuaded to seek assistance when grappling with new information technology and legal research tools. Librarians have to be innovative in seeking opportunities to provide this service and then savvy enough to make sure that concise and beneficial instruction is rendered in either individual or group settings.

Presentations and Publications–Spreading the Message

As an advocate for taking a proactive approach to teaching legal research, I believe in using innovative and creative ways to reach out and touch our customers.[48] At Kentucky, reaching through teaching has been a recurring theme we have developed and nurtured during the past few years. Many of our librarian presentations and publications have focused on legal research instruction to a variety of state, regional, and national audiences.[49]

Presentations and publications have helped spread the message that University of Kentucky College of Law librarians are knowledgeable legal information experts who have an important message to share.[50] Teaching legal research is a vital part of that message.

CONCLUSION

Law librarians should view the opportunity to teach legal research as a win-win proposition. As information brokers, librarians are skilled professionals who provide the keys to unlock a storehouse containing a wealth of legal research treasure. Unlocking the legal information storehouse, however, is not enough. Librarians also serve as mediators between customers and legal research tools and methodology. Teaching legal research, in its most expansive form, is what law librarians do best.

This article has dealt with proactive approaches to teaching legal research. The MacCrate Report and ABA Standards provide some good reasons why librarians should teach legal research. Possibilities to strengthen and develop librarians, as well as an opportunity to keep an organization thriving, are others. In the end, it is up to each law librarian to decide what is important to the survival of his or her own institution. I stand with those who believe that librarians who fail to respond to the metamorphosis in the information environment face extinction.[51] Taking a proactive approach to teaching legal research is one step down the road to survival.

NOTES

1. Helene S. Shapo, *The Frontiers of Legal Writing: Challenges for Teaching Research,* 78 L. Libr. J. 719, 725 (1986). Based on ABA surveys, Shapo concluded that "in most law schools, legal research is no longer taught by law librarians." While I have not seen data that contradicts this assessment, other information seems to confirm it. *See* Jill J. Ramsfield, *Legal Writing in the Twenty-First Century: A Sharper Image,* 2 Legal Writing: J. Legal Writing Inst. 1, 4 (1996). Ramsfield indicates that a 1994 Legal Writing Institute survey determined that from 1990 to 1994 the number of law schools which taught legal research as a separate course apart from legal writing dropped from one-half to less than a third. When legal research and writing courses are combined, law librarians are less likely to offer the legal research instruction.

2. Joan S. Howland & Nancy J. Lewis, *The Effectiveness of Law School Legal Research Training Programs,* 40 J. Legal Educ. 381, 383-391 (1990).

3. Donald J. Dunn, *Why Legal Research Skills Declined, or When Two Rights Make a Wrong,* 85 L. Libr. J. 49, 52 (1993).

4. *Id.* at 56.

5. Herbert E. Cihak & Judith Morgan, *Using Change to Beat "The Grisham Factor,"* 12 Marketing Libr. Services, June 1998, at 1. The authors analyze John Grisham novels and illustrate the attacks made on law librarians, law libraries, and legal research. One example dealing with legal research is cited at page two: "'We've reviewed your writing sample and it's quite impressive.' 'Thank you. I enjoy research.' They nodded and acknowledged this obvious lie. It was part of the ritual. No law student or lawyer in his right mind enjoyed research, yet, without fail every prospective associate professed a deep love for the library." John Grisham, *The Firm* 6 (1991).

6. This opinion has been expressed by numerous law librarians including Thomas A. Woxland, *Why Can't Johnny Research? Or It All Started with Christopher Columbus Langdell,* 81 L. Libr. J. 451 (1989).

7. An amusing story illustrates this point and was provided via e-mail correspondence from Robert C. Berring, Librarian and Professor of Law, School of Law (Boalt Hall), University of California, Berkeley, to Herb Cihak on November 10, 1999: "I often tell an anecdote about interviewing the fellow who was head of our research and writing program a few years back. . . . I asked him how he wanted to handle research training. He looked at me and said, 'Research, Wow, I don't know. I hadn't thought about that. Is that something that the library does or something?'" Even if legal writing instructors are legal research experts, they often give short shrift to research instruction. *See* Michael J. Lynch, *An Impossible Task but Everybody Has To Do It–Teaching Legal Research in Law Schools,* 89 L. Libr. J. 415, 431 (1997).

8. *See* Marjorie Dick Rombauer, *Regular Faculty Staffing for an Expanded First-Year Research and Writing Course: A Post Mortem,* 44 Alb. L. Rev. 392 (1980).

9. Robert C. Berring & Kathleen Vanden Heuvel, *Legal Research: Should Students Learn It or Wing It?* 81 L. Libr. J. 431, 438 (1989).

10. Joyce Manna Janto & Lucinda D. Harrison-Cox, *Teaching Legal Research: Past and Present,* 84 L. Libr. J. 281 (1992), reinforce the opinion that law librarians are uniquely qualified to teach legal research. Teaching legal research has been a focus of discussion in American law schools for years. For an early overview of this topic *see* John R. Austin & Carmencita K. Cui, *Teaching Legal Research in American Law Schools: An Annotated Bibliography,* Legal Reference Services Q., Spring 1987, at 71.

11. This article is directed at academic law librarians, but private law librarians certainly deal with legal research instruction on a daily basis. I do not suggest that academic law librarians are uninterested in teaching legal research, but many seem to have become very cynical. The annual private and academic teaching research conferences sponsored by the LEXIS Publishing Librarian Relations Group are certainly examples of proactive approaches to teaching legal research that should be encouraged.

12. *See* Arturo López Torres, *MacCrate Goes to Law School: An Annotated Bibliography of Methods for Teaching Lawyering Skills in the Classroom,* 77 Neb. L. Rev. 132 (1998), for an instructive bibliography of publications which deal with the lawyering skills enumerated in the MacCrate Report.

13. American Bar Association, Section of Legal Education and Admissions to the Bar, *Report of The Task Force on Law Schools and the Profession: Narrowing the*

Gap, Selected Excerpts from the MacCrate Report, Legal Education and Professional Development–An Educational Continuum 1, 15-18 (July 1992) <http://www.abanet. org/legaled/publications/onlinepubs/maccrate.html>.

14. *Id.* at 16. Skill 3 deals with legal research.

15. Lydia M. V. Brand, *The MacCrate Report and the Teaching of Legal Research: A Justified Scenario for Educational Malpractice,* 2 Tex. Wesleyan L. Rev. 123 (1995).

16. American Bar Association, *Standards for Approval of Law Schools,* 1, 41 (1999).

17. Having served as a member of an ABA site evaluation team, I can attest to the fact that these teams are encouraged to closely examine legal skills programs.

18. Recently I have concentrated on developing support staff. See *Coaching Library Support Staff: The Three R's That Count,* Library Mosaics, Mar.-Apr. 1999, at 10. During the past year, these non-law librarians have also been involved with teaching legal research to a number of our customers.

19. The full mission statement reads: "The Law Library's primary mission is to support the College of Law's academic programs as well as to provide the highest quality of service, in a hospitable environment, to its faculty, students, and alumni. As the Law Library's most valuable resource, the library team strives to exceed the expectations of all clients by providing creative and flexible solutions to their diverse and evolving information needs."

20. Louis Sirico has given some timely advice and suggestions to legal writing instructors as to ways that they might gain more respect. His suggestions take the expansive approach to teaching that I advocate. See *Getting Respect,* 3 Legal Writing 293 (1997).

21. Peter Senge et al., *The Dance of Change: The Challenges of Sustaining Momentum in Learning Organizations* 16 (1999).

22. While this comment has been published in several places, *see* Warren Bennis & Patricia Ward Biederman, *Organizing Genius: The Secrets of Collaboration* 21 (1997).

23. Arthur Martinez, Chairman and CEO of Sears, Roebuck & Co., is credited with stating "You can't shrink your way to greatness." *See* Tom Peters, *The Circle of Innovation* 19 (1997).

24. Herbert E. Cihak, *The Changing World of Legal Research,* Ky. Law., 1999-2000, at 6.

25. Robin K. Mills, *Legal Research Instruction in Law Schools, The State of the Art or, Why Law School Graduates Do Not Know How to Find the Law,* 70 L. Libr. J. 343, 345-46 (1977), chronicles these obstacles and presents a concise history of the state of legal research instruction as it existed nearly twenty-five years ago.

26. E-mail from Lamar Woodard, L. Libr. & Prof. L., Stetson Univ. College L., to Herb Cihak (Nov. 15, 1999).

27. Such a program existed at the University of Kentucky College of Law in 1971. *See* Kenneth B. Germain, *Legal Writing And Moot Court At Almost No Cost: The Kentucky Experience, 1971-1972,* 25 J. Legal Educ. 595 (1973).

28. I am referring to the suggestion that instruction be delayed until the second semester of the first year, or moved to the second year, after law students have framed

a context in which to place legal research. Dunn, *supra* note 3 at 64, favors a model that places legal research instruction in the week before fall classes begin.

29. The sequence of the articles is as follows: Christopher G. Wren & Jill Robinson Wren, *The Teaching of Legal Research,* 80 L. Libr. J. 7 (1988); Robert C. Berring & Kathleen Vanden Heuvel, *Legal Research: Should Students Learn It or Wing It?* 81 L. Libr. J. 431 (1989); Christopher G. Wren & Jill Robinson Wren, *Reviving Legal Research: A Reply to Berring and Vanden Heuvel,* 82 L. Libr. J. 463 (1990); and Robert C. Berring & Kathleen Vanden Heuvel, *Legal Research: A Final Response,* 82 L. Libr. J. 495 (1990).

30. During the past eight years, I have used one of three textbooks for my first-year legal research class: *Finding the Law, The Process of Legal Research,* and *Legal Research in a Nutshell.*

31. For a description of one interesting instructional method *see* Perry M. Goldberg & Marci Rothman Goldberg, *Putting Legal Research into Context: A Nontraditional Approach to Teaching Legal Research,* 86 L. Libr. J. 823 (1994).

32. A good article on PowerPoint usage has been written by Alison Sulentic, *Adventures in PowerPoint,* 7 L. Tchr, 1 (Fall 1999). I moved to PowerPoint in order to capture the interest of a varied group of adult learners. *See also* Eileen B. Cohen, *Teaching Legal Research to a Diverse Student Body,* 85 L. Libr. J. 583 (1993).

33. The instructional approach I utilize, including a script, is very similar to that proposed by Donald Dunn. *See* Dunn, *supra* note 3 at 64.

34. E-mail correspondence from Penny A. Hazelton, Professor of Law and Law Librarian, University of Washington, to Herb Cihak (Nov. 16, 1999). Professor Hazelton confirmed her opinion that since first-year law students will use CALR anyway, why not just "Teach them CALR whenever they want in the first year. . . . "

35. S. Blair Kauffman provides an early review of this topic in *Advanced Legal Research Courses: A New Trend in American Legal Education,* 6 Legal Reference Services Q. 123 (1986).

36. Goldberg & Goldberg, *supra* note 31 at 823, indicated that only a small percentage of law students could be accommodated with advanced legal research classes. I will be able to overcome this hurdle by offering my class to about one-third of the third-year class.

37. Joan S. Howland, *Survival in Cyberjungle,* Trends in L. Libr. Mgmt. & Tech., Apr. 1998, at 1.

38. For an informative address on this topic, *see* Morris L. Cohen, *Research in a Changing World of Law and Technology,* 13 Dalhousie L. J. 5 (1990).

39. Richard Warner et al. *Teaching Law with Computers,* 24 Rutgers Computer & Tech. L. J. 107, 110-13 (1998).

40. *See* Herbert E. Cihak, *Buying and Using Hardware & Software for Presentations,* Marketing Libr. Services, June 1996, at 5.

41. Two articles about this "smart building" were written by John Mayer: *Chicago-Kent's Smart Building: Using Technology to Enhance Legal Education, Part 1,* Trends in L. Libr. Mgmt. & Tech., Sept. 1991, at 1; *Chicago-Kent's Smart Building: Using Technology to Enhance Legal Education, Part 2,* Trends in L. Libr. Mgmt. & Tech., Oct. 1991, at 3.

42. These technological advancements were installed, in part, because the University of Kentucky College of Law agreed to house the Kentucky Prosecutor's Institute sponsored by the Kentucky Attorney General's office. This equipment is used by the institute for training one week per year.

43. Herbert E. Cihak, *Marketing CD-ROM and Other Electronic Library Services*, Computers in Libr., June 1997, at 73.

44. Terry Ballard, *Escape From the Tower,* Computers in Libr., Oct. 1999, at 71.

45. Librarians could take a cue from what Professor Peter Martin, of Cornell, has done with teaching via the Internet. *See* Steven Keeva's article about Martin, *Stars of the Classroom,* A.B.A. J., Dec. 1997, at 18.

46. It is encouraging that the ABA has been working on the development of guidelines for distance education, under the direction of Professor Arthur Gaudio of Wyoming. ABA Section of Legal Education and Admissions to the Bar, Distance Education Conference, "Distance Education: A Program of Law Professors Talking with Law Professors" (ABA, Nov. 1999).

47. *See* Harriet Richman & Steve Windsor, *Faculty Services: Librarian-Supervised Students as Research Assistants in the Law Library,* 91 L. Libr. J. 279 (1999), for details of their program at the University of Houston Law Center.

48. I am indebted to the late Colonel Harlan Sanders, of Kentucky Fried Chicken Fame, for providing me with some creative marketing insight. While on a 1995 tour of Sanders original Kentucky Fried Chicken Restaurant, at Corbin, Kentucky, I picked up a booklet entitled, "1990: A Year to Restore, a Year to Remember." I have tried to apply one bit of advice that Colonel Sanders gave in that booklet–"To grow you must innovate."

49. University of Kentucky College of Law Library support staff have also made presentations. Four of our law library support staff members (Janice Cox, Antoinette Fiske, Sharon Harrod and Heather Harbett) accompanied me to the Annual Conference of the Academic Library Association of Ohio, held at Columbus, Ohio, in November 1999, and to the COLT Convention in Chicago in July 2000. Parts of these presentations focused on the types of legal research instruction support staff gets involved in.

50. Examples of legal research centered presentations that I have made include: a CLE presentation at three sites in Kentucky entitled, "Kentucky Lawyers Online: The Internet and the Practice of Law"; a CLE presentation to the state government bar titled, "New Directions in Legal Research–Yesterday, Today and Tomorrow"; a presentation to our state library association called, "Electronic Library Resources: Using the Marketing Bridge"; a presentation to a regional library association conference (with Carol Parris) entitled, "Legal Research for Non-law Librarians: Tips, Tools, and Treasures"; and a national presentation to a computers and libraries conference titled, "Marketing Electronic Library Services." Other University of Kentucky law librarians have made presentations with a legal research bent. Shaun Esposito has made several presentations to medical librarians on the use of the Internet for legal research. Shaun Esposito and Kurt Metzmeier have also spoken at several CLEs dealing with ethical web use by attorneys. Dee Wood and Carol Parris have appeared before state library groups to present material about legislative histories in various

formats. Shaun Esposito and Carol Parris presented a well-received basic legal re-search skills program to the inmate trustees at La Grange, Kentucky.

Publications that I have authored with a teaching legal research focus include: "Reaching Through Teaching," "Marketing CD-ROM and other Electronic Library Services," and "The Changing World of Legal Research." Other University of Ken-tucky law librarians have published articles with a legal research basis. Kurt Metzmeier wrote: "Kentucky Legal Research on the Internet." Amy Osborne au-thored, "Internet Reviews: The U.S. House of Representatives Law Library." Dee Wood penned, "Easy Ways to Market Government Documents." Sue Burch and Ebba Jo Sexton published, "Library Laws of Kentucky." Kurt Metzmeier, Shaun Es-posito and Amy Osborne are working on a forthcoming book entitled, "Kentucky Legal Research."

51. Howland, *supra* note 37, at 2.

Teaching Legal Research
in a Government Library

Judith Meadows
Lisa Mecklenberg
Stephen Jordan

SUMMARY. Law libraries that serve the public have diverse clientele, types of reference and research requirements, and opportunities for contact that firm and academic law libraries seldom experience. This article explores these opportunities, which the authors take advantage of for providing a "teachable moment." *[Article copies available for a fee from The Haworth Document Delivery Service: 1-800-342-9678. E-mail address: <getinfo@ haworthpressinc.com> Website: <http://www.HaworthPress.com> © 2001 by The Haworth Press, Inc. All rights reserved.]*

The subtitle of this article could easily be the over-used term, "the teachable moment." In our library, we see almost every reference contact as an

---

Judith Meadows has been State Law Librarian of Montana since 1984. She has served in a number of leadership positions for the American Association of Law Libraries, including being President from 1997 to 1998. She received her MLS from the University of Maryland in 1979.

Lisa Mecklenberg, Electronic Services Librarian for the State Law Library of Montana since 1997, received her JD from the University of North Dakota in 1996 and her MLIS from the University of Washington in 1997.

Stephen Jordan received his JD from Memphis State University in 1980 and his MLS from the University of Tennessee in 1987. He was Reference Librarian for the State Law Library of Montana from 1988 to 1999, when he returned to Tennessee to work at Vanderbilt University School of Law as Reference Librarian.

[Haworth co-indexing entry note]: "Teaching Legal Research in a Government Library." Meadows, Judith, Lisa Mecklenberg, and Stephen Jordan. Co-published simultaneously in *Legal Reference Services Quarterly* (The Haworth Information Press, an imprint of The Haworth Press, Inc.) Vol. 19, No. 3/4, 2001, pp. 41-46; and: *Teaching Legal Research and Providing Access to Electronic Resources* (ed: Gary L. Hill, Dennis S. Sears, and Lovisa Lyman) The Haworth Information Press, an imprint of The Haworth Press, Inc., 2001, pp. 41-46. Single or multiple copies of this article are available for a fee from The Haworth Document Delivery Service [1-800-342-9678, 9:00 a.m. - 5:00 p.m. (EST). E-mail address: getinfo@haworthpressinc.com].

41

opportunity to teach something. The specific subjects are diverse: the legislative process, summary dissolution, arbitration rules, or how to use a keyboard's mouse. Our constant goal is to teach or show that libraries and librarians are still an integral part of today's commercial and legal arenas, and to demonstrate that a government agency can actually be a beneficial tax-supported institution.

A public law library, such as the State Law Library of Montana, differs from academic and firm libraries in many ways. The primary difference is that over half of our users are non-law trained. They are, however, highly motivated and deeply involved in their research issues, many of which apply directly to their daily lives. They might be seeking the correct papers to file for dissolution, exploring their options for remedy under the Montana Lemon Law, or trying to determine whether their mining claim is still valid. We do not work in a closed environment where we will have the same students for three years, or the same associates and paralegals for an even longer period. Granted, our judges and their law clerks have specific terms to fill. But they represent a very small portion of those who seek our assistance.

Our library's customers come from all walks of life. They are servicemen stationed overseas. They are grandparents fighting for visitation rights. Seeing state government workers searching for federal regulations is as common as seeing practicing attorneys from small firms looking up adoption procedures. Tax protesters, government protesters, and malcontents who are anti-everything are not uncommon customers. All types of people can come into the library. Or, more often than not, they access us remotely via telephone, fax or e-mail. Our web site generates a large portion of our business. People from all over Montana, and elsewhere, use it to access Montana Supreme Court decisions, the Montana Code, specific forms for the state, and a host of other resources.

The Clerks of Court from all of our judicial districts refer people to the State Law Library, as do the public libraries. We offer workshops for the public libraries in order to help them determine when they can provide reliable legal information or when they should refer their patrons to us. Several years ago we installed a toll-free telephone line for public libraries in order to make it more affordable for them and their patrons to reach us. In a large, basically rural state such as Montana that does not have a system of county law libraries, frequently the State Law Library is the only avenue available for those seeking legal information. With the loss of major funding for Legal Services, low-income citizens' access to the law has been reduced dramatically over the past several years. In order to address this crisis, we established a *pro bono* legal clinic in the law library a couple of years ago. In conjunction with this program, we help teach the state agency attorney volunteers family law and legal clinic procedures.

Taking into account all of the above, one of our biggest challenges is knowing when it is appropriate to actually teach someone a facet of legal research and when it is easier, or just more appropriate, to locate the relevant information ourselves and serve it up on a platter. We frequently don't know–and can't very well ask–when a customer is going to give us repeat business. However, we have discovered that often, if we help someone in a way which she deems as successful, that individual will come back to us the next time with a similar legal question. As we all know, this can be both a blessing and a burden–but we are doing what it is that we've been trained to do, which is helping people with their information needs.

The risk we have in simply answering a question or providing a form is that we trivialize what we do. If someone e-mails us a vague request for a speech presented to the United States Senate in the 1970s, and we then fax her the relevant pages from the Congressional Record, she has no idea how difficult it was to wade through the microfilmed indices to find what she wanted. But we'd be damned if we didn't do it. If we looked at a request like that and decided that it was beyond the scope of our service because of lack of a correct citation or the inordinate amount of time it will take to find the information, then we doom ourselves, as well as other librarians, to the growing pile of intermediaries who are no longer needed. And, more importantly, we have not helped our patron.

The structured classes that we offer at the State Law Library do not have the seasonal imperatives that private and academic libraries experience. Rather, our classes are taught periodically and on demand. Generally there is a prerequisite that each student a basic foundation in legal research. Thus, for many classes only attorneys, paralegals, and legal secretaries are taught.

For lay people, we recommend our publication, *A Guide to Montana Legal Research, 6th Edition, 1999*. This research guide is updated after every legislative session so that all statutory references are accurate. The *Guide* includes explanations of our state's court structure, how to locate opinions, an explanation of our previous and current statutory law sources, a selective legal bibliography for our state, and finding aids for sources of legal information. These include our library, the State Bar, and the law school in Missoula. The *Guide* is written for those who have had legal research training but do not know anything about Montana's specific legal structures and resources. However, a lay person can learn a great deal about process and procedure by using it.

Lay people present a special teaching challenge for us, particularly when we are assisting them via the Internet. On our web page[1] we have an e-mail link allowing people to ask us questions or offer input concerning the page. It is rare that we don't get at least one question per day. And the majority of those questions are from lay people. Typically, their questions can be answered by directing the individual to the Montana Code online. But directions, from us, have to be given as to how to find the Code on the Internet, and the best search terms to use when searching for the information in the Code. It is also not unusual for us to e-mail full cases to individuals who need them and do not have access to them through other means. We are now providing more and more Internet training on demand for customers who call in. The usual scenario is that they have their computers on, but in using the generic search browsers such as Yahoo, they can't find what they are looking for. We lead them through the process, encouraging them to start with our home page, and show them how to locate a specific web site. We then demonstrate for them how the search engine for something like the *United States Code* or the *Montana Code Annotated* works. In helping these remote users with their online reference questions, we are providing them with valuable information, which they can then use themselves the next time they have a similar question. We call this an "online teachable moment."

The formal classes we teach in the library include LEXIS and Westlaw (frequently presented by the companies' representatives), primary and secondary legal authority, legislative intent, legal research using CD-ROMs and the Internet, and lobbying protocols. Scope of coverage, Boolean searching, pricing options, and subject-specific issues are the focus of our Westlaw and LEXIS training. Montana does not have any state-based field representatives, which is the reason why we answer the occasional request for training. And people seem to be comfortable coming to us; a trend we try to encourage. We act as a liaison for a Montana-wide contract with both online vendors, so it could be that people see us as having especially developed knowledge of these products.

For teaching the use of CDs, our emphasis is on how to format a search based on the requirements of each specific product. Internet classes are designed for researchers doing work in specific fields, such as the environment. When holding Internet classes, we highlight our web site, and encourage Montana's researchers to use it as their home page. As our computer lab is quite small, we are forced to keep our electronic media classes limited in size. We discourage more than two students from using a workstation. And, of course, much of our "electronic" teaching is done one-on-one with an individual explaining to us what he is looking for and us showing him the quickest, easiest way to find that specific information, which is frequently online.

Manual research classes are held in our conference room. In teaching primary authority, we cover federal and state case law, statutes, administrative regulations, and sources that are used to find them. Secondary authority classes include topics such as legal encyclopedias, ALRs, legislative history, legal journals and periodicals, treatises, and looseleaf services. Many of our formal classes target state government employees. We notify the legal departments of upcoming classes by contacting the chief legal counsel for the agency and asking that the announcement be distributed among that department's legal staff. For attorneys and paralegals in the private sector, we post a sign-up sheet in the law library

We are also frequently asked to host legal research teaching sessions for college and secondary school students. We combine tours of the library with a brief explanation of the sources and structure of the law. We tailor these sessions to the educational level of the students and the instructional goals of the teachers. We have learned very painfully over the years that it is much easier for us to do the research instruction on the front-end than for us to mistakenly rely on the teacher to provide it. Too often we had students descending on us *en masse* a few days before their assignments were due and not having a clue as to how to proceed. This still happens to some extent; thus it becomes a one-on-one teachable moment.

For any of our formal classes, we draft an individual teaching plan, prepare and distribute handouts, and encourage questions and comments at any point during the class. We are very appreciative of the materials prepared by the American Association of Law Libraries' Research Instruction and Patron Services Section for the annual teach-in that is timed to coincide with Law Day. We invariably use most of these materials in some way, although it may not be in May.

Another method of teaching legal research we have employed has been instructing law firm administrators through distance education classes. This was begun before the advent of the web and involved videotaped lectures augmented by weekly classes conducted through telephone connections. It was not at all unusual to have eight sites participating simultaneously, spread around our large state, with hundreds of miles separating the instructor from the students. The challenge in teaching this way was that, except for the students in Great Falls, Missoula, and Helena, there is no access to a law library. As we all must remember from our reference classes in library school, it is the hands-on exposure to resources that determines how well students learn to use the tools, so this was far from an ideal situation.

If appropriate, we refer our in-library customers to the standard textbooks or guides to specific legal subject matter. One that we find particularly helpful for a lay person is *West's Encyclopedia of American Law*.[2] But often we have found that our average customer is driven by a specific transaction, such as how to "fill-in the blank": file a lien, change a name, etc. For attorneys who want a refresher, we spend an hour or two with them reviewing the sources of federal statutory law. If they don't know it because it bored them in law school, they certainly are not about to spend a quiet evening with *The Lawyer's Research Companion*[3] or even *Legal Research in a Nutshell*.[4]

These customers come to us because they trust us to (1) make it easy and understandable, and (2) keep it confidential that they could not pass "Go" in the game of Legal Research of the 21st Century.

We continually stress that one research source is not inherently better than another by explaining that the appropriate tool to be used will depend on the particular issue being researched. We feel this is especially important to emphasize given the growing prominence of electronic research and the tendency among so many younger researchers to rely solely on electronic tools even when print sources could be more beneficial.

Finally, we occasionally are asked to teach workshops for various legal organizations at their locations. The State Bar's Annual Meeting, local bar associations, paralegal groups, and legal secretaries have asked us to be the featured speaker at their monthly and annual meetings. We trot out our laptops, overhead projectors, transparencies, and the old fashioned books for historical humor, and hit the road. It is a very rare occasion that we decline a speaking opportunity. Each one, no matter who the audience is or what the topic might be, is an opportunity to advertise the strengths and talents of the law library's resources.

Teaching legal research in a public, government library is unique because you seldom know what you are going to be called on to teach or to whom you will teach it. Our staff is committed to doing the public good, and we believe that that means teaching and training any and all who come to us, through any means, how to access and use today's legal information. Accordingly, the opportunity for personally and professionally satisfying "teachable moments" is endless.

NOTES

1. *See* <www.lawlibrary.state.mt.us>.
2. West Group. *West's Encyclopedia of American Law* (1998).
3. *The Lawyer's Research Companion: A Concise Guide to Sources* (Joanne Zich & Gary McCann, eds., 1998).
4. Morris L. Cohen & Kent C. Olson, *Legal Research in a Nutshell* (6th ed.1996).

Teaching Legal Research in the Law Firm Library

Amy J. Eaton

SUMMARY. This article proposes several ways to initiate or update legal research training for attorneys in a law firm library. It is written from the perspective of the solo librarian and focuses on small, doable projects. Large-scale programs are introduced with some issues that need to be addressed by the librarian and the firm administration. *[Article copies available for a fee from The Haworth Document Delivery Service: 1-800-342-9678. E-mail address: <getinfo@haworthpressinc.com> Website: <http://www.HaworthPress.com> © 2001 by The Haworth Press, Inc. All rights reserved.]*

INTRODUCTION

Teaching legal research in a law firm library has been compared to herding cats. The "teachers" are librarians, knowledgeable about resources and often not formally trained to teach. The "students" are attorneys who are not required to take the class, who do not receive grades based on performance, and who have a strong incentive to use the time on billable tasks instead. As difficult as herding cats may be, the challenge of getting the attorneys to agree to come to the class, to actually show up, to stay in the class, and to pay attention as well makes herding cats seem preferable. Yet the plethora of information and resources available makes the teaching and training of attorneys critical to the law firm's success.

Amy Eaton, MLS, was, until recently, the Law Librarian at Stokes Lawrence, Seattle, WA. She is currently an independent contractor.

[Haworth co-indexing entry note]: "Teaching Legal Research in the Law Firm Library." Eaton, Amy J. Co-published simultaneously in *Legal Reference Services Quarterly* (The Haworth Information Press, an imprint of The Haworth Press, Inc.) Vol. 19, No. 3/4, 2001, pp. 47-54; and: *Teaching Legal Research and Providing Access to Electronic Resources* (ed: Gary L. Hill, Dennis S. Sears, and Lovisa Lyman) The Haworth Information Press, an imprint of The Haworth Press, Inc., 2001, pp. 47-54. Single or multiple copies of this article are available for a fee from The Haworth Document Delivery Service [1-800-342-9678, 9:00 a.m. - 5:00 p.m. (EST). E-mail address: getinfo@haworthpressinc.com].

Ten years ago the primary training concerns in law firm libraries revolved around the use of computer assisted legal resources. New associates needed to be taught about cost-effective research, and senior attorneys needed to be taught the advantages of the new systems. Although these issues still exist today, we also have to cover CD-ROM, the Internet, and a multitude of fee-based databases. Today's new associate may be a skilled Internet searcher but lack the means to use the West Digest system. Experienced attorneys are comfortable with the resources they use frequently but lack time to learn the new systems that may offer more. Legal research continues to be a patchwork of electronic and print sources. It is the librarian's job to make sure training is provided that will meet the needs of the firm's attorneys.

Teaching and training have been recurring topics on the law librarians' listserv, law-lib, as well as in newsletters and journals. After reviewing many of the published articles, I checked the archives on law-lib back through June 1998. Topics ranged from how to structure a class to how to draw an audience. I then posted a message on law-lib asking for a brief description of the training programs firms are currently using. I received many responses that had specific, helpful information. I will include some of the examples below. This paper will be a practical demonstration of some of the possible ways a training program can be established or updated in your library.

TRAINING GOALS

The firm librarian has two goals in mind when she begins a training program. First is to teach the users how to best use the available resources. Second is to demonstrate the unique skills of the library staff. An effective training program will do both. Part of fulfilling these goals is monitoring new resources, which includes evaluating how a product will fit a particular firm's needs, informing attorneys of the availability of the product, and, once acquired, training them to use the new resource. Further, once a product is acquired, librarians should regularly remind the attorneys that the source is in the library.

Point-of-Need Training

In the law firm environment, the attorney needs to understand very specific issues. Thus, unlike the academic world, firm librarians don't usually spend time covering all aspects of an issue. We want to solve a defined problem. It is in the client's best interest to limit the time spent on research and to do what is needed to find the resources that will address the attorney's particular problem. We commonly find ourselves introducing attorneys to new resources at their point-of-need. Sometimes called the "teachable moment," such point-of-need contact gives us the opportunity to teach when the attorney most needs the information. Retention will be higher when the resource is actually used for a specific problem.

Although large law firm libraries are more likely to offer structured training programs, the librarians still find point-of-need training to be the most effective. It is, however, time consuming, and individual librarians may find their time monopolized by individual attorneys. In order to alleviate this problem, some firms assign subject area specialties to the library staff. If an attorney needs help learning how to find intellectual property information on the Internet, then the librarian with that expertise will provide assistance. Another method used is to have one librarian specialize in desktop training. The proactive trainer will meet frequently with individual attorneys to review Westlaw and LEXIS research strategies, review the available CD-ROM products and cover new Internet resources.

In small law firm libraries, point-of-need training is often the only training the solo librarian can manage. The librarian does it all: check-in, routing, invoices, budget control, cataloging, reference, and training. He must always be available to answer reference questions and provide assistance using the resources. At my current firm, with thirty attorneys, my three-day workweeks are stretched to the fullest, and it is not feasible to develop and schedule a range of training courses. Instead I rely on the help of vendors and try to meet with each practice group annually. At the practice group meetings, I use the opportunity to cover supplementation costs, efficient use of Westlaw and LEXIS, and the best Internet resources for that specific group. Although these meetings do not teach everything there is to know, they do help the attorneys become aware of some of the research tools and techniques available. If nothing else, attorneys trained in this way will call me and say that they cannot remember what it was, but didn't I mention a resource that might help them with this project? The net result is not only effective library marketing but also another opportunity to teach about a new resource.

Another challenge facing the solo librarian during point-of-need training is leaving the library unstaffed (and therefore empty) while assisting an attorney in his or her office. My library has an extra PC for attorneys to use while doing research, so, if possible, I train the attorneys on this PC so that I may be available for walk-in assistance. However, there are attorneys who function much better at their desks, and I find the training is more successful if we can do it in their environment. This also helps me uncover any installation or printing problems that might otherwise be unaddressed. I rely heavily on our receptionist to inform people where I might be found when I am not in my office. This helps promote the library without walls concept and yet lets users know I will soon be available. I also find that as I walk around the firm, I am frequently stopped to assist individuals with search questions. Proponents of "Management by Walking Around" suggest that time spent in informal interaction is key to the success of the manager. In a like fashion, I suspect that "Training by Walking Around" may be one of the most effective methods for the solo librarian.

Formal Legal Research Training

Structured classes are the most common form of formal legal research training in law firms. The classes range from brief overviews to detailed reviews and cover all manner of topics. The initial teaching usually occurs during the attorney's orientation. The prevailing theory is that if you can train the first-year associate to use the library efficiently, you will have a library supporter for life. A typical orientation includes a detailed tour of the library including a map of the collection layout and an overview of the classification system. Basic procedures should be explained including how to check out books, make copies, and contact the reference desk. A quick introduction to secondary resources is also helpful. To make the orientation an active session, the session should include walking around the library as collection highlights are pointed out, lots of eye contact with the attorneys, and frequent smiles. A key objective of the tour is to make the new attorneys comfortable enough that they will not hesitate to ask for help the next time they come into the library.

I rarely touch on Westlaw and LEXIS searching during this first meeting. The effectiveness of the orientation session is lost if too much information is given at once. Instead I set up a second meeting, one on one, when I give them their passwords and discuss the specific costs of each service. I usually have a series of cheat sheets to distribute that demonstrate the varying costs of each service and when to use which password. I also schedule individual sessions with the appropriate vendor representatives before they are permitted to use their passwords. After attorneys or paralegals join the firm, I review their online bills very closely for a few months. If I notice any problems, I bring it to their attention immediately. As a rule, everyone appreciates it. They would much rather hear from me and approach the assigning partner directly than hear about it when the client bills are submitted.

Some firms have a more structured approach. Incoming associates are required to attend training sessions of one to two hours. These sessions review where to find codes, regulations, and cases, and how to use the digest system and Shephard's. Other classes may focus on secondary tools and major looseleaf services. Often, sample research questions are handed out and the associates are required to complete the exercises. If you can get the classes scheduled before new associates or paralegals are given particular assignments, they have the time and energy to participate. They are still eager to learn about the firm, and this may be your single best opportunity to train them.

The largest firms sometimes have computer training labs where attorney/student and librarian/teacher can meet for formal classes. Such labs offer each trainee a hands-on experience and greatly increase the participation rate. However, this classroom setting is not without drawbacks. An inexperienced student can create havoc if the teacher stops to help him catch up. When possible, having a teaching assistant available can allow the teacher to move on while the assistant helps the "lost" searcher. The ready availability of the online resource may tempt some students to tune out during portions of the class that do not apply to them directly. Keeping the class focused and together is a continual challenge to the teacher. Professional trainers often break the training sessions into discrete portions. At the end of each section, a small exercise is given to the students. This gives the teacher an opportunity to provide additional help to those who need it, while the others move ahead and reinforce the concepts learned through the exercises. Of course, as always in a law firm, any break will permit the attorneys to leave "just to check voice mail" and not return.

If librarians elect to develop a strong orientation program, it is critical that they receive the support of firm management. If the programs are not fully supported by management, the associates will quickly lose interest as they become involved in billable projects. The training will be lost in the chaos of the first week if attendance is not required or if appropriate time is not allotted to the new associates. Management must also give librarians time and support to prepare and conduct the sessions. If they are under a billable hour quota, this needs to be adjusted to reflect the time spent teaching and training. Without management support, a formal orientation program will fail.

Although many firm librarians have orientation training sessions in place, few continue with a training program throughout the year. Demands on the librarian's time contribute to the demise of training, but generally the reason training falters is the tight time constraints under which the experienced attorney labors. To provide ongoing training, librarians must face this primary challenge. As one librarian mentioned to me, it is difficult to overcome the "incredibly-valuable-worth-five-times-as-much-as-yours-time" modus operandi of many attorneys. There are several ways to handle this. First, if you can arrange to obtain CLE credit for your classes, do so. This will certainly increase attendance. Secondly, try developing mini-sessions limited to specific practice areas. Offer the sessions early in the morning or over lunchtime. Provide food and you are sure to have increased participation. Whenever possible, be flexible. If last minute cancellations frustrate you, remember that the attorney's day is often not her own. I frequently tie ten-to-fifteen minute sessions in with departmental meetings. In that short period of time, I can demonstrate several great Internet sites, discuss new books or periodicals we have added to the collection, or mention new developments on Westlaw and LEXIS. Our departmental meetings require all attorneys within that group to attend, and I find my brief snippets of information well received.

External Training Resources

If a staff is stretched to the fullest, librarians might look outside the library for session leaders. Some firms have experienced attorneys participate in the training sessions. This has many benefits including helping establish relationships between the newer and more experienced attorneys and strengthening relationships between the librarians and the attorneys. If an attorney recently taught at a CLE seminar, ask him to give a shortened version of his presentation to new associates and paralegals. Look to the local bar associations for help. Our bar association offers one-hour seminars at noon. I attend those sessions and report back to our attorneys.

Take advantage of opportunities that arise, even if time is short. For example, one Seattle firm's management invited the library to participate in teaching Internet skills at the firm-wide partner retreat. Along with other administrative departments, librarians were asked to prepare a training session to be offered to the spouses while the attorneys attended morning meetings as well as a second class for the attorneys in the afternoon. Two librarians and the firm webmaster teamed to meet the challenging task of designing and creating multiple classes for diverse audiences. They found that, while the subject and site content differed widely, the core skills for Internet proficiency were the same for attorneys and spouses alike. By changing the class's subject and site content to appeal to the target audience, two general classes were expanded to four audience-pleasing sessions that offered both essential skills and useful sites for research. This unique opportunity had two serendipitous results. First, it demonstrated the skills and expertise of the library staff to a group who seldom uses the library directly. Secondly, by offering a class to the spouses, it also reached those partners who did not attend the afternoon session. The spousal class was well received and commented upon.

Many of us rely on vendors to help with our training programs. For the pay-per-use services like Westlaw and LEXIS, this is a necessity; otherwise the librarian spends firm money to train on these services. There are both advantages and disadvantages to this system. The vendor representatives are expert searchers and provide free on-site training, often at the attorneys' convenience. Some services (for example, Courtlink) also provide CLE credit for on-site courses. A Portland, Oregon, librarian reported to me that she was able to obtain CLE credit for a presentation by a BNA tax attorney. The class was well attended, and the attorneys received an easy CLE credit.

When dealing with vendors librarians may occasionally encounter a heavy-handed sales approach, insufficient knowledge of research techniques, or poor teaching style. When any of these occur, librarians should not hesitate to call the regional manager. In my experience, it is often possible to get a different sales representative. I also follow the vendors' presentations with my own comments and use the opportunity to compare services or resources.

Librarians should use contract negotiations with Westlaw and LEXIS to improve their local training or representation. When I joined my current small firm, I found that we were not eligible for free on-site training. When contract negotiations came up, I made that a requirement of the new contract. Even if a firm has a flat rate contract, it is critical to keep attorneys trained and efficient researchers. When contract renewal approaches, costs will be lower if the firm's gross rates have stayed within reasonable limits.

Library Publications

Written materials continue to have a place within the training program of a law firm library. These materials may be posted on the firm intranet or printed on paper and distributed by the library. They may include pathfinders, practice area guides, or a librarian's PowerPoint demonstrations. Thus, every time a librarian leads a brown-bag session and uses PowerPoint, she should subsequently load the presentation on the firm intranet. If the firm has a newsletter, the librarian might ask to have a column and use this to introduce research tips or nifty new web pages. I e-mail Westlaw tips as I discover them and send out a weekly "Fun Web Page of the Week" message. Heavy Westlaw and Internet users set up folders and save my tips. I could also load them on the intranet with other library research tips. Cheat sheets are a favorite in my firm. I have found that they should be highly focused and easy to read. I cover only one topic on each sheet and use color or tabs to organize them. Some of my most requested topics are–Transactional or Hourly Pricing: Which Should I Use?; Finding a Known Citation; and Document Delivery Services. The cheat sheets are particularly helpful since I work part-time and am a solo librarian.

Evaluating Training

Qualifying the success of a training program can be difficult. After training attorneys on a new service, librarians should watch usage numbers to see if they increase. They should also ask themselves, "Am I receiving more questions about the new service?" If so, then they can consider their training session a success. After running a training program for a year, librarians should consider sending out a user satisfaction survey to find out if the program is perceived as being successful. I found that the attorneys at my firm rate the one-on-one training as excellent but give the vendor training a much lower rating. As a result of this response, I set a goal for the next year to improve our vendor training.

CONCLUSION

Teaching legal research in the law firm library is not a linear process. I like to think of it more as a spiral. We often touch on the same point many different times and many different ways. The varying methods reach each attorney according to his or her learning style and his or her point-of-need. Like most library related tasks, teaching legal research is never finished. There is no point when a librarian can cross it off her list of "to-do" items. Instead, her ongoing focus on establishing a continuing, positive relationship with her attorneys will create learning opportunities for them and library marketing opportunities for her.

Perspectives on Teaching Foreign and International Legal Research

Jean Davis
Victoria Szymczak
Katherine Topulos
Stefanie Weigmann

SUMMARY. This article discusses various models for teaching international and foreign legal research. In some law schools, international and foreign legal research is a semester-long course. In other law schools, international and foreign legal research is a component of an advanced legal research seminar or an international law course. Stefanie Weigmann presents an overview of teaching international legal research and describes her experience teaching in various formats. Katherine Topulos outlines some of the resources that are helpful for those who want to begin teaching foreign and international legal research. Jean Davis and Victoria Szymczak discuss teaching techniques and class activities for a semester-long course. *[Article copies available for a fee from The Haworth Document Delivery Service: 1-800-342-9678. E-mail address: <getinfo@ haworthpressinc.com> Website: <http://www.HaworthPress. com> © 2001 by The Haworth Press, Inc. All rights reserved.]*

Jean Davis is Reference Librarian, International Law Specialist, and Adjunct Associate Professor of Law at Brooklyn Law School

Victoria Szymczak is Electronic Information Specialist and Adjunct Associate Professor of Law at Brooklyn Law School.

Katherine Topulos is Foreign and International Law Librarian and Lecturing Fellow at Duke University School of Law.

Stephanie Weigmann is Reference Librarian in Foreign and International Law at Harvard Law School. At the time of this writing, she was Reference Librarian at the Pappas Law Library, Boston University School of Law.

[Haworth co-indexing entry note]: "Perspectives on Teaching Foreign and International Legal Research." Davis, Jean et al. Co-published simultaneously in *Legal Reference Services Quarterly* (The Haworth Information Press, an imprint of The Haworth Press, Inc.) Vol. 19, No. 3/4, 2001, pp. 55-69; and: *Teaching Legal Research and Providing Access to Electronic Resources* (ed: Gary L. Hill, Dennis S. Sears, and Lovisa Lyman) The Haworth Information Press, an imprint of The Haworth Press, Inc., 2001, pp. 55-69. Single or multiple copies of this article are available for a fee from The Haworth Document Delivery Service [1-800-342-9678, 9:00 a.m. - 5:00 p.m. (EST). E-mail address: getinfo@haworthpressinc.com].

TEACHING INTERNATIONAL LEGAL RESEARCH
IN A LAW SCHOOL

Stefanie Weigmann

The teaching of international law has entered the mainstream of the law school curriculum slowly; indeed its proper role is still being discussed.[1] The general perception is that students, as future lawyers, would benefit from exposure to international law. The Dean of Southern Methodist University School of Law has said that "[s]ervicing the global community will require new approaches for practicing law and for training lawyers."[2] International law courses, however, are still moving toward complete acceptance: a recent ABA survey found that while law schools are increasing their offerings, students have not been taking complete advantage of those offerings.[3] The ABA perspective is that all law students should have some familiarity with both public and private aspects of international law. In the midst of this debate about the teaching of international law, it is hardly surprising that the teaching of international legal research–which involves teaching students about international and foreign legal resources–has been largely ignored.

International legal research is now at the stage traditional legal research was thirty years ago. At that time legal research was taught haphazardly, with much of the instruction taking place informally within the context of orientation to the library.[4] As traditional legal research instruction entered the formal law school curriculum, such instruction moved outside of the influence of the library. Some believe that legal research should have stayed in the library and should be taught by librarians. Arthur Miller, a Harvard Law School professor and advocate of law librarians, has said librarians should be teaching legal research.[5] Building on his remarks, I believe that the teaching of international legal research should be the responsibility of librarians and is best situated in the formal curriculum of the law school.

The teaching of international legal research fits naturally into the ambit of libraries with significant international curricula and library holdings. These libraries will have a reference librarian who specializes in international and foreign reference. Students, especially if there is an international journal at the law school, have many questions regarding treaties, United Nations documents, and European Union documents. Most researchers who do not specialize in international law have only a vague idea of how to go about researching an international law topic.[6] Reference librarians are ideally situated to teach international legal research because they are required to familiarize themselves with the resources available in a library and on the Internet in a systematic way and across many subject areas to help their patrons. At the moment, librarians also appear to be the only group interested in international legal research instruction. Most law school legal research courses never touch any aspect of the sources of international law, including the teaching of treaty research–an important part of U.S. law. Librarians should take the current situation, with librarians as the primary instructors of international legal research, and formalize that role making instruction in this area a permanent part of the role of every foreign and international reference librarian.

A survey of how international legal research is currently taught at various law schools shows a range of instructional models. Many law schools offer subject-specific instruction, such as researching the law of the European Union or researching United Nations documents. These are offered as individual sessions either through the library or in conjunction with a particular substantive course and are not reflected in the formal curriculum. For example, every year two professors at Boston University Law School asked me to present research sessions in their courses on refugee and asylum law and EU law. Both of these courses require a research paper, and the professors felt that they got better papers when the students understood research in these areas. This is a useful means of research instruction because it provides the students with a context; however, it has two significant drawbacks: it relies on the interest and cooperation of the professor, and it is not systematic. An alternative model is seen in schools that offer international legal research as a component of advanced legal research.[7] Examples of these include: Cardozo School of Law, Yale Law School, Fordham University School of Law, Northwestern University School of Law, and Cornell Law School. Some of these schools require advanced legal research for all upper-class students while others offer it as an elective. The advantage of including such instruction in an advanced legal research class required for all upper-class students is that all students get some exposure to international legal research. Finally, some law schools offer courses in international legal research for credit. These include the University of Washington School of Law,[8] Harvard Law School,[9] Brooklyn Law School,[10] Duke University School of Law,[11] University of Houston Law Center,[12] Boston University School of Law,[13] and the University of Virginia School of Law.[14] Librarians teach all of these courses.

My own experience of introducing instruction in international legal research at Boston University Law School followed an evolutionary path. First, I was asked to teach an international legal research component of an advanced legal research course. Then, having had that experience, I thought that students would be interested in improving their research skills and offered open sessions on particular topics. Next, the law school approved a stand-alone three-credit international legal research course, which I taught. The following year this course was integrated into a substantive international law course. This evolution from one class to a full course was interesting and taught me a number of things about how research, particularly international legal research, is best taught.

As a component of an advanced legal research course, the teaching of "international legal research" is a misnomer. Because the time the teacher is allotted–one lecture–is so limited, she is forced to choose a subject to present. Should she teach treaty research, certainly the most useful thing for students to learn, or should she teach something else? I opted to teach a problem-based class in an attempt to show students what international and foreign questions they might encounter in day-to-day practice. The advantage to this approach is that students can see the potential relevance of the lecture to their future work. It is not hard to think of situations in day-to-day practice where a student might encounter a treaty or need to understand the law of a foreign jurisdiction. I used a child abduction case where the non-custodial parent takes the child to another jurisdiction. I demonstrated in the class how this problem could be approached from a research perspective. The problem with this approach is that there is too much material for such a short period. To actually instill in students a sense of the tools available and a research methodology would require much more time. So, given the limited amount of time available in a single advanced legal research session, it might be best to focus on treaty research. Most students will encounter at least one treaty in their careers, and if they do not take an international law course, they may never even hear the word "treaty" mentioned in any of their other legal courses.

The next format, research lectures offered to students on a voluntary basis, was more or less a failure. The bottom line is that no one is going to take a research course unless he has to. Law students have enough work to do and generally do not see the value in building up their research skills. I, myself, only realized the importance of research once I was actually practicing law. I offered a series of lectures focusing on treaties, the UN, the WTO, commercial arbitration and the EU, some of which supplemented courses offered at Boston University Law School. Attendance was poor even where I tried to get the professor who taught the substantive course to announce my course in his classes. I realized that without a formal link to those courses or an independent mechanism for compelling attendance, there would be little point to the sessions, so I approached my director and asked him to lobby the administration for a course on international legal research. He did so happily and was successful. I presented a proposal together with a syllabus developed with the help of Virginia Wise who has taught international legal research at Harvard as an independent course for a number of years. The proposal was approved, and I proceeded to develop the course.

The course was a success overall; the only drawbacks were that the students taking the course were all third-year students, and there were only seven of them. Third-year students are less likely to need a library-centered course for research papers than second year students, so the value of a course that deals with some of the more esoteric subjects–like customary international law–is limited if only directed at third-year students. The course itself was two-and-a-half hours a week. Weekly readings, five problem sets, three writing assignments, and a presentation were required. Over the course of the semester, I introduced researching multilateral treaties, researching bilateral treaties of which the U.S. is a party, customary and other sources of international law, the United Nations, human rights (as an example of UN research plus that of other international entities), trade law, international litigation and arbitration, international business, the EU, common law jurisdictions, and civil law jurisdictions. I attempted to cover all of the sources of public international law, some of the major international institutions, some aspects of private international law, the EU as an example of regional integration, and provide some sense of researching foreign jurisdictions. Students commented that they felt they gained an understanding of the structure inherent in the international system as well as some knowledge of how to research questions with an international dimension.

Although the full-fledged course had many advantages over my earlier attempts, it also presented problems. Because international, foreign, and comparative legal research is an area not taught in the traditional legal research curriculum, there is no textbook. I found that many of the materials I wanted to use could only be reproduced at great expense. Therefore, I put those readings with copyright protection on reserve and created a course pack for those materials without copyright protection. A few publications might serve as textbooks. For example, NYU Law Library's 1998 publication, *An Accidental Tourist on the New Frontier*, covers a number of topics one might want to include in an international legal research course. The books generated from the AALL-sponsored institutes on foreign and international law can also be reproduced and used as a group to cover quite a number of research areas.[15] The teacher of a free-standing three-credit course, for example, can comfortably assign readings that cost $50 plus; however, if she teaches a one-credit course or integrates her course into another class that also assigns books, she needs to have a text available that is less than $50. What is needed is a textbook, complete with problems and with the structure of a traditional legal research course book that can be used to teach international legal research.

Which leads to the next problem–how to ensure that students get practice in the skills they are learning. A problem set, questions created with the purpose of using important research tools, is time consuming to create. Ideally, a problem set is centered on an interesting area of research, uses all the relevant resources, and takes a certain amount of time for the students to finish. Other courses use other models: students can be assigned a pathfinder, forcing them to think of the uses of resources; or there can be an exam. In one of my classes, I gave writing assignments where the students started with only a fact pattern. All of these models have their drawbacks: problem sets are repetitive and can be uninteresting; pathfinders do not force the students to use the materials; exams mean the students need never even touch the materials; and writing assignments can be confusing and difficult to grade. Some combination of these models would be ideal, and a good textbook could touch all the bases.

The other problems I encountered were traditional research course problems: generating class discussion and integrating the readings. Because there is no textbook in this area, I focused most of my energy on covering the large amounts of material I was trying to include and devoted little attention to teaching methods that would involve the students more. Helpful in this regard is the portion of this article written by Jean Davis and Victoria Szymczak, which focuses on the methods they have used in teaching international legal research.

My course evolved one step further. Because I felt that the course was not reaching the students who were most likely to do research in this area, the second-year students on the *Journal of International Law,* and because I hoped to get a larger number of students, I approached a professor who teaches a substantive international law course. We joined his substantive law class and my research class with the intention that it became a requirement for those journal students who had not taken international law in the first year. We proposed our course to the administration, and it was accepted. Our four-credit course met three times a week, and I had the students on one of those days for one hour and twenty minutes. While this format was not completely satisfactory because the substance and research portions of the class functioned independently, it could work quite well with a true introductory class.

The ideal with regard to international legal research is that it continue to be taught by librarians who have an interest in maximizing the use of the collections in their libraries. To legitimize the study of international legal research, however, it needs to be integrated into the formal law school curriculum as a full-credit course. Having one lecture in an advanced legal research course is not adequate. To ensure student participation, it should be either a required portion of a substantive international law course, or required of all students on international journals or participating in an international moot court competition. Finally, some effort should be made to put together a course book complete with problems so that such a course could be taught without the work of improvising an entire syllabus and all the practical course work. Given the extensive offerings of international law at many law schools and the increase of international law journals, there is clearly a need for systematic instruction in researching international law.

HOW TO GET STARTED TEACHING FOREIGN AND INTERNATIONAL LEGAL RESEARCH

Katherine Topulos

You are faced with the prospect of teaching international and foreign legal research for the first time, either an entire course or several lectures in an advanced legal research class. Where do you begin? This section of the article is based on my experiences teaching a semester-long course meeting once a week on research methods in international, foreign, and comparative law. The class is required for students pursuing an LL.M. degree in international and comparative law at Duke Law School. When such a course is taught for a full semester, there is ample opportunity to cover a wide range of international and foreign legal research topics, from treaties to the European Union, from comparative law to international arbitration. Not so when the teacher is limited to giving a few lectures as part of a larger course and must make decisions about what topics to include based on the rest of the curriculum and student interest.

The course begins with classes on researching international law (how to find treaties, the law of international organizations, etc.), followed by classes on comparative and foreign legal research, and ends with classes on international business transactions and dispute settlement. These last two topics help students pull together research strategies they have learned during the semester because they involve researching a variety of materials, from treaties to the regulations of international organizations (such as the World Trade Organization) to the laws of other jurisdictions.

I used the classic definition of the sources of international law from the Statute of the International Court of Justice as a framework for planning the curriculum. (I was lucky I had the syllabi and advice of my predecessors at Duke to guide me.) Article 38(1) of the Statute states that disputes submitted to the court should be decided by applying treaties, international customs, general principles of law, judicial decisions, and the teachings of international law scholars.[16]

We devote a class early in the semester to learning how to research treaties and other international agreements, the first source in the Statute. Students learn about U.S. sources (such as *Treaties in Force*), multinational sources (like the *United Nations Treaty Series*), and prepare a short treaty-finding exercise for class.

The next source of international law listed in the Statute is international custom, in other words, rules that are derived from the general practices of states and international bodies. International practices are documented in a wide variety of sources, including international and national judicial decisions, state papers, and the documents of international organizations (such as resolutions of the U.N. General Assembly). Classes designed to teach students how to find this information include sessions on U.S. practice in international law (focusing on publications from the Department of State) and the law of international organizations (focusing on the United Nations and the European Union).

The third source of international law listed in the ICJ Statute is general principles common to the major domestic legal systems (for example, the notion of procedural due process). Classes on comparative law in general, as well as on researching specific legal systems, teach students where to find legal materials from other jurisdictions. In addition, students do short (fifteen minute) presentations on the law of a foreign jurisdiction; the presentations include an overview of the legal system, an explanation of the students' research strategies, and the most important sources (in print and electronic formats) a researcher would use to learn about this jurisdiction.

Judicial decisions and teachings of international law scholars are the final sources listed in the Statute. Judicial decisions include those of both international and national courts. In classes on selected international organizations and on foreign and comparative legal research, the students learn how to find decisions of various international tribunals, such as the International Court of Justice and the European Court of Justice (the courts of the U.N. and E.U.) and decisions of national courts (e.g., England and France).

The writings of international law scholars are useful research aids as well as sources of international law. They are especially useful starting points for international legal research. They not only discuss legal issues, but they often provide references to the sources of international law–important since international law is not conveniently indexed and organized.

Secondary sources are good starting points for foreign legal research as well. They explain the basic arrangement of a legal system so researchers will know where to look for the documents they need and be able to understand their significance once found. Secondary sources in the vernacular will acquaint researchers with the specialized legal vocabulary they will need to do research successfully. Included on the research guides I hand out in class are the titles of some of the most important treatises for each subject, along with advice for finding others (such as the most efficient subject searches in the online catalog).

Students need to know that they should not limit themselves to the law library when researching international and foreign law. To teach them about other resources on the Duke campus, we visit the international documents collection in our main library. That library is a depository for the U.S. and the European Union and has a comprehensive collection of U.N. documents. I also introduce them to less obvious resources on campus, especially "people" resources. For example, I tell them about bibliographers with area specialties, such as East Asian, Slavic, and Latin American studies, who can help them with their research projects.

Assignments are designed to teach students to use both print and electronic sources. This year there were several ungraded exercises that we went over in class, including three document-finding exercises designed to teach students to find treaties, U.N., and E.U. publications. The graded assignments included two short projects, an evaluation of the web site of an international organization, a class presentation on a foreign legal system, and an annotated bibliography (about ten to fifteen pages) on some aspect of international law or about a foreign legal system. The final paper was organized into three sections: a concise abstract of the topic, a discussion of research methodology, and an annotated bibliography of sources. Students enjoy the chance for class participation and the opportunity to work on topics that we do not cover in class.

A new teacher of international and foreign legal research should not attempt to reinvent the wheel. There are many resources that can help the novice learn about the most useful tools for foreign and international legal research as well as help him or her to design a syllabus. During the 1990s, the American Association of Law Libraries (AALL) sponsored a series of five institutes designed to train foreign and international law librarians. The institutes focused on a variety of topics, from foreign and international law to transnational legal transactions and international business law. Each institute was memorialized by a book with articles written by instructors at the institute.[17] These books provide a brief overview of the substantive issues as well as a wealth of bibliographical sources.

Another resource is the Teaching Foreign, Comparative and International Legal Research Interest Group of the Foreign, Comparative and International Law Special Interest Section (FCIL-SIS) of AALL. This group, which provides a forum for exchanging ideas about teaching international and foreign legal research, meets each year during the AALL annual meeting to talk about what works (and what does not), share activities and exercises that have been particularly effective, and discuss common problems and issues. Members range from directors to new librarians, and everyone interested in the subject is welcome to attend the meetings. The FCIL-SIS member, Christine Corcos, Associate Professor of Law at the LSU Law Center, has created a web page that includes both syllabi and research guides for international, foreign and comparative law research.[18]

TEACHING TECHNIQUES AND ACTIVITIES
FOR AN INTERNATIONAL
AND FOREIGN LAW RESEARCH SEMINAR

Jean Davis
Victoria Szymczak

The Davis and Szymczak Credo: Master your material. Be a dynamic, entertaining speaker. Encourage class participation. Use hypotheticals featuring your students. Devise group exercises and gaming activities.

The Students' Credo: Snacks are *good!*

Our International and Foreign Law Research seminar requires each student's active involvement. We engage pupils through various teaching techniques, including visits to large research libraries, presentations by seminar participants, guest lectures by energetic colleagues, and our popular, interactive games.[19]

Guidelines for Assignments

In Fall 2000, we required mid-semester presentations on foreign legal systems and end-of-term research guides on international organizations. In our 1998, 1999 and 2000 IFLR seminars, students understood and ably performed these requirements. The key–post instructional guidelines for each assignment on your course page. If possible, train student assistants to hold "office hours" in the library's IFLR collection during the weeks preceding project deadlines. (Anticipate temporary lulls in patrons and assign the student worker a research task, such as evaluating new acquisitions for a bibliography.)

Tours of Research Libraries

Before this semester's presentations on foreign legal systems, our class toured New York University School of Law Library. Mirela Roznovschi and Jeanne Rehberg highlighted subject-oriented sets covering many jurisdictions and sources focusing on students' countries. We asked students to compare the print *Tax and Commercial Laws of the World* (available at New York University School of Law) to *Foreign Tax and Commercial Laws on CD-ROM* (available at Brooklyn Law School). Students also searched the online version of the *Index to Foreign Legal Periodicals: A Subject Index to Selected International and Comparative Law Periodicals and Collections of Essays.* Following the tour, we remained and as students used this opportunity to evaluate hard-to-find materials on their jurisdictions. As a result, students who returned to New York University School of Law Library throughout the semester were more confident researchers.

Student Presentations

Prior to addressing the class, Fall 2000 students attended and *enjoyed* a Corel Presentations training session led by Brooklyn Law School's software trainer, Barry Reichman. He taught the students how to create slide shows, to link Internet sites to slides, and to add graphics and sounds to slides. We will invite Barry to return for a 2001 command performance.

Building on their training, most students chose to create slides on re-searching a legal topic in a foreign jurisdiction. Displaying slides and linking to web sites is time-consuming. In the classes preceding presentations, instructors must emphasize that each student will have only fifteen minutes to speak. If the most useful web site is inaccessible, the presentation goes on. If a student's laptop freezes, the presentation continues. We frequently remind students: "*You* are your own best visual!" Our warnings pay off. When the library laptop crashed as one student linked from a slide to the *Europa* web site, this student directed the audience to a photocopy of the web page and continued his analysis. Meanwhile, Victoria addressed the technology problem.

If students wish to use their laptops for presentations, insist that they (1) schedule advance appointments to test equipment and slides in the class-room and (2) arrive twenty minutes prior to the designated class to conduct a final run-through. On presentation dates, schedule these students first, or im-mediately after a mid-class break. You do not want to lose class time as they set up. Some students might prefer to distribute handouts and to display a few web sites with the library's equipment. In advance, require these students to submit the Internet addresses. Bookmark the sites on the library's laptop.

Guest Speakers

Invite guest speakers to address your class. Tempt speakers with dining adventures to follow their appearances. This semester, Jeanne Rehberg, Spe-cial Assistant to the Director/Reference Librarian for International and For-eign Law at New York University School of Law Library,[20] illustrated GATT/WTO research with Internet and depository sources. Students were thrilled to meet the editor of their textbook, *Accidental Tourist on the New Frontier: An Introductory Guide to Global Legal Research*.[21] In fall 1999, Kate McLeod, Associate Law Librarian for Public Services at Fordham Uni-versity School of Law Library, honed our pupils' European Union research skills.[22] Emphasize that students must prepare for classes featuring guest lecturers. We take note of and commend pupils who interact with a visiting information professional. We also credit active class participation.

Library Exercises

Course evaluations reveal that students expect a research seminar to begin with a library tour and to include many "hands-on" exercises throughout the semester. Students prefer to prowl the stacks when completing exercises, but this might not be feasible if one has a large enrollment. This semester, Victoria conducted a Canadian legal research exercise in the library's foreign law collection area. Students used the *Canadian Abridgment* to "note up" a case and to find articles on international trade. Weeks in advance, Victoria posted notices in the library announcing the upcoming session and warning of possible disruptions.

In our Fall 2000 opening class, each student "selected a stumper" from a grab bag. The stumper required use of a designated research tool, such as *Treaties in Force: A List of Treaties and Other International Acts of the United States in Force on January 1, [ ]*.[23] During the library tour in the following class, we highlighted the sources that students used to answer the stumpers and asked each student how a particular tool led to an answer.

Interactive Games

Played in teams, Mission Made Possible creates bonds among students and stimulates interest in our course. Before our first class meets, we ask students to complete a public international law reading. During the first class, we play Mission Made Possible. We base our questions on the reading assignment. As the game progresses, we highlight pertinent sources.

We knew that our end-of-semester adaptation of "Who Wants To Be a Millionaire. . . . " was a hit when students wished to continue playing through the mid-class break. "So You Want To Pay Off Your Law School Loans. . . . " was our send-off. Chairs ringed the room. All eyes focused on the "hot seat" in the center of the circle. The theme to "Mission Impossible" punctuated our explanation of the rules. Qualifying and game questions covered topics discussed throughout the semester. During the game, we allowed each player to choose two of the following "life lines": access one Internet site, review sources on the book cart,[24] ask the professors to eliminate two answers, or poll the class. Students urged each contestant to consult the class. They lobbied for a fifth option–to call a librarian. A player had three minutes to answer a question. We encouraged students to explain their responses. When a contestant did not select the correct answer, we described the source(s) that would have led to a better response. Some questions were tough. We did not want one student to monopolize the hot seat. Once a student had completed a turn, the student could no longer answer qualifying questions. The students raved about the game; it combined learning and laughter.

Learning from Colleagues

We benefit from collaborating with enthusiastic, skilled colleagues. Instructing Palmer School of Library and Information Science students with Radu Popa, Jeanne Rehberg, and Mirela Roznovschi of New York University School of Law Library sharpens our international law research skills. In partnership with Marci Hoffman, International and Foreign Law Librarian at Georgetown University Law Library, we maintain a list of Internet sources described in the April 2000 presentation, "A New Vision for International Law Instruction: Changing Roles/Relationships of Professors, Librarians and Students."[25]

For creative approaches, we review the web page of the FCIL-SIS interest group on teaching foreign and international law research.[26] Combing legal periodicals also yields pearls like Laura J. Orr-Waters' article, "Teaching English Legal Research Using the Citation Method."[27] Our version of Orr-Waters' discussion questions appears on the Fall 2000 course home page. Attending vendor training sessions also increases our understanding of new sources. We recommend Stephanie Stoudt-Hansen's and Michele Spencer's presentation, "The British Legal System and United Kingdom Materials on Westlaw®." On July 15, 2001, Victoria and John Nann[28] will demonstrate many techniques at their fast-paced, fun AALL Annual Meeting program: "Mastering THE MATRIX: Teaching with Technology." They will then lead a discussion at the AALL FCIL-SIS "teaching" interest group meeting.

The authors hope that the sources, techniques, and experiences described in this article will aid others in developing international and foreign law research training sessions and courses.

NOTES

1. *Roundtable on the Teaching of International Law*, 85 Am. Soc'y Int'l. L. Proc. 102 (1991).

2. Louis F. Del Duca and Vanessa P. Sciarra, *Developing Cross-Border Practice Rules: Challenges and Opportunities for Legal Education*, 21 Fordham Int'l. L. J. 1109, 1123 (1998).

3. John A. Barrett, *International Legal Education in U.S. Law Schools: Plenty of Offerings but too few Students*, 31 Int'l. Law. 845 (1997).

4. Joyce Manna Janto & Lucinda D. Harrison-Cox, *Teaching Legal Research: Past and Present*, 84 Law Libr. J. 281, 283 (1992).

5. According to Arthur Miller, legal research is being taught "in a crazy quilt, half-assed way." He says, "I view that as a tremendous vacuum that you people [law librarians] should just go out and seize." *Towards a Renaissance in Law Librarianship* (Richard A. Danner ed., 1997) at 41.

6. *Modern Technology and Its Effect on Research and Communication,* 86 Am. Soc. Int'l. L. Proc. 604 (1992).

7. This model is recommended by Lucia Ann Silecchia, *Designing and Teaching Advanced Legal Research and Writing Courses,* 33 Duq. L. Rev. 203 (1995).

8. Mary A. Hotchkiss, *University of Washington School of Law, Course Home Pages, International and Foreign Research* <http://www.law.washington.edu/courses/hotchkiss/E579A/syllabus.html>.

9. Virginia Wise, *Harvard Law School, Courses by Professor, Legal Research: International, Foreign and Comparative* <http://www.law.harvard.edu/students/catalog/catalog.php?op=show&id=303>.

10. Jean Davis & Victoria Szymczak, *Brooklyn Law School, Introduction to International and Foreign Law Research* <http://www.wcbcourses.com/wcb/schools/LEXIS/law06/vszymcza/19/>.

11. Katherine Topulos, *Duke University School of Law, Course Home Pages, Research Methods in International, Foreign, and Comparative Law* <http://www.law.duke.edu/curriculum/courseHomepages/380_01>.

12. Timothy F. Mulligan, *University of Houston Law Center, Research in Foreign and International Law* <http://www.law.uh.edu/librarians/tmulligan/f&isyllabus2001.html>.

13. Daniel G. Partan & Stefanie Weigmann, *Boston University School of Law, International and Foreign Law in United States Courts.*

14. Xinh Luu, *University of Virginia School of Law, Course Home Pages, International and Foreign Legal Research.*

15. *See* further discussion in Katherine Topulos' section below where full citations are referenced.

16. For a copy of the syllabus *see supra* note 11.

17. The books, all published by Oceana, are titled *Introduction to Foreign Legal Systems* (Richard A. Danner & Marie-Louise H. Bernal eds., 1994); *Introduction to International Organizations* (Lyonette Louis-Jacques & Jeanne S. Korman eds., 1996); *Introduction to Transnational Legal Transactions* (Marylin J. Raisch & Roberta I. Shaffer eds., 1995); *Introduction to International Business Law: Legal Transactions in a Global Economy* (Gitelle Seer & Maria I. Smolka-Day eds., 1996); and *Contemporary Practice of Public International Law* (Ellen G. Schaffer & Randall J. Snyder eds., 1997).

18. You can link to this web page from the FCIL-SIS site <http://www.lawsch.uga.edu/pcil/pcil.html> by clicking on "Collection of FCIL-related Course Descriptions and Syllabi."

19. Our International and Foreign Law Research course home page appears at <http://www.webcourses.com/web/schools/LEXIS/law06/vszymcza/19/>. This site includes an introductory slide show, the "Mission Made Possible" game, and the "U.N.derstanding" game. We further discuss our classroom games in a later section of this article. To view the slide show, select: **Handouts and Links > Links:**

Introduction to the Course. To access the games, select: **Handouts and Links** > **Lessons: Research Skills**. Regarding Millennium Madness game category, "National Pride": audio files for national anthems are not loaded on Brooklyn Law School Library's server. *See* <http://www.imagesoft.net/flags/flags.html> (flag images and national anthems), <http://www.fg-a.com/flags.htm> (flag images), and <http://www.lengua. com/hymnen.htm> (national anthems). The course finale, "So You Want To Pay Off Your Law School Loans . . . ," is available through <http://www.idrive.com/vszymczak/ files/Shared/>. Check off a file to download and click on: **Download**. Click on the file name. You need Corel Presentations software to view this game (qualifying questions: **qualifying.shw** and game: **payoff.shw**). The first time a visitor downloads a file with the extension .shw, the browser offers the choices: **Pick App** or **Save File**. To open the file, select: **Pick App** > **Browse** > **Corel Presentations**. To save the file, select: **Save it to disk** and choose the folder on your computer in which you want to save the file.

20. Ms. Rehberg supervises the library's WTO depository collection and is the author of *WTO/GATT Research* <http://www.law.nyu.edu/library/wto_gatt.html>.

21. Jeanne Rehberg and Radu D. Popa, eds., 1998.

22. Previously, Ms. McLeod was our colleague in the Joint International Law Project (JILP) among Brooklyn Law School, City University of New York School of Law, Queens College, Flushing, and New York Law School. In the JILP program, New York Law School collects the majority of European Union materials. Ms. McLeod is an expert EU researcher.

23. Treaty Affairs Staff, Office of the Legal Adviser, U.S. Dept. of State, Pub. No. 9434.

24. Sources included *Introduction to Transnational Legal Transactions* (Marylin J. Raisch & Roberta I. Shaffer, eds., 1995) and the International Bar Association, *I.B.A. Rules on the Taking of Evidence in International Commercial Arbitration* (1999).

25. *See* "A New Vision for International Law Instruction: Changing Roles/Relationships of Professors, Librarians and Students," at <http://brkl.brooklaw.edu/screens/pubs.html> and at <http://www.ll.georgetown.edu/intl/presentations/teachingintlaw. htm>.

26. *See supra* note 18. Christine Corcos (ccorcos@isu.edu) welcomes submissions (syllabi, research guides, and exercises) for this page.

27. Persp.: Teaching Legal Res. & Writing, Spring 1998, at 108.

28. Mr. Nann is Educational Technology Specialist/Legal Reference Librarian at Boston College Law Library.

Making the Connection:
Learning Style Theory
and the Legal Research Curriculum

Kristin B. Gerdy

SUMMARY. The author discusses the application of three different learning style models to successful teaching in legal research courses. *[Article copies available for a fee from The Haworth Document Delivery Service: 1-800-342-9678. E-mail address: <getinfo@haworthpressinc.com> Website: <http://www.HaworthPress.com> © 2001 by The Haworth Press, Inc. All rights reserved.]*

INTRODUCTION

Whether in the formal classroom, at the reference desk,[1] or one-on-one, law librarians teach every day. There has been much discussion about what legal research topics should be taught, but substance is only half the battle. What do we do about the student who simply cannot understand the material presented in the textbook? Or the student who understands the concepts and is able to locate resources in a group but is unable to do so independently? Or

Kristin B. Gerdy is Visiting Assistant Professor of Law, Temple University Beasley School of Law, Philadelphia, PA, on leave from the Brigham Young University J. Reuben Clark Law School and Howard W. Hunter Law Library. She teaches first-year Legal Research and Writing, Advanced Legal Research, and Advanced Appelate Advocacy, and is the 1999-2000 Chair of the Research Instruction and Patron Services Special Interest Section of the American Association of Law Libraries.

[Haworth co-indexing entry note]: "Making the Connection: Learning Style Theory and the Legal Research Curriculum." Gerdy, Kristin B. Co-published simultaneously in *Legal Reference Services Quarterly* (The Haworth Information Press, an imprint of The Haworth Press, Inc.) Vol. 19, No. 3/4, 2001, pp. 71-93; and: *Teaching Legal Research and Providing Access to Electronic Resources* (ed: Gary L. Hill, Dennis S. Sears, and Lovisa Lyman) The Haworth Information Press, an imprint of The Haworth Press, Inc., 2001, pp. 71-93. Single or multiple copies of this article are available for a fee from The Haworth Document Delivery Service [1-800-342-9678, 9:00 a.m. - 5:00 p.m. (EST). E-mail address: getinfo@haworthpressinc.com].

the student who seems to grasp the material easily and has no problem solving example problems or in-class exercises but is unable to transfer that knowledge to a hypothetical fact situation? With each of these students the problem is not the substance being taught. Rather, there is a disconnect between the substance and the student–complete learning is not occurring. As legal research educators, we must examine how we teach and how we might adapt our teaching methodology to best reach our "students" and enhance their learning experiences.

Learning has been described as the "process of progressive change from ignorance to knowledge, from inability to competence, and from indifference to understanding."[2] The way learners progress through the spectrum from ignorance to knowledge is often referred to as a learning style. In his leading work on learning styles, educational theorist James W. Keefe defined learning style as "characteristic cognitive, affective, and psychological behaviors that serve as relatively stable indicators of how learners perceive, interact with, and respond to the learning environment."[3] Learning style does not reflect upon a person's intelligence, and one style is not superior to another. While learning style is likely to be relatively stable throughout a person's life, it is not unalterable and often must be adjusted to enable the student to learn in a less than ideal environment.

The idea that people learn in different ways emerged in educational literature as early as 1892; however, the specific phrase "learning style" was probably first used in the 1950s by Thelan in his discussion of the dynamics of work groups.[4] Since that time many educational theorists and researchers have explored the concept of learning style leading to the creation of numerous models and theories. This multiplicity of theories all categorized under the same descriptor often leads to confusion. In order to comprehend learning style theory more accurately, it is necessary to understand that learning style theories exist on four different levels. The deepest layer of learning style focuses on personality models. Learning style at the personality level tends to be the most stable throughout a person's life. A second layer assesses how students process information while learning. The third layer is behavioral and focuses on how students interact in learning settings. The fourth layer explores learners' instructional preferences–the ways in which they like to be taught. The four levels are not isolated as each influences the others.[5]

Although learning style is linked to the individual student, understanding the concept of learning style is arguably as important to the teacher, and its application can dramatically improve teaching. Traditional theories of education were based on the model that teachers, as repositories of information, were simply responsible for dispensing that information to their students. If the students did not learn the material it was viewed as their fault entirely. Adapting teaching style to facilitate learning when students did not learn was not a part of that paradigm; students alone were expected to adjust. With the introduction and acceptance of learning style theories, this paradigm has shifted, and overall education is improving–beginning with the individual student's recognition of how he or she learns and progressing to the teacher's ability, if not responsibility, to adjust teaching style to best facilitate learning.[6]

While understanding and adapting teaching to accommodate different learning styles is advisable, taking the concept to the extreme can be detrimental. Allowing a student to learn only in a way that is preferred because it feels comfortable can seriously hinder the student's ability for future learning and development. Students can, and should, learn to use different learning strategies, but they are most comfortable with assignments within their learning style preference. Students can feel alienated if they are forced to stay out of their comfort zone too long, and this discomfort may be significant enough to interfere with their learning. Thus, one of the objectives of true education should be to teach students to learn in both their preferred and less preferred styles.[7]

Law librarians likely realize that people learn differently and that adapting our teaching, whether in the classroom or one-on-one, would enhance learning, but achieving such results may seem like a daunting task. Formal assessment of a learner's style is unrealistic in many situations in which librarians teach.[8] Either contact with the "student" is too brief or sporadic, as would be the case with a patron seeking assistance at the reference desk, or time pressures preclude any "unnecessary" activity, as would be the case with many first-year legal research classes, which already seem to require instruction that far exceeds the time allotted.

Fortunately, merely acknowledging and understanding that there are different learning styles is the first step in accommodating those styles. The remainder of this article will summarize the educational theory behind three different learning style models representing theories from three of the four learning style levels–adult learning styles, instructional preference styles, and information processing styles–and will illustrate instructional techniques that can be used to foster learning in each style.

ANDRAGOGY–PRINCIPLES OF ADULT LEARNING

In the early 1970s, Malcolm Knowles introduced adult learning theory.[9] Called andragogy, his theory outlined the distinct characteristics distinguishing how adults learn from traditional pedagogical theory used with children–*andra* meaning adult as opposed to *peda* meaning child. Andragogy is based on four main premises. First, adult learners are self-directing. Knowles labeled this self-concept. The premise asserts that adults prefer to make their own decisions and manage themselves rather than having the will of the teacher imposed upon them. Thus, adult learning is enhanced by mutual inquiry by student and teacher.

One means of including self-direction in the legal research curriculum is by providing flexibility and options when possible, thereby allowing individual students to decide for themselves the option that works best for them. In my legal research class, students are required to write research reports explaining their research strategies and results. The report accompanying the first legal problem is quite rigid in its requirements—the students must work together in groups of three and must produce a formal document addressing a series of specific questions. However, the requirements for the second report are very loose and permit students to work in the way that best suits their personalities and learning styles. Two major elements of this assignment include options. First, students are permitted to work alone or in a small group. This option allows the students who need to discuss what they are learning with other students the ability to do so, but it also allows the students who best learn independently to function in that way. Second, the format of the submitted report is left wide open. The only criteria are that the report be complete and that I be able to identify the material addressing each question area. Some students choose to write a narrative research report while others opt for a chart/checklist supplemented with a few paragraphs describing their strategy. By allowing this type of flexibility, the students feel they are "in charge" of the assignment and, consequently, they take the assignment seriously rather than viewing it as "busy work" required by the teacher. Flexibility that allows the student to be self-directed enhances adult learning.

The second premise of andragogy is that adults learn best experientially. Adults' greater reservoirs of past experience form the most effective basis for new learning, and they learn most efficiently and effectively when material is introduced sequentially—taking them step-by-step from simple concepts through complex concepts while relating those concepts to their experience. Students encounter more learning difficulties when new information is presented without such context. The best way to provide context is to begin with an overview of the material to be presented and end with a summary of how it all fits together. But context within the scope of the material to be covered in the class is not enough; adult learners need a framework tied to information or experience already within their grasp in which to place the information they receive. With such a framework, the learner can see how each individual skill or concept fits into the overall structure or "big picture" that extends beyond the scope of the course itself and how it fits into their existing experience.

Tapping into law students' experiences when teaching legal research occurs on at least two levels. First, the new information must somehow be connected to the students' previous research experience. Beginning a class with a short discussion of the research projects and processes the students experienced in their undergraduate education provides a good foundation from which to begin a discussion of the particularities of legal research. Not only does such a discussion provide the teacher with background information about the students and their existing knowledge, the students also have the opportunity to consciously consider their past experiences putting them fresh in their minds to be built upon. As the semester progresses and resources and strategies are introduced, the teacher can draw connections back to the first day's discussion and the knowledge shared. For example, when introducing legal encyclopedias it is helpful to compare and contrast them to the general encyclopedias students have used in the past.

Another level of context and experience that legal research teachers must tie into is the framework the student has formulated to understand such things as where law comes from. A general understanding of the three branches of government is such a framework most students have already acquired from junior high school civics class. Beginning a discussion of the sources of law with a review of the three branches of government and their different roles and functions helps refresh students' memories and prepares them to learn about the laws generated by each branch.

Providing context and tying into students' experiences can also add an element of fun to the legal research class. When I teach legislative sources of the law, I always begin my class with a review of the legislative process–how a bill becomes a law. After several semesters of struggling through a Socratic dialog or delivering a dry lecture, I asked myself where I first learned about the legislative process. The answer was simple and immediate: Schoolhouse Rock on Saturday morning television. The singing bill "sittin' on Capital Hill" was engrained in my memory, and I found myself almost singing aloud as I recalled the lyrics. I located a video of the segment and decided to take a chance and show it in class–not knowing if the students would find it too juvenile. It was a complete success. After asking the teaser question, did anyone remember the steps of the legislative process, and getting no real response, I showed the video. The students loved it; many of them sang along. It provided a nice break from the normal law school routine, but most important, it reminded the students of their experience with legislation and set out a context for learning about bills, slip laws, and codes. Small and insignificant as they may seem, examples or questions that cause students to examine their experience and recall a context into which new information can be placed is a key to successful adult learning.

The third premise of andragogy is that adults must be "ready to learn." Knowles asserts that curriculum must be timed to coordinate the subjects or skills taught with the concurrent tasks facing the student. Adults learn best when they understand the importance of material they are learning and see that it is linked to performance that is expected of them in their social role. They must be motivated in order to learn, and that motivation comes from a belief that what they are learning is relevant and important to their lives–both short-term (in preparing for and succeeding in the current course) and long-term (in their future professions).[10]

The concept of readiness is perhaps best illustrated with seemingly mundane subjects, like citation format. Most legal research instructors would agree that lecturing on the Bluebook is wasted time and breath. Students retain very little of what they are taught. While some would argue that the subject matter itself leads to this lack of retention, I believe it is more a factor of timing and readiness than subject matter. Students will not really "learn" citation format until they recognize its importance and until they need to–until it is expected of them. Unfortunately, for many students this means that they learn citation format, especially the picky rules governing abbreviations and introductory signals, by themselves sometime between midnight and two in the morning the night before their first legal writing assignment is due–sometimes weeks after they were "taught" citation format in class.

Recognizing this reality, I tried something new in my legal research class. Instead of lecturing or even discussing Bluebook citation in class beyond the basics of format that were introduced with the major sources (cases, statutes, etc.), I distributed a worksheet with citation issues about a week before the students' first major research memorandum was due. I told the students that I based the problems on the kinds of citation issues I knew would arise in their memoranda. The students did their best to complete the assignment before class. When they came to class many were frustrated. They had spent hours with their Bluebooks wading through the minutia and inconsistency attempting to create the citations. Despite their frustrations, they were eager to go through the problems and be taught because they finally recognized this was not something they could easily learn on their own when putting the polishing touches on their papers. They were ready to learn, and they did.

The final premise of andragogy concerns the concept of orientation to learning, which stresses the presentation of material in the context of problems students are likely to face in the "real world"; thus, instruction becomes problem-centered rather than subject-centered. This aspect of adult learning may explain why many attempts at solely teaching legal research bibliographically fail. Rather than focusing on the subject matter–the particular resources in the legal research arsenal–legal research instruction could focus on solving legal problems with the resources introduced as tools to be used in solving the problems.

Orientation to learning may also explain the dissatisfaction with and inferior results produced by "treasure hunt" exercises, which often cause students to feel the information is trivial or overly steeped in minutia–but not particularly relevant. To overcome this barrier and to lead students to an appreciation of the importance of legal research, teachers must devise opportunities for legal research in "real world" contexts of importance to their students. For instance, teachers could allow students, when feasible, to complete research assignments in the jurisdiction where they want to practice. This way the students are researching in an area that they care about–taking the information into reality. In so doing, students recognize that their research may relate to a problem they will have to research for a client some day, or at least it uses sources they will be using when they conduct "real" research.

Additionally, questions posed by patrons at the reference desk can provide examples of the "real world" component to legal research. One law librarian begins each meeting of her advanced legal research course with a five-minute discussion of a legal research question posed at the law school's reference desk during the previous week. The students brainstorm resources that could be used to answer the question and then debate the strengths and weaknesses of the different approaches. In so doing the students see the practical value of the material covered in class.

The results of a survey of graduate students conducted in the early 1990s confirm these principles. When asked about their preferred learning methods, the students involved cited orderly presentation of material interspersed with drill and practice.[11] They did not like to read textbooks but preferred discussion where they could listen to other students' ideas. Application-type essays were the preferred method of evaluation.

By keeping the four premises of andragogy in mind when designing the objectives and content of a legal research class, instructors will better serve their students and enhance learning.

INSTRUCTIONAL PREFERENCES

Perhaps the most familiar learning style theories are those relating to instructional preference or students' penchant for particular teaching modes and methods. While instructional preference can be as specific as a preference for reading a textbook over a casebook, the most meaningful categories are more broad: verbal, visual, and tactile/kinesthetic. The key to applying instructional preference learning styles in the classroom is variety. Excellent teachers reach out to all learning styles as each new piece of information is presented. Not only does this insure that each student receives some instruction in his or her preferred style, it is the way to best stretch all students. The following sections introduce the instructional preferences of verbal, visual, and tactile/kinesthetic learners and provide examples of legal research teaching techniques for each.

Verbal

Students whose instructional preferences categorize them as verbal learners learn best when dealing with words, either written or spoken. The majority of legal instruction is oriented toward verbal learners. Within the realm of verbal learners are aural/verbal learners and visual/verbal learners.

Students with aural/verbal preferences learn best when information is presented orally–in either lecture or discussion format–so they can hear it. When trying to remember information, they can often "hear" the way the information was originally presented. This group of learners includes the student in seemingly every class who has to talk the problem through for himself. This student seems to have his hand in the air constantly, and when called on seems to ramble on and on, never really making a point, or making points that are not "on point." For this student the talking is only a way to get to the end and understand the information. Unless a teacher understands this instructional preference, she may become frustrated with this student who seems to talk simply to hear the sound of his own voice. In a legal research context aural/verbal learners would benefit from lectures and discussions of legal resources and methodology. Guest speakers, particularly law firm librarians brought in to discuss "real world" legal research, are also favorites of aural/verbal students. These students often benefit from study groups because they find discussing and explaining new ideas to other people help them learn the material themselves.

Visual/verbal learners learn best when new material is presented in writing. While they may not remember what they hear, they do remember what they read. Students with visual/verbal preference would benefit from legal research instruction that focused on readings, lecture notes, and manuals. Distributing lists of essential points of a lecture or an outline to follow along with during a lecture would also enhance these students' learning, as would summaries of key information, headings, definitions, and other verbal handouts. While some teachers may be hesitant to distribute outlines or summaries of class material for fear students will pay less than full attention in class and rely on the notes alone, I have found the opposite to be true. When I post or distribute an outline or other guiding handout, the students tend to be more involved in the class and are diligent in fleshing out the handout with more details.

Another group of verbal learners learns best when they process new information by writing about it. Research journals are a traditional method that would serve these students well. With increasing access to technology and the Internet, threaded discussion groups provide a new outlet for students who learn by writing. Online discussion lists also allow students who are uncomfortable speaking in class the opportunity to "discuss" ideas with their classmates in writing. Teachers can require students to participate in class listservs and may assign students discussion topics to further explore material presented in class. For example, first-year legal research students could be assigned to find two sources that would shed light on a problem and to evaluate those sources and explain why they are useful in solving the problem.

Visual

Students with visual instructional preferences learn best what they see. These students need visual components to complement verbal presentations. For example, a student I had in a first-year legal research class was experiencing considerable difficulty in completing her research assignment. She came to my office feeling very frustrated and seeking advice. In trying to understand her difficulties, I asked her to tell me about her experience looking for case citations in a regional digest. A bewildered look crossed her face–"Are those the green books or the blue books?" she asked. At first I thought she was asking simply to refresh her memory between the state digests and the regional digests; however, after further conversation I realized that she was identifying different sources by the color of their covers rather than by their content. She did not seem to understand the difference between a digest–state or regional, an annotated code, or a reporter beyond the differences in their appearance. She had "learned" the sources by committing them to her visual memory. No wonder she was confused.

Students with visual preferences often dislike and are frustrated by lecture, textbooks, handouts, and other "word-dominated" instructional methods. Instead they learn best when these verbal methods are supplemented with visual aids. Visual representations are particularly useful in helping students see organization and connections between ideas. Visual learners tend to like material exhibited on an overhead projector or chalkboard, non-verbal handouts, colors, pictures, diagrams, flow charts, graphs, time lines, films, and demonstrations. Limiting the amount of information presented on visual aids assists the visual learner, who tends to take a mental picture of the information.

A high visual instructional preference can cause difficulties for students, especially in the law school environment where the majority of information is presented verbally–either through lecture or Socratic method or through casebook readings. However, most students do have some visual preference and learn more when visual presentations are used to complement lectures and readings, and all students learn better when material is presented both verbally and visually.[12]

One example of the many visual aids that can be used to teach legal research is the flowchart. Flowcharts illustrating the legal research process are particularly useful for visual learners. Available in many textbooks, or easily created, these charts help the visually-oriented student organize the many resources and strategies involved in even the most elementary research problem.

Tactile/Kinesthetic

Students whose instructional preferences center on activity are called tactile or kinesthetic learners. These students often remember what they write, draw, or doodle, and often feel the need to move around while learning and to work with materials they can handle and touch. Tactile/kinesthetic learners learn best with physical representations like index cards, maps, games, and puzzles. Hands-on and trial and error approaches like labs, field trips, role plays, and simulations are also favored instructional methods for these students. Solutions to problems, examples of previous exam papers, and practice answers also enhance tactile/kinesthetic learners' experience.

Legal research instruction lends itself easily to tactile/kinesthetic methods. Perhaps the two most obvious tactile/kinesthetic methods involve bringing books into the classroom and teaching electronic legal research online–with the students at the keyboard actually going through the steps rather than watching the teacher work. Merely passing around volumes of the digest or reporter series so students can handle them and leaf through them to see the different divisions discussed does a lot to solidify information in the mind of the tactile/kinesthetic learner. One legal research teacher I know introduces her students to the *Federal Register* by distributing daily issues to each student, having the students locate the various sections as they are discussed, and asking them to provide examples from their volumes.

When I teach practice materials, rather than lecturing on the different types of materials and illustrating them with sample volumes, I bring a book cart filled with books to the classroom. As the students enter they are instructed to pick up two volumes that look interesting to them. I encourage them to look through the books as they wait for class to begin. When class begins I spend about five minutes introducing the different categories of practice materials. Then the students have ten minutes to go through their books to determine which category each fits into and to discover something interesting in the book. We then go around the class and have each student report on his or her books by describing their content, fitting them into a category, and explaining how they would be useful to an attorney in practice.

Although bringing sources into the classroom can do a lot to reach tactile/ kinesthetic learners, there is nothing better for these students than physically moving into the library. When I introduce a new source in my first-year legal research class I begin with a short lecture (no longer than twenty minutes) supplemented with visual aids like handouts or PowerPoint. The class then moves en masse to the law library where the students are given sample problems to solve using the sources. The students enjoy the chance to use the sources while I am with them and am able to answer questions. They comment that they finally "understand" the material presented in the classroom only after they actually use the source in the library. If physically moving into the library is not feasible, similar results could be achieved by bringing a series of pre-selected sources to the classroom and allowing students to use the sources to find answers, perhaps moving from station to station around the room.

Advances in technology also help the tactile/kinesthetic learner understand and apply new material. Such things as computerized exercises, interactive CD-ROM, video discs, and web sites enhance these students' learning.

Tactile/kinesthetic learners need hands-on experience at all stages of their learning–not only when information is initially presented. A final exam preparation tool I have used for several years now caters to the tactile/kinesthetic learner who needs to physically move through the library and handle the sources in order to review the material presented in class. Beginning with secondary sources and moving through each branch of government and its finding tools and primary sources, we walk through the library and review each source. We take volumes off the shelves and pass them around, looking at the different divisions in each, and talking about how they are accessed and where they would fit naturally in a research strategy. Although none of the material presented is new, each year several students comment that they "finally" learned the material as we walked around the library.

Acknowledging the fact that each legal research class will likely include students from all three major instructional preference groups, our aim as instructors should be to reach out to all three preferences. In order to do this successfully we must examine our current teaching to see if there is a style bias. Then we must consciously add variety, specifically focusing on visual and tactile/kinesthetic preferences.

KOLB'S LEARNING CYCLE–
INFORMATION PROCESSING MODEL

Old Chinese Proverb:
Tell me and I forget
Show me and I remember
Involve me and I understand

Basing his theory of experiential learning on the work of three earlier educational researchers including Dewey, who saw "learning as a dialectic process integrating experience and concepts, observations, and action," Lewin, who placed emphasis on experience to test abstract concepts and on feedback processes, and Piaget, who believed the key to learning "lies in the mutual interaction of the processes of accommodation of concepts or schemas to experience in the world and the process of assimilation of events and experiences from the world into existing concepts and schemas," David A. Kolb's learning theory emphasizes the central role of experience in the learning process.[13] According to Kolb, true learning combines experience, perception, cognition, and behavior. Under this theory, "knowledge is continuously derived from and tested out in the experiences of the learner."[14]

The impact of experience in the learning process is multidimensional. First, according to Kolb, all learning is really *"relearning"*–in other words, each student comes to the learning experience with some idea about the topic at hand. Some students' preexisting ideas will be inaccurate or inarticulate, but they will have them if their experience has presented the topic previously. With this background, one important responsibility of a teacher is to dispose of or modify preexisting ideas–not merely to present new ideas. Therefore, the most effective teaching will begin by exploring the learner's preexisting beliefs and theories about a topic, will examine and test them, and then will "integrate the new, more refined ideas into the person's belief system[]."[15]

The Four Learning Modes

Kolb's experiential learning model is best described as a cycle through which the learner passes numerous times as she progresses from novice to expert. The cycle revolves around two axes that represent fundamental elements of the learning process: perception, or the way the student perceives or grasps the new information, and processing, or the way the student adapts the information to meet his or her needs and realities.

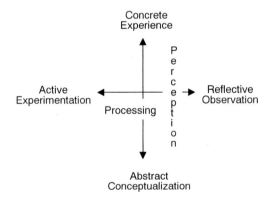

The four axis-points represent the four basic learning modes: the two predominant manners of perception: feeling, which Kolb called "concrete experience," and thinking, which he called "abstract conceptualization" and the two predominant manners of processing: watching, called "reflective observation," and doing, called "active experimentation."

The first mode of perception, "concrete experience" or feeling, focuses on human interactions and students' involvement in their learning. This mode is often characterized as "artistic" and "intuitive" because it emphasizes feeling over thinking and favors systematic over intuitive approaches to problem solving. Learners who prefer this mode of learning tend to be social and to excel in interpersonal relations. They also tend to function well with little structure.[16] Learning is enhanced by personalized feedback from the teacher and from other students, sharing feelings, activities designed to apply skills to real-life problems, and opportunities for self-direction and autonomy. Learning in this mode is hindered by reading assignments that are more theoretical than concrete.[17]

The second predominant perception mode is "abstract conceptualization" or thinking, which is placed opposite "concrete experience" on the axis. This mode is logical and focuses on ideas and concepts. In this mode learners think through material and derive general theories rather than solving specific problems. Scientific, systematic approaches are favored over intuition. Students with an orientation toward this mode tend to appreciate structure and neatly conceptualized presentations.[18] Learning in this mode is enhanced by theoretical readings, case studies, and thinking through problems alone, but is hindered by group projects. Learners with this orientation tend to avoid sharing personal feelings and to dislike personalized feedback.[19]

The first predominant processing mode is "reflective observation" or watching. Here students learn by careful observation and description, focusing on impartiality and "truth." A person with this orientation is more interested in knowledge for knowledge's sake than in the pragmatic applications of that knowledge. These learners often excel at identifying differing perspectives and drawing implications from ideas and situations.[20] Learning in this mode is enhanced by "authoritative information" presented by lecture, guided or limited discussion, and reading. Learning is hindered by focusing information on solving problems or accomplishing tasks.[21]

The second processing mode, "active experimentation" or doing, is opposite "reflective observation" on the axis. This is the mode we most often think of when we think of "active learning." An orientation toward this learning mode emphasizes the practical application of knowledge rather than the appreciation of knowledge for the sake of intellectual curiosity or fulfillment in finding "truth." These students are often risk-takers who strive to see results.[22] Learning in this mode is enhanced by active application of skills and concepts to "real world" problems. Methods including peer feedback, practice problems, and small-group discussions facilitate this learning mode. Learning is hindered by focus on content without application, lectures, and evaluations based on "right or wrong."[23]

While the modes are not exclusive and excellent learners are able to perceive and process information in all four modes, learners tend to have a natural affinity for one or more learning mode. Each learner has preferred modes of perception and processing. The combination of these preferences forms the basis of a learning "style." According to Kolb, "As a result of our hereditary equipment, our particular past life experience, and the demands of our present environment, most people develop learning styles that emphasize some learning abilities over others."[24]

The Four Major Learning Styles

In Kolb's formulation there are four major learning styles, each incorporating preferred modes of perception and processing. The four learning styles are labeled "divergent," "convergent," "assimilative," and "accommodative."

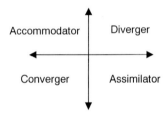

Learners categorized as "divergent" perceive information through concrete experience and process it through reflective observation. Divergent learners' greatest strength is their imagination and ability to formulate alternatives, to perceive situations from a variety of perspectives, and to draw conclusions about principles and relationships that apply to the whole. They also tend to be people- and feeling-oriented.[25] Although there is currently no published research assessing law students' dominant learning style on the Kolb scale, it is likely that the divergent style is well represented because Kolb's research indicates that undergraduate students concentrating on history, English, political science, and psychology (popular majors for students who later attend law school) tend to cluster in this style.[26]

Learners categorized as "convergent" lie on the opposite end of the spectrum from divergers. They perceive information through abstract conceptualization and process it through active experimentation. Convergent learners excel in the practical application of ideas. They are most comfortable working in situations where there is a single correct answer or solution because they focus their knowledge on deducing the "answer" to the specific problem posed. These learners tend to be reserved in their expression of emotion, preferring to deal with tasks and problems rather than with people.[27]

Learners categorized as "assimilative" perceive information through abstract conceptualization and process it through reflective observation. These learners are called assimilators because of their ability to assimilate multiple observations into an integrated theory or principle. Inductive reasoning and theoretical modeling are tools of the assimilative learner–it is more important that the theories derived be logically sound and precise than that they have practical application. Assimilators are more concerned with abstract ideas than with people.[28]

Learners categorized as "accommodative" lie on the opposite end of the spectrum from assimilators. They perceive information through concrete experience and process it through active experimentation. As their learning modes would indicate, these learners tend to approach problems intuitively through trial and error and have strengths in risk taking and action. However, in situations where the theory does not "fit the facts," accommodators tend to discard the theory rather than discount or reexamine the facts. Although they enjoy and are at ease in social situations, accommodators are often viewed as impatient or "pushy."[29]

Learning Around the Cycle

Rather than focusing their learning experiences in the particular quadrant of their preferred learning styles, effective learners move around the cycle in each learning experience. Excellent learners who develop skills in all four quadrants of the cycle can move through the cycle rapidly, ultimately enabling them to learn independently.

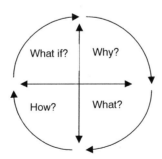

Moving around the cycles is accomplished by answering the summarizing question in each quadrant: *why?* (concrete experience), *what?* (reflective observation), *how?* (abstract conceptualization), and *what if?* (active experimentation).

Kolb and educational researchers who have critiqued his work recommend that teachers use the modes and styles as a guide when they design course objectives and specific learning activities, thereby enabling students to progress through the cycle with the information to be learned. Ideally, as a student travels around the learning cycle she begins by having a "concrete experience" (*why?*); she then reflects upon that experience from different perspectives in the "reflective observation" phase (*what?*). From the different observations, she is able to create general principles and theories; this is the "abstract conceptualization" phase (*how?*). Finally, she is able to test her newly created theories in different situations, thereby engaging in "active experimentation" (*what if?*). In so doing, a course is responsive to all four styles and provides experiences in all four modes, producing the most effective learning experience. According to one study, "[l]earning is enhanced as more of the modes are used, increasing from 20 percent retention if only abstract conceptualization is used to 90 percent if all four modes are used."[30]

Failure to move around the cycle leads to gaps in knowledge and inability to apply concepts to practical situations. For example, some students are very good at the mechanics of legal research–they can find anything in an index if they are given the topic to research; however, they are unable to recognize the legal problem presented by a fact situation. Other students may be unable to transfer the skills learned in one problem setting to another problem setting–they are able to use an index to find statutes but are unable to use the descriptive word index to find topic and key numbers in a digest. Still others are able to use their new research skills to find solutions to problems when they are given specific guidance about where to look for information, but flounder when they have less direction or have to make judgments about sources. Thus, in order for our students to learn legal research effectively and completely, we must guide them around the learning cycle.[31]

Quadrant 1: Why?

The first quadrant of the learning cycle provides the "concrete experience." Here the teacher introduces the subject matter and begins to answer why the material is being taught. Answering *why?* is enhanced by providing the "big picture" and giving relevance to the subject by showing the learners how the new knowledge or skills will be important to their lives now and in the future. The enthusiasm generated in this phase of the cycle will see the student through the remaining three phases.

Stories from the teacher's own experiences in the law library or in practice, or those shared by a guest speaker, are an effective means of generating enthusiasm and helping students recognize the importance of legal research to both their law school experience and later careers. Panels of upper-class students discussing the importance of their legal research training in their summer work are another excellent motivational tool.

Quadrant 2: What?

The second quadrant allows students the opportunity for "reflective observation." When learning *what?*, students are looking for facts. Teachers need to provide information to the students; they need to organize and integrate new material by showing how it fits into the big picture; and they need to provide time for thinking and reflection.

The information dissemination necessary in the second quadrant should be provided through a variety of methods, as discussed previously in the instructional preference section of this piece. In addition to the actual information, in this second quadrant students must be given the opportunity to think about and to reflect upon what they have learned. Research journals and reports provide such an opportunity. In more advanced cycles, discussions of legal research strategy also allow reflection.

Although the four quadrants of the cycle build upon each other, the cycle is not completely rigid. Reflective observation can effectively take place multiple times during the cycle, including after abstract conceptualization but preceding active experimentation.

Quadrant 3: How?

The third quadrant, "abstract conceptualization," requires that learners apply their new knowledge to answer *how?* Here the teacher is transformed from an information disseminator to a coach.[32] The focus of this quadrant is on both the application of knowledge and on the acquisition of problem solving skills. A safe environment in which to experiment with both strategy and specific skills is essential to learning in this quadrant.

Class discussions of legal research process and strategy are appropriate at this phase of the learning cycle. As students discuss the sources they plan to use to solve a problem and the process by which they will use them, they are able to turn the abstract concepts introduced in the second quadrant into useful tools.

Opportunities to apply their new knowledge in a "safe" environment can be created by using problems with "correct" answers. For example, after discussing strategies for finding state statutes, students could be asked to locate a specific statute in the state code. Because the teacher knows in advance that the statutory provision exists, the environment is safe and students will not fail in their first attempts to apply their abstract knowledge.

Quadrant 4: What If?

Finally, in order to complete the cycle and the learning experience, the learners must move to the fourth quadrant, "active experimentation," where they apply the material learned to their own lives by solving "real" problems thereby synthesizing their theoretical knowledge and answering *what if?* This experimentation is essential to completing the learning process and provides the foundation for more advanced experiences. Finally, using their new legal research skills to solve a hypothetical problem is the best way to complete the learning cycle and to solidify the new knowledge in the students' minds.

Kolb's Learning Cycle in a Full-Semester Legal Research Course

Kolb's learning cycle can be completed in a single class period or topical unit, or it may take several weeks or an entire semester to complete. In my first-year legal research and writing class I attempt to take the students around the cycle three times, each building upon the last, while incorporating the premises of andragogy and instructional preference. The semester is organized around three problems, beginning with a simple state-law problem with a "right" answer, moving to a more difficult federal-law problem, and ending with a complex problem.[33] Each problem is structured to include a complete learning cycle.

After an introduction to the importance of legal research in law practice and a review of the legal system, the three branches of government, and the lawmaking functions of each branch, I distribute the first research problem. With a fact scenario in hand and an assignment to write a memorandum, which is due one week later, the students are motivated to learn the research skills necessary to solve the problem. During the next two class periods, through a series of short lectures, PowerPoint presentations, and readings, I introduce students to secondary sources and the basics of state law research. To get the students to think about their research strategies and the work they will soon be doing, I continuously ask questions about how they think the information might be useful in solving their problem.

At the end of the second class the students are divided into groups of three and given a series of questions designed to guide their research. They must go to the library as a group, conduct their research, and write a formal report answering the questions and detailing their research processes and results. I give the students a schedule of the hours I will be in the library to assist them. I try to be available at least two hours each of the three days they are researching. I tell the students that I will not do the research for them, but will be available to answer their questions and give them guidance. Most of the students learn the material the best while they are in the library with their group trying to find articles in the legal encyclopedias, use the *American Law*

Reports, find the applicable statute, use the annotations and state digest to find relevant cases, and Shepardize their authorities.

After the research is completed, the students write group research reports. The reports are designed to make the students reflect upon their re-search–both the strategies they used and the results they achieved. Some of the questions they are asked to respond to are result oriented–for example, were they able to find an ALR Annotation on their topic; others are process oriented–where did you begin your legal research? Why did you choose to begin there? List some considerations you took into account. Writing the reports as a group forces the students to discuss their answers, allowing them to look at their research from different perspectives.

On the day the reports are due, class time is spent discussing the experi-ences students had with the research and discussing the substantive law they gleaned from the research. In this way the entire class is able to benefit from the experiences of each group. The reports are returned with comments and suggestions addressing both the strategy and result elements of the students' research. At the end of this sequence the students feel comfortable using major secondary sources and finding tools, state primary sources, and She-pards' citators. Not only do they know what the sources are and the logistics of using them, they have used their new research skills to solve a "real" problem. Their solutions are presented in an office memorandum.

The second phase of the legal research course builds upon the foundation provided in the first problem. After a new fact scenario is distributed and the students have had a chance to read it, class discussion focuses on the types of resources needed to solve the problem. Federal primary materials, finding tools, and legal periodicals are introduced. We then have a short discussion about the advantages and disadvantages of beginning research on the prob-lem in several different sources. The research report facet of this problem provides options. First, the students can work in groups of two or three or they can do the research and write the report individually. Second, they can submit a narrative report of their research strategies and results, or they can submit a checklist/chart of their results complemented by a narrative describ-ing their strategy. Again, the reports are returned with comments focusing on the research completed for the problem and with suggestions for future re-search experiences. After the research is finished an entire class period is devoted to a discussion of the results. The students then write more complex predictive memoranda conveying the results of their research and analysis.

The capstone of the research for the semester comes with the third prob-lem, which culminates in the final predictive memorandum and which is graded on both its research and writing components. Rather than the guided research of the earlier problems, the third research problem is almost entirely self-directed. Although we spend a few minutes of class time brainstorming potential sources, the students are not given research questions to guide them. This time the students are required to work independently, with prohibitions against collaboration. Rather than submitting a narrative report or checklist, the students are required to submit preliminary lists of citations so I can make sure they are on the right track. Specific feedback is given only if a student is missing essential information. Having had three opportunities to hear, see, and read the material presented, three opportunities to reflect upon the information and their experience with it, and three opportunities to apply their new skills, each in an increasingly more difficult context, the research the students produce for the final problem is generally excellent. They have completed the learning cycle three times and are empowered to take their new knowledge on to further independent experimentation.

CONCLUSION

Because the ability to perform complete and accurate legal research is critical to success in law practice, it is vital that our students be taught in the most effective way possible. It is not necessary that each law librarian teaching legal research become an expert in educational theory, but what is necessary is that law librarians who teach recognize that their students learn in different ways and that they as teachers can help or hinder learning by the way they teach. With an understanding of the different facets of the learning cycle and a recognition that students learn in different ways, law librarians can adapt their teaching methods to enhance their students' learning experiences and help them to become capable practitioners.

NOTES

1. While many of the teaching techniques discussed in this paper could be adapted to the reference desk, reference service poses some additional challenges that can be addressed through educational theory; however, they are beyond the scope of this piece. *See generally,* Bibliography, *Brief Encounters: Using Techniques from Psychology and Education to Improve the Effectiveness of Reference Service* (Education and Behavioral Sciences Section of the Association of College and Research Libraries of the American Library Association, CA, June 1992).

2. Cameron Fincher, *Learning Theory and Research, in Teaching and Learning in the College Classroom* (Kenneth A. Feldman & Michael Paulson, eds., 1994) (Ashe Reader Series).

3. James W. Keefe, *Learning Style Theory and Practice* 5 (1987).

4. *Id.* at 7.

5. Charles S. Claxton & Patricia H. Murrell, *Learning Styles: Implications for Improving Educational Practices,* 7 (ASHE-ERIC *Higher Education Report* No. 4, 1987).

6. Keefe, *supra* note 3, at 31-32.

7. Richard M. Felder, *Matters of Style,* ASEE Prism, Dec. 1996 at 18-23.

8. For a similar discussion of the hindrances to assessment in library research instruction, *see* Andrea Wayman, *Learning Style: Its Place in Library Instruction* (U.S. Department of Education Office of Educational Research and Improvement, ED # 318 478, 1989).

9. Malcolm S. Knowles, *The Modern Practice of Adult Education: From Pedagogy to Andragogy* 41(1970); Malcolm S. Knowles, *The Adult Learner: A Neglected Species* 39-63 (1990).

10. John Dewey, *How We Think: a Restatement of the Relation of Reflective Thinking to the Educative Process* (1971).

11. Samuel Hinton, Presentation, *The Learning Style Preferences of Students in Graduate School* (Annual Meeting of the Mid-South Educational Researchers Assn., Nov. 1992 (available from the U.S. Department of Education Office of Educational Research and Improvement, ED # 354 807).

12. Richard M. Felder & Barbara A. Soloman, *Learning Styles and Strategies* <http://www2.ncsu.unity/lockers . . . /f/felder/public/ILSdir/styles.htm> (accessed Aug. 31, 1999).

13. David A. Kolb, *Experiential Learning: Experience as the Source of Learning and Development* 20-21 (1984).

14. *Id.* at 27.

15. *Id.* at 28.

16. *Id.* at 68.

17. *Id.* at 200.

18. *Id.* at 69.

19. *Id.* at 200.

20. *Id.* at 68-69.

21. *Id.* at 200.

22. *Id.* at 69.

23. *Id.* at 200.

24. *Id.* at 76.

25. *Id.* at 77-78.

26. *Id.* at 85.

27. *Id.* at 77.

28. *Id.* at 78.

29. *Id.*

30. Claxton & Murrell, *supra* note 5, at 33.

31. For description of the use of the Kolb learning style in an undergraduate research class, *see* Sonia Bodi, *Teaching Effectiveness and Bibliographic Instruction: The Relevance of Learning Styles,* 52 C. & Res. Libr. 113 (1990). For a list of excellent ideas for "teaching all types" *see* Richard M. Felder, *Matters of Style,* ASEE Prism, Dec. 1996, at 18-23 (Ideas for teaching all types: (1) teach theoretical material by first presenting phenomena and problems that relate to the theory. Don't jump directly into the details–perhaps give the students an idea of the problems that can be solved with the theory and see how far they can go before they get all the tools to solve them; (2) balance conceptual information with concrete information; (3) make

extensive use of visuals in addition to oral and written explanations and derivations in lectures and readings; (4) provide class time for students to think about the material being presented and for active student participation; (5) encourage or mandate cooperation on homework–hundreds of studies show that students who participate in cooperative learning experiences tend to earn better grades, display more enthusiasm, etc.; and (6) demonstrate the logical flow of individual course topics, but also point out connections between the current material and other relevant material in the same course or other courses in the same discipline, in other disciplines, and in everyday experience).

32. Kolb, *supra* note 13, at 202.

33. This is the basic structure and assignment content of all first-year legal research and writing courses at Temple University Beasley School of Law. Many thanks to Jan M. Levine, Susan DeJarnatt, Elena Margolis, and Kathryn Stanchi. The schema for teaching research embedded in the Temple program (also used at Virginia and Arkansas) is described in print in several places. The overall conception was first described in Jan M. Levine, *Analytical Assignments for Integrating Legal Research and Writing* (1991) (yearly 1993 to 1996, the 1995 and 1996 editions were written with Kathryn A. Sampson). *See also,* Jan M. Levine, *"You Can't Please Everyone, So You'd Better Please Yourself": Directing (Or Teaching In) a First-Year Legal Writing Program,* 29 Val. U. L. Rev. 611, 622-23 (1995). The Temple LRW faculty also presented this system as part of its 1998 Legal Writing Institute presentation, *The Death of the Closed Universe, Farewell to the Easter Bunny, and Other Cosmological Myths of LRW–or–the Total Integration of Legal Research, Legal Writing, and Legal Analysis* (PANEL: Susan DeJarnatt, Jan Levine, Ellie Margolis, Michael Smith, Franklin Snyder, & Kathryn Stanchi).

REFERENCES

Learning Theory Generally

Charles S. Claxton & Patricia H. Murrell, *Learning Styles: Implications for Improving Educational Practices* (ASHE-ERIC Higher Education Report No. 4, 1987) (addresses many approaches to learning style at adult levels: (1) personality; (2) information processing; (3) social interaction; and (4) instructional methods, and discusses how this information has improved student learning).

Barbara Gross Davis, *Tools for Teaching* (1993) (chapter on learning styles and preferences provides a concise overview of learning style models, suggestions for helping students to recognize their own learning styles, and accommodating different learning styles in the classroom).

J. N. Harb & R. E. Terry, *Teaching Through the Cycle: Application of Learning Style Theory to Engineering Education at Brigham Young University* (2d ed. 1995) (discusses the theory and implementation of the Kolb Learning Cycle as a teaching model).

James W. Keefe, *Learning Style Theory and Practice* (1987).

David A. Kolb, *Experiential Learning: Experience as the Source of Learning and Development* (1984).

Profiling and Utilizing Learning Style (James W. Keefe, ed., 1988) (NASSP Learning Style Series).

Teaching and Learning in the College Classroom (Kenneth A. Feldman & Michael Paulson, eds., 1994) (ASHE Reader Series).

Learning Theory and Legal Education

Paul Bateman, *Toward Diversity in Teaching Methods in Law Schools: Five Suggestions from the Back Row,* 17 Quinnipiac L. Rev. 397 (1997).

Robin A. Boyle & Rita Dunn, *Teaching Law Students Through Individual Learning Styles,* 62 Alb. L. Rev. 213 (1998).

Steven I. Friedland, *How We Teach: A Survey of Teaching Techniques in American Law Schools,* 20 Seattle U. L. Rev. 1 (1996).

Gerald F. Hess, *Listening to Our Students: Obstructing and Enhancing Learning in Law School,* 31 U.S.F. L. Rev. 941 (1997).

Paula Lustbader, *Construction Sites, Building Types, and Bridging Gaps: A Cognitive Theory of the Learning Progression of Law Students,* 33 Willamette L. Rev. 315 (1997).

William Wesley Patton, *Opening Students' Eyes: Visual Learning Theory in the Socratic Classroom,* 15 L. & Psychol. Rev. 1 (1991) (discusses effective teaching methods other than the pure Socratic method).

Sarah E. Thiemann, *Beyond Guinier: A Critique of Legal Pedagogy,* 24 N.Y.U. Rev. L. & Soc. Change 17 (1998).

Learning Theory and General Research Instruction

Sonia Bodi, *Teaching Effectiveness and Bibliographic Instruction: The Relevance of Learning Styles,* C. & Res. Libr., Mar. 1990 at 113 (describes Kolb's theory of experiential learning and introduces a pattern of bibliographic instruction using experiential learning theory).

Diane Nahl-Jakobovits & Leo A. Jakobovits, *Learning Principles and the Library Environment,* Res. Strategies, Spring 1990 at 80.

Nancy O'Hanlon, *Begin at the End: A Model for Research Skills Instruction,* Res. Strategies, Summer 1991 at 116 (describes a research instruction model incorporating learning style theory).

Andrea Wayman, *Learning Style: Its Place in Library Instruction* (U.S. Department of Education Office of Educational Research and Improvement. ED # 318 478, 1989).

Learning Theory and Legal Research Instruction

Eileen B. Cohen, *Teaching Legal Research to a Diverse Student Body,* 85 L. Libr. J. 583 (1993) (provides an overview of different learning styles and advocates creating several program options to offer students choice in selecting a learning program that matches their learning patterns).

Eileen B. Cohen, *Using Cognitive Legal Theories in Teaching Legal Research,* 1 Persp.: Teaching Legal Res. & Writing 79 (1993).

David W. Whampagne, *Improving Your Teaching: How Students Learn,* 83 L. Libr. J. 85 (1991).

Success at the Reference Desk:
Helping Patrons Overcome
Computer Anxiety

Suzanne Miner

SUMMARY. Even though computer use is prevalent, there are still many library users who are uncomfortable using computers to do legal research. Reference librarians can assist patrons in lowering their computer anxiety by being reassuring, giving patrons hands-on experience, not using technical words, explaining why using a computer to find information will be helpful, anticipating areas of difficulty, and checking back with them. *[Article copies available for a fee from The Haworth Document Delivery Service: 1-800-342-9678. E-mail address: <getinfo@haworthpressinc. com> Website: <http://www.HaworthPress.com> © 2001 by The Haworth Press, Inc. All rights reserved.]*

As more legal information becomes available electronically, reference librarians are increasingly referring patrons to computers to locate what they need. Even though computer use is prevalent in the cyberworld we live in, it is surprising how many library patrons seem reluctant to research using computers. Further, showing patrons how to use a computer to search databases can be laborious–both to teach search strategies and to allay fears. However, using print resources is not always an option. Almost ten years ago, law librarian James Hoover wrote about legal scholarship and the electronic

Suzanne Miner is Head of Information Technology at the University of Utah S. J. Quinney Law Library. She received her JD from Brigham Young University in 1989 and her MLS from the University of Washington in 1990.

[Haworth co-indexing entry note]: "Success at the Reference Desk: Helping Patrons Overcome Computer Anxiety." Miner, Suzanne. Co-published simultaneously in *Legal Reference Services Quarterly* (The Haworth Information Press, an imprint of The Haworth Press, Inc.) Vol. 19, No. 3/4, 2001, pp. 95-103; and: *Teaching Legal Research and Providing Access to Electronic Resources* (ed: Gary L. Hill, Dennis S. Sears, and Lovisa Lyman) The Haworth Information Press, an imprint of The Haworth Press, Inc., 2001, pp. 95-103. Single or multiple copies of this article are available for a fee from The Haworth Document Delivery Service [1-800-342-9678, 9:00 a.m. - 5:00 p.m. (EST). E-mail address: getinfo@haworthpressinc.com].

revolution: "It will not be possible or logical to have most legal sources in both print and electronic forms."[1] With most libraries experiencing shrinking physical space and budgets, this is becoming a reality. Therefore, reference librarians must know how to help patrons feel comfortable using computers to retrieve information.

The adage that "[l]egal research instruction is most effective at the point-of-need"[2] is widely accepted in the law library field. Reference librarians have golden opportunities each day to reinforce concepts learned by law students and attorneys in their legal research classes. For other library users, the informal training that takes place at the reference desk can be an invaluable way to provide hands-on learning and lessen the stress patrons feel when using computers to research.

MANY LIBRARY USERS EXPERIENCE COMPUTER ANXIETY

At the publicly accessible academic law library where I work there are a variety of patrons–law students, law faculty, attorneys, students from other university classes, students from community colleges, non-law faculty, runners from law firms, and people from the general public trying to research their own legal issues. The majority of these are students. Research studies[3] have shown that up to one-third of college students suffer from "technophobia."[4] While it is true that many of the younger students feel comfortable using computers, they still may not know how to find and efficiently search the database they need. Nontraditional students have increased by 80% since 1969 and are faced with learning new computer skills.[5] Last year, my law school had a seventy-two-year-old in the entering class who was willing to learn but still anxious when using computers.

Faculty are even more technologically stressed with 67% of 34,000 faculty surveyed in 1998-99 reporting that they felt regular stress in trying to keep up with technology.[6] While there are some technologically savvy faculty who use computers proficiently, many come to the reference desk seeking assistance with basic searches of the automated library catalog or document retrieval from systems such as LEXIS and Westlaw. For many faculty, skilled computer use is not directly tied to tenure and, therefore, they are not motivated to spend time learning computer skills. However, faculty still have to retrieve information from computers periodically and since they do not have the skills to do it quickly, they feel anxious.

Those in the legal community have not been the leaders in embracing technological change.[7] Law firms have been slow to purchase office computers for each attorney, and when CD-ROMs were first gaining prominence, the production of law-related CD-ROMs lagged several years behind other subject areas. Consequently, many practicing attorneys using the library also experience stress trying to locate information electronically.

Even though electronic library catalogs have been available for well over ten years, many patrons in our library still walk into the reference room and ask for assistance in finding books because they do not feel confident using the computer to find what they are looking for. While some people head straight to the reference desk because they want to save time by "asking a librarian," some truly do not know how to use the computers or do not feel comfortable figuring out how to find and search the database they need. Even students who are technologically competent may feel intimidated by the law library itself. Daily, at least one non-law student or public patron will hesitantly come to the reference desk and preface their request for assistance with the statement, "I've never been in a law library before," or "I'm not a law student." These library users suffer from anxiety.

COMPUTER SELF-EFFICACY

Self-efficacy is the confidence an individual has in his ability to perform a task. "[I]ndividuals who judge themselves able to perform certain tasks will more often attempt and successfully do the tasks."[8] Studies evaluating computer self-efficacy show that the higher the self-efficacy, the higher the chance that students will decide to engage in a computer task and the longer they will persist in accomplishing the task.[9] If a reference librarian can help alleviate a library user's computer anxiety, then confidence will build and chances are high the patron will be successful in his use of the computer. Even though the amount of time reference librarians spend with patrons is usually short, reference librarians can assist in raising patrons' computer self-efficacy.

Factors Affecting Self-Efficacy

A number of factors affect the computer user's level of self-efficacy. Just being aware of these is a first step in approaching the patron.

Ownership of Computers

People who own computers are less anxious and have more confidence in their computer skills.[10] This is logical because as individuals use computers they become more comfortable with them, thus reducing anxiety. Studies also show that experience with computers results in lower anxiety levels.[11] Each year, our library surveys all entering 1Ls and while most students own at least one computer, there are usually one or two students a year who do not own a computer (and do not want to own one). If some law students do not own a computer, then it is especially important to recognize that not all library patrons own a computer either.

Socioeconomic Status

Librarians should be aware that patrons with low socioeconomic status may be experiencing more computer stress than others. A study of accounting students using information retrieval systems found that those from low socioeconomic backgrounds have higher computer anxiety and poorer computer performance than those with higher socioeconomic status.[12] Since those who come from a lower socioeconomic status are less likely to own a computer, this is a group of whom librarians should be especially aware.

Gender, Ethnic Origin and Age

While older studies indicate that males experience less computer anxiety than females, a recent study indicates that gender makes no difference on levels of anxiety, attitude and self-efficacy experienced by students.[13] When measuring levels of computer anxiety, ethnic origin also seems not to matter.[14] In general, older adults have less computer confidence than younger adults but one study found that computer experience matters more than age in measuring computer anxiety.[15]

Learning Style

Librarians who assist reference patrons soon see that when "faced with mastering new and difficult information or tasks, individuals have unique learning styles."[16,17] Only a brief discussion of learning styles will be attempted here and only in the context of computer usage. David A. Kolb, well-known authority, described four learning styles based on the ways individuals create knowledge through the transformation of experience.[18] The four learning style types are divergers, assimilators, convergers, and accommodators.[19] Divergers learn by concrete experience and reflective observation; they tend to view situations from many perspectives, are very imaginative and people-oriented. Assimilators learn by abstract conceptualization and reflective observation; they excel at inductive reasoning and developing logically-sound ideas. Convergers learn by abstract conceptualization and active experimentation; they are problem solvers, skills-oriented and are able to easily make decisions. Accommodators learn by concrete experience and active experimentation; they are problem solvers, people-oriented and like getting things done. Of the four learning style types, convergers have the lowest levels of computer anxiety overall.[20]

One college study found that students with these different learning styles have no significant differences in the level of computer anxiety before computer instruction but that after computer instruction, the level of anxiety decreases depending upon the learning style type.[21] This same study, however, indicates that if the training is brief then the level of anxiety after computer instruction lessens equally for all learning styles.[22] Since reference librarians usually only have a short period of time with a patron, trying to accommodate specific learning styles when helping patrons use computers does not seem necessary. On the other hand, if training is extensive, learning styles become more significant. More studies need to be done in this area.

Ways Reference Librarians Can Assist Computer-Stressed Patrons

If library users have successful experiences with computers, they will feel more comfortable coming to the library and doing research on computers. Investing a little time now in boosting patrons' self-confidence will save the reference librarian time in the future. Here are some ways to promote computer self-efficacy.

Be Reassuring

If you reassure library patrons that they will be able to navigate the computer to find what they are looking for, they will be more willing to try. Assuring them that the computer will not break if they hit a wrong key and that all patrons feel a little apprehensive at first will go a long way in relieving computer stress. Be sensitive to your user groups–patrons such as law faculty or practicing attorneys are reassured if they know it will not take much time to locate the information they need on the computer.

Give Patrons Hands-On Experience

Many people learn by doing. Hands-on in computer learning increases positive attitudes about computers and reduces anxiety.[23] Instead of describing what button to press when they get to the computer or showing them what button to press from your computer, walk with patrons to the computer, have them sit down and as you describe the action, have them do it. This may take longer but having a successful hands-on experience raises computer self-efficacy.

Do Not Use Technical Words or Jargon

Most library patrons do not know what ILP, RLG, ILL or WorldCat stand for, or even the name of the library catalog. If you use an acronym, technical computer term, or terms of art such as "stacks," use simple language to explain what you mean.[24]

Explain Why Searching a Particular Database Will Be Helpful

Many people learn better if they know why they are doing a certain task. Students are more interested in learning computer skills if they know how the computer will be useful to them.[25] Likewise, adults will spend time learning a particular database if they know why it will help them[26] Even attorneys will spend time learning something new if they see it as adding value to their practice.[27]

If you feel that searching the full text of the *United States Code* would be more helpful in researching a particular issue than using the paper index, explain why. For example, if the researcher is looking for a unique phrase, it will be much easier to find electronically than by using a paper index categorized by subject and not phrase.

A few years ago, an older man came to the reference desk and wanted to use the paper version of the *Index to Legal Periodicals*. I explained that he was welcome to use it but I also explained why he might want to search it electronically. Once he understood that he could save time by searching the author, title, and subject fields simultaneously and that he did not have to search year by year, he was more willing to venture into the wonderful world of electronic searching.

Give Patrons Information About the Databases You Are Suggesting

If you suggest two or three sources for finding what they are looking for, explain the differences; e.g., more law reviews are indexed in the *Index to Legal Periodicals* than are found full-text on LEXIS or Westlaw. You may want to tell them about date coverage. I once saw a law student spend over an hour trying to find a *Utah Law Review* article that turned out to be too old to be in the Westlaw database. Also, let the patron know which databases are full-text and which ones are not. Some of our library patrons have wasted an inordinate amount of time trying to bring up the full-text of the law review article in the *Index to Legal Periodicals*.

Encourage Patrons to Come Back to the Reference Desk for Assistance if Needed

"If you have any problems, please come find me at the reference desk." This helps patrons feel like an avenue is open to obtain more assistance and that you will not think they are stupid or too imposing if they do come back for more help. Some patrons too freely seek assistance at the reference desk but the majority try to be self-sufficient.

Check Back

If you are out and about in the library and walking past a patron, a quick inquiry like "How are things going?" gives patrons an opportunity to ask questions and helps them feel like you care. Most patrons using the library are under stress, whether it is a law student clerking at a firm, an undergraduate researching for a paper that is due tomorrow, or a *pro se* user who has been evicted from her apartment. Feeling that there is a person who is available and willing to help means a lot to library users.[28]

Anticipate Areas of Difficulty

It you know that a patron might have problems with a particular computer feature, such as using a mouse or navigating Windows, give a few instructions. Even regular Windows users may learn something if you show them how to change the size of the window or toggle between two windows. They may already know this, but if not, they will appreciate the information.

Employ Law Students at the Reference Desk

One thing to consider in assisting law students is that it may be beneficial to have law students work at the reference desk. Students learn computer skills primarily on their own or from their peers and seem more comfortable consulting peers than anyone else.[29] Law students employed by Westlaw and LEXIS are a good example of this. Law students will seek assistance from these student representatives more regularly than they will consult a reference librarian.

Help Avid Users Refine Techniques

Another thing to consider is that some law students may be completely unafraid of computers and rely too much on LEXIS and Westlaw (in fact, you have probably been thinking this throughout the article). Reference librarians can help law students have successful computer experiences by emphasizing what the students have learned in their legal research classes, including date coverage, reliability of source, best connector(s) to use, etc. One-on-one instruction and reminders will build confidence in their searching abilities.

CONCLUSION

In the electronic world that we live in, library users cannot avoid using computers to do research. In 1991, as James Hoover was discussing the transition of law libraries from a print-based place to one of multi-formats, he wondered what law libraries' instructional and reference responsibilities to database users should be.[30] We can no longer just wonder but must take an active role in training that contributes to patron success in their electronic research.

Studies show that if individuals feel computer anxiety, their experience in using computers will not be as successful. However, if reference librarians reassure patrons, give them hands-on experience, do not use technical words or jargon, explain the usefulness of a database, encourage them to come back to the reference desk for more assistance, and check back, they can help all library users raise their computer self-efficacy. This self-efficacy enables library patrons to have positive experiences retrieving legal information electronically, empowering them to feel confident using computers in future research situations.

NOTES

1. James L. Hoover, *Legal Scholarship and the Electronic Revolution,* 83 L. Libr. J. 643, 648 (1991).

2. Ellen M. Callinan, *Research Protocols in Reference Service: Informal Instruction in Law Firm Libraries,* 82 L. Libr. J. 39, 50 (1990).

3. Studies referred to in this article pertain to computer classes and focus on students enrolled at educational institutions. While these studies are not specific to reference desk interactions, I believe they provide useful information.

4. Yixin Zhang & Sue Espinoza, *Relationships Among Computer Self-Efficacy, Attitudes Toward Computers, and Desirability of Learning Computing Skills,* 30 J. Res. Computing in Educ. 420, 420 (1998).

5. Ratna Sinha, *Teaching Computer Applications to Nontraditional Students,* Bus. Educ. F., Dec. 1998, at 46, 46.

6. Anjetta McQueen, *Report Finds Majority of Faculty Technologically Stressed,* Black Issues in Higher Educ., Sept. 30, 1999, at 35, 35.

7. Mark Grossman, *Waiting for the New Age Lawyer,* Legal Times, May 31, 1999, at 29.

8. Philip A. Houle, *Toward Understanding Student Differences in a Computer Skills Course,* 14 J. Educ. Computing Res. 25, 28 (1996).

9. Zhang & Espinoza, *supra* note 4, at 420-21.

10. Houle, *supra* note 8, at 43.

11. James R. Necessary & Thomas S. Parish, *The Relationships between Computer Usage and Computer-Related Attitudes and Behaviors,* 116 Educ. 384, 385 (1996); *see also* David J. Ayersman, *Effects of Computer Instruction, Learning Style, Gender, and Experience on Computer Anxiety,* 12 Computers in the Schools, 15, 26 (1996).

12. Dana Gibson & James E. Hunton, *The Effect of Socioeconomic Background on Computer Anxiety and Performance: Evidence from Three Experiments,* 4 Advances Acct. Info. Sys. 11, 41 (1996).

13. Ayersman, *supra* note 11, at 17, 22; *see also* Houle, *supra* note 8, at 40; Sinha, *supra* note 5, at 45.

14. Gibson & Hunton, *supra* note 12, at 41.

15. Jennifer L. Dyck & Janan Al-Awar Smither, *Age Differences in Computer Anxiety: The Role of Computer Experience, Gender and Education,* 10 J. Educ. Computing Res. 239, 246 (1994).

16. For an excellent discussion on dealing with learning styles in general legal reference work, *see* Kristin Gerdy's *supra.*

17. Gene Geisert et al., *Reading, Learning Styles, and Computers,* 6 J. Reading, Writing, & Learning Disabilities Int'l 297, 298 (1990).

18. David A. Kolb, Experiential Learning: Experience as the Source of Learning and Development 41-42 (1984).

19. *See id.* at 77-78.

20. Ayersman, *supra* note 11, at 25-26.

21. *Id.* at 25.

22. *Id.*

23. Caroline Presno, *Taking the Byte Out of Internet Anxiety: Instructional Techniques that Reduce Computer/Internet Anxiety in the Classroom,* 18 J. Educ. Computing Res. 147, 150 (1998); *see also* Zhang & Espinoza, *supra* note 4, at 428; Ayersman, *supra* note 11, at 16; *see generally* Trudi E. Jacobson & Beth L. Mark, *Teaching in the Information Age: Active Learning Techniques to Empower Students,* in *Library Instruction Revisited: Bibliographic Instruction comes of Age* at 105, 109 (Lynne M. Martin ed., 1995). Published simultaneously in Reference Libr., No. 51/52 at 105, 109 (1995).

24. Jane Thompson, *Teaching Research to Faculty: Accommodating Cultural and Learn-Style Differences,* 88 L. Libr. J. 280, 281 (1996).

25. Zhang & Espinoza, *supra* note 4, at 428.

26. Sinha, *supra* note 5, at 46.

27. Jim Feuerstein, *Keeping Up with the Changes: How Technology Can Transform Your Legal Practice,* LegalTech Newsl., July 1999, at 4.

28. Callinan, *supra* note 2, at 51-52.

29. Philip Davis, *How Undergraduates Learn Computer Skills: Results of a Survey and Focus Group,* THE J., April 1999, at 68, 71.

30. Hoover, *supra* note 1, at 649.

Electronic Research Beyond LEXIS-NEXIS and Westlaw: Lower Cost Alternatives

Susan Lewis-Somers

SUMMARY. Lower-cost alternatives to LEXIS-NEXIS and Westlaw have entered the scene to give users without deep pockets access to electronic legal and congressional research. Loislaw.com, V., Congressional Universe and CQ.com on Congress may open up electronic research to new users and lure away some of the big legal research services' customers as well. *[Article copies available for a fee from The Haworth Document Delivery Service: 1-800-342-9678. E-mail address: <getinfo@haworthpressinc.com> Website: <http://www.HaworthPress.com> © 2001 by The Haworth Press, Inc. All rights reserved.]*

Legal research in the computer age has come to be defined by the dominant electronic legal research services LEXIS-NEXIS and Westlaw. We turn to these research giants because they allow us to update beyond what our manual research can achieve; they allow us to search the full texts of legal resources for keywords and phrases; they retrieve these materials quickly; and they contain resources that many of us do not have in our libraries.

But we pay dearly for these conveniences: to say that LEXIS-NEXIS and

---

Susan Lewis-Somers is Senior Reference and Educational Services Librarian at the American University Washington College of Law Library in Washington, DC, and has been an academic law librarian since 1989. She has a BA from the University of California at Los Angeles (UCLA), a JD from Southwestern University, and a MLibr from the University of Washington.

[Haworth co-indexing entry note]: "Electronic Research Beyond LEXIS-NEXIS and Westlaw: Lower Cost Alternatives." Lewis-Somers, Susan. Co-published simultaneously in *Legal Reference Services Quarterly* (The Haworth Information Press, an imprint of The Haworth Press, Inc.) Vol. 19, No. 3/4, 2001, pp. 105-118; and: *Teaching Legal Research and Providing Access to Electronic Resources* (ed: Gary L. Hill, Dennis S. Sears, and Lovisa Lyman) The Haworth Information Press, an imprint of The Haworth Press, Inc., 2001, pp. 105-118. Single or multiple copies of this article are available for a fee from The Haworth Document Delivery Service [1-800-342-9678, 9:00 a.m. - 5:00 p.m. (EST). E-mail address: getinfo@haworthpressinc.com].

Westlaw are expensive may be an understatement. Many smaller law firms and public law libraries go without them because they cannot afford them, although both services now offer more affordable, limited packages. Even those in more well-endowed firms, public libraries, and educational institutions with flat-rate contracts may feel some pressure to conduct LEXIS-NEXIS and Westlaw research quickly and sparingly to avoid a larger flat-rate fee the following year due to increased use.

So it is with some appreciation that we consider a few of the other fee-based legal and law-related research services as lower-cost alternatives, or at least supplements, to LEXIS-NEXIS and Westlaw for primary legal and legislative materials. This article will take a critical look at two full-text legal research services, Loislaw.com and V., and two full-text services for congressional research, CQ.com on Congress and CIS Congressional Universe.[1]

CASE LAW, STATUTES, AND OTHER PRIMARY LAW RESOURCES

Two publishers have developed web-based collections of state and federal primary law that have begun to chip away at the dominance of LEXIS-NEXIS and Westlaw. Law Office Information Systems, Inc., offers Loislaw.com, which provides full-text access to federal and state cases, statutes, regulations, and other primary law. Versuslaw, Inc. produces V., a federal and state case law research system.

Of the two new upstarts, it is Loislaw.com that is taking on LEXIS-NEXIS and Westlaw most directly. In its growing collections of federal and state law from all fifty states, Loislaw.com offers access to many of the same libraries of primary legal materials that the two giants have called their own. While V. is only now beginning to go beyond case law, as it adds state statutes, it does provide case law for federal and all fifty state jurisdictions that reaches farther back than the case law on Loislaw.com.

Thus, while Loislaw.com offers much more breadth for each federal and state jurisdiction in its collection of cases, statutes, regulations, and other primary law, V. offers a deeper archive of case law. Even those libraries that prefer to use LEXIS-NEXIS and Westlaw may find it cost effective to supplement research on these more expensive systems by turning to Loislaw.com and V. to print or download legal materials found on the more established services. Loislaw.com and V. charge no additional fees for printing and downloading.

Loislaw.com <loislaw.com>

Loislaw.com[2] is an affordable web-based research service that aims squarely at the higher-priced LEXIS-NEXIS and Westlaw market. It offers searchable full-text case law from all federal appellate jurisdictions (but not from federal district courts) and from all states and the District of Columbia; the *U.S. Code,* the U.S. Constitution, and state statutes from all states and D.C.; and session laws from almost all states.[3] Loislaw.com also features the *Code of Federal Regulations,* the *Federal Register,* and administrative regulations from all states, D.C., and New York City; federal and state court rules from all states; and attorney general and other administrative agency opinions from a growing number of jurisdictions.

Case law on Loislaw.com reaches back to 1899 for the U.S. Supreme Court and 1971 for the federal appellate courts. State case law archives vary. Loislaw.com adds new cases and legislation within twenty-four to seventy-two hours of their receipt from the courts, legislatures, or other official bodies.

Loislaw.com provides an especially useful feature in its currency scope notes for every title in its system. These currency notes allow a user to easily determine the currency and archival range of any title to the date. Thus, on November 4, 1999, the currency note told the user that the Arizona Court of Appeals database began on February 2, 1965, and was current through October 19, 1999, and the *U.S. Code* was current through Public Law 106-64, enacted on October 5, 1999.

Searching on Loislaw.com is relatively simple. Users must initially choose between two approaches to searching: type of law or jurisdiction. Types of law include case law, statutes and acts, administrative regulations, attorney general opinions, and jury instructions. This approach is useful for searching across jurisdictions; thus, a user may search for all state and federal case law within a particular federal circuit. She may also use this approach to search across all court decisions within a jurisdiction, such as across all appellate courts within a state.

On the other hand, searching by jurisdiction requires a user to narrow a search to a particular state or federal jurisdiction and, within that jurisdiction, to a specific court's decisions, to a specific code, or a specific set of court rules. This approach is useful to narrow a search to a known case, statute, or other specific document.

If a user is looking, more generally, for appellate case law for a particular state, the better approach is to search by type of law rather than by jurisdiction. While counterintuitive, with this approach, she may search all of a state's appellate case law, regardless of the court; with the jurisdiction approach, she may search only *one* court's decisions. After choosing the type of law option, the user may select any or all of the available courts for one or more jurisdictions.

Loislaw.com provides an easy-to-use case law search screen, tailored to the particulars of court decisions. There is a dialog box for each searchable field, including official citation, docket number, party names, and the opinion's author, as well as an option to "search entire document." In this way, the Loislaw.com search screen is much more user-friendly than the V. case law search screen, which does not provide separate dialog boxes for each field but requires a rather specialized field searching syntax, within the single dialog box provided, to limit a search by field.

A user may search on Loislaw.com by word or phrase, and it offers Boolean and proximity connector searching to tie words and phrases together. The "/n" connector will look familiar to users of LEXIS-NEXIS and Westlaw, and it works the same way: it searches for words within a prescribed number of spaces of each other and in either order. There is no connector on Loislaw.com that allows a user to specify the order in which the words in proximity should appear, however, as V., LEXIS-NEXIS, and Westlaw provide.

A search for cases on Loislaw.com retrieves a citation list of cases in reverse chronological order. Each citation includes the official summary as an abstract. The full text of each case offers the official citation and the West regional reporter citation, where they are different, and the page breaks for the official reporter. Page breaks for the West reporter appear only where that reporter is the official reporter. Because Loislaw.com offers the official reporter pagination, its cases have no paragraph numbering.

Citations to cases, statutes, regulations, and other primary law appearing within full text documents on Loislaw.com are hyperlinked to the cited documents' full text, allowing a user to jump back and forth between a case and related law cited within. This makes it more competitive with LEXIS-NEXIS and Westlaw and gives Loislaw.com a definite advantage over V., which currently offers no hyperlinks to other kinds of primary law cited in the text of a case. Footnote references are hyperlinked to a list of footnotes at the end of the case, as they are in V.

As with case law, a Loislaw.com user may choose to search for statutes, regulations, and other primary law across jurisdictions or within a state or federal jurisdiction. A search of the *U.S. Code* offers a search template with fields appropriate to a statute and buttons to retrieve helpful currency information and a table of contents. The search retrieves a list of federal statute citations with abstracts taken from the text of the statute, although not necessarily from the beginning of the statute or near the search terms. The list appears by code section number in descending order.

The full text of the federal statute is the official text and includes all official notes and references. Loislaw.com offers hypertext links to other statutes referred to in the text but not to related public laws, the full text of which are not included in Loislaw.com's database (although Loislaw.com integrates them into the *U.S. Code* expeditiously). If a user searches by statute citation, Loislaw.com gives her the option of browsing from one section to the next and back by always retrieving the table of contents for the *U.S. Code* chapter, of which the section is part, as one of the found documents; each section listed in the contents is hyperlinked to its full text.

While Loislaw.com does not include a citator, such as LEXIS-NEXIS' *Shepard's* or Westlaw's KeyCite, it does give instructions in its useful online tutorial for using Loislaw.com as a citator to find cases that cite to a particular case, statute, or other legal document on Loislaw.com. A user must enter citation or party name information in the "search entire document," "text of majority opinion," or "text of dissenting opinion" fields. While there are no editorial references, Loislaw.com will find the judicial history and treatment of a case or other primary text, at least as far back as its case law archive goes.

As with other Loislaw.com searches, the full text display will open at the place where the search terms appear highlighted only if opened from the citation list and not from the "next result" and "previous result" buttons. This requires the user to go back and forth to the citation list, a minor annoyance.

Other features on Loislaw.com include its LawWatch service, which will automatically run a user's saved searches on a periodic basis, and its Client Billing Timer, which will track the amount of time a user spends on Loislaw. com and calculate the amount to bill a client based on a specified rate per hour supplied by the user.

All in all, Loislaw.com is to be applauded for its chutzpah in taking on LEXIS-NEXIS and Westlaw and for creating a reasonably-priced alternative that is easy to use and suitable for most basic legal research.

V. <versuslaw.com>

V.[4] is a web-based research service that offers the full text of federal and state case law from all fifty states and the District of Columbia. V. is not a comprehensive legal research service in the mold of Loislaw.com, LEXIS-NEXIS, and Westlaw because it does not offer much beyond case law, at least for now.[5] But if it is inexpensive electronic access to case law you are after, V. fits the bill nicely.

V's archive of federal cases includes U.S. Supreme Court cases back to 1900 and federal appellate court decisions for all circuits, dating back to 1930 for most of the circuits. V. has also begun to add case law from the federal district courts, currently offering cases back to 1997 for the Eastern District of Pennsylvania and the Northern District of Mississippi. (Loislaw.com does not provide any case law from the federal district courts.) Newly-released U.S. Supreme Court decisions are added to V. within a few hours of their release. Other new federal cases are added as they are received from the federal courts.

The depth of V.'s state appellate case law archive varies with each state; coverage for fourteen states goes back to 1930, while for others its vintage is more recent. Newly issued state case law is added as it is received from state courts.

For those with experience using LEXIS-NEXIS and Westlaw, searching on V. looks vaguely familiar. Instead of initially selecting a library and file or a database, a user first chooses a jurisdiction, such as "Federal Circuits," "State Appellate," or "4th," which includes state and federal case law within that circuit. The next step offers a user who has chosen anything other than a U.S. Supreme Court search the option of narrowing her jurisdictional choice. Thus, she may choose to search within one or more federal circuits, within one or more states, or within a particular federal circuit and only one of its states. Alternatively, a user may search across all federal circuits and the U.S. Supreme Court or across all state appellate courts and the U.S. Supreme Court.

After making a jurisdictional selection, the user must enter a search query in a special dialog box. The query may be either a word or phrase (V. calls its exact phrase searching "natural language" searching) or formulated as a Boolean search. For those users uninitiated in Boolean searching, V. provides a helpful "Search Buddy" that formulates sample searches in a number of selected subject areas as a teaching tool.

V. offers "shortcut searching," which is essentially field searching, for more experienced users to search the fields that appear before the text of a case, such as the party, docket, and citation fields. It would have been helpful, though, if V. had provided more user-friendly search boxes for each field, as Loislaw.com has done, instead of only one dialog box that requires a specialized syntax for field searching.

For experienced LEXIS-NEXIS and Westlaw users, V.'s use of the proximity connector "w/n" to mean the equivalent of "pre/n"on LEXIS-NEXIS and Westlaw (the words searched for must appear within a prescribed number of words of each other and the first word must always appear before the second) may be confusing. V. uses the proximity connector "near/n" for words that must appear within a specific proximity to each other and in either order.

After entering a search query, the next step is to select a date range, if any, and to specify the number of results, or documents, desired; the default is 50 documents but a user may alternatively select 25, 100 or 200. V. uses a relevancy ranking algorithm to display those cases more likely to be relevant at the top of the list.

The cases retrieved have paragraph numbering to allow citation to V.'s own citation format, which is "[year].[jurisdiction abbrev.].[V.'s case no.],[para. no.] <http://www.versuslaw.com>." Thus, a V. case citation may appear as 1997.MD.4, P.18 <http://www.versuslaw.com>.

V. now also displays the more familiar official and West reporter parallel citations in the citation list and at the top of the full-text decision; it is in the midst of converting from a less useful display to this new format. Footnote references within the text of a case and the footnotes themselves, which appear at the end of the text, are hyperlinked to each other. Unfortunately, references to cited cases are not yet hyperlinked to the full text of those cases, as they are on Loislaw.com, LEXIS-NEXIS, and Westlaw.

V. may be used as a citator to find the history and treatment of a case. It offers a step-by-step explanation of how to use V. as a citator in its online "FAQ" (frequently asked questions) document. As on Loislaw.com, there are no handy editorial references, but a user may approximate *Shepard's* and KeyCite on V. to find the judicial history and treatment of a case or other primary document.

By initially limiting its product to case law, V. has not attempted to directly compete with LEXIS-NEXIS and Westlaw, although this may change as it adds statutes and regulations. Yet it does well what it modestly sets out to do: provide inexpensive searchable electronic access to a sizable archive of federal and state case law.

CONGRESSIONAL RESOURCES

LEXIS-NEXIS and Westlaw are also major providers of primary congressional materials that researchers use to conduct legislative history research and to track pending legislation still making its way through Congress. However, two established publishers that specialize in congressional research services offer alternatives to the major legal research services.

Congressional Quarterly, Inc., now known as CQ, Inc., and Congressional Information Service, Inc. (CIS) provide electronic access to a wide range of congressional information and documents via CQ.com On Congress and CIS Congressional Universe. LEXIS-NEXIS now owns CIS, so much of the content of Congressional Universe is derived from content on LEXIS-NEXIS. Similarly, many of the databases in CQ.com On Congress are also included in Westlaw, although they are not available on Westlaw academic accounts.[6]

CQ.com On Congress <oncongress.cq.com>

CQ, Inc.,[7] formerly known as Congressional Quarterly, Inc., has been a leading publisher of all things Congress for many years. Its *Congressional Almanac, CQ Report* (formerly *Congressional Quarterly Weekly Report*), many congressional guides and directories, and electronic CQ Washington Alert have been staples of current information and background reporting on Congress.

CQ has moved beyond its CD-based CQ Washington Alert into a web-based research service with the awkward name CQ.com On Congress. It provides a researcher with current full-text bills; committee documents, such as reports and hearings transcripts; floor debate from the *Congressional Record*; bill tracking reports; voting analysis; member and committee information; and congressional news and analysis, including the in-depth *CQ Weekly* and *CQ Monitor News*.

CQ.com's coverage of these materials goes back to the beginning of the 104th Congress in January 1995. In addition, it provides the text of the *Federal Register* back to 1997 and links to the *Code of Federal Regulations* at the GPOAccess web site[8] and to the dated official version of the *U.S. Code* at the U.S. House of Representatives Office of Law Revision Counsel.[9]

Older documents are available from the new CQ Archives, whose material is culled from the former CQ Washington Alert and the defunct Legi-Slate database, part of which CQ, Inc., purchased in 1999. CQ Archives provides access to congressional voting records back to the 98th Congress (1983-84), bill tracking reports back to the 99th Congress (1985-86), bill texts and the text of the *Congressional Record* back to the 100th Congress (1987-88), committee reports and hearings back to the 101st Congress (1989-90), and the *Federal Register* back to 1990.

Unfortunately, these archival databases are incompatible with the current CQ.com files and must be searched separately. In contrast, CIS Congressional Universe offers its extensive archive of full text congressional materials and the *Federal Register*, the *Code of Federal Regulations*, and the current *U.S. Code Service* as part of its primary service, so that one search will cover current and archival materials.

CQ.com's searchable files are updated daily. New documents are usually added within twenty-four hours of their release by Congress and bill tracking reports are updated within twenty-four hours of the latest action. Current news sources, such as the *CQ Daily Monitor*, are updated several times a day, and the *CQ Weekly* is published on CQ.com forty-eight hours before its print counterpart is published.

The search screens for CQ.com On Congress are logically organized into "areas" by category of material or function, with research areas for bills, committees, floor action, vote analysis, committee schedules, member information, news and analysis, the *Federal Register*, and useful reference resources. The search templates offer search fields that are appropriate to the particular topical area and allow a user to enter word, phrase, or simple Boolean queries. Each template offers helpful search examples and hyperlinks to relevant search tips beside each query box. CQ.com's immediate links to its search tips are much more obvious than Congressional Universe's tips, which are not noted near the query boxes but are hidden down below the search screen.

A search in the "Bills" area will retrieve full-text bills, bill analyses and digests, and bill tracking reports. These bill tracking reports are manually derived from material in the *Congressional Record* and compile most *Congressional Record* mentions of an action or document related to a bill or public law in chronological order. They offer hyperlinks to the full text of documents referenced, including various versions of the bill and related resolutions, activity related to the bill in the *Congressional Record,* committee reports and hearings, voting records, detailed narrative reports about committee markup sessions, and *CQ Weekly* articles. CQ.com's bill tracking reports do not include references to floor remarks by individual members, however, as Congressional Universe does.

A minor annoyance is that these bill tracking reports do not include at the top of a report, as Congressional Universe's bill tracking reports do, a reference to the last date on which there was action on a bill. A user must scroll all the way through the document to find this information at the end. CQ.com bill tracking reports do provide the names of all bill sponsors at the beginning, while sponsors appear at the end of bill tracking reports on Congressional Universe.

Search terms are highlighted in the full-text bills, committee reports, hearings transcripts, and *Congressional Record* floor debate that may also be retrieved from CQ.com. In addition, CQ.com provides extensive news and analysis in its BillWatch treatment of each bill, its coverage of committee markup sessions and other committee action, its House Action Reports and SenateWatch that cover floor proceedings, its custom vote analysis, and its *CQ Weekly* and other publications that cover Congress and the White House. Congressional Universe, which hired many former Legi-Slate reporters and editors, also offers current news and analysis of Congress and the White House in the *National Journal* and *CongressDaily.*

CQ.com uses a cluttered-looking and hard-to-use frames format in its search screens to present sidebar links to collections of material that are related to the topical area being searched. Some of the material in the left-hand sidebar frame simply duplicates what can already be found on the main area search screen. But in most cases, the related frame provides "Quick Views," which are links to browsable (but not searchable) resources not available from the search screen. Thus, in the "Bills Area," Quick Views offers links to references related to the bills topic, such as "Recently Introduced Bills," "Bills with Recent Action," and "Appropriations Bills."

In the "Committees Area," a user can find handy membership lists for all congressional committees via Quick Views, although in mid-November 1999 and again in early December, its joint committee rosters reversed the offices of committee members so that all senators on joint committees were incorrectly listed as members of the House and all House members were listed as senators. It appears that CQ does not tend to its sidebar information with much care.

Finally, CQ.com offers several convenient custom searching options that make searching much easier. A user can design custom lists of bill numbers, search terms, member names, and vote numbers that can be quickly retrieved at a search screen to avoid having to enter this information for each search. In addition, a user can create a custom search to use repeatedly when the same search is conducted often. Moreover, as on LEXIS-NEXIS and Westlaw, CQ.com's "Custom Alerts" feature will run a custom search at specified intervals to retrieve any new results available since the last search and deliver the results via E-mail or to the CQ.com login screen. "Custom Vote Analysis" allows a user to run customized vote-tracking reports on particular members of Congress.

CQ.com creates a significant stumbling block for its users by requiring them to use older versions of Netscape (4.08) and Internet Explorer (5.0) to get the best results with its busy frames format. The time it took for the screens to load with Netscape 4.5 was excruciatingly slow. Unlike CQ.com, Congressional Universe creates the same kind of dynamic sidebars without frames by using a relational database design, which allows its screens to display more quickly with any reasonably current browser. In addition, the CQ.com hyperlinks on its bill tracking reports do not work at all with some browsers. While they worked with my colleague's Netscape 4.7, the links were dead with my Netscape 4.5, apparently due to an incompatibility between CQ.com's Java Script and the 4.5 browser. CQ.com will unveil a new version in 2000; one hopes that it will resolve these vexing technical problems.

What sets CQ.com apart is its excellent congressional news and analysis, long a hallmark of CQ, Inc., publications. But as an electronic research tool, it is still rather rough around the edges and needs some improvement. Maybe its new version in mid-2000 will meet this challenge.

CIS Congressional Universe <www.lexis-nexis.com/cis>

Like its competitor CQ, Inc., Congressional Information Service, Inc., (CIS)[10] has been a publisher of congressional materials for many years. Its *CIS Index* indexes and abstracts congressional committee reports, hearings, documents, and prints; its companion microfiche set reprints the full text of all documents in the *CIS Index*.

The *CIS Legislative Histories* compiles a broader range of legislative history references by public law number, including references to the public law and related bills, various committee documents, floor debate from the

Congressional Record, presidential statements, and references to legislative materials for related bills from the same and previous congresses. CIS has published the *CIS Index* and *CIS Legislative Histories,* covering legislative materials from 1970-, on CD-ROM as Congressional Masterfile 2.

Several years ago, LEXIS-NEXIS purchased CIS and combined its own database of full-text congressional bills, committee documents, the *Congressional Record,* U.S. public laws, the *U.S. Code Service,* the *Federal Register,* and the *Code of Federal Regulations* with the *CIS Index* and *CIS Legislative Histories* to create the electronic Congressional Compass. Congressional Compass was soon renamed Congressional Universe and made part of a larger stable of LEXIS-NEXIS products in its LEXIS-NEXIS Universe.

In addition to its full-text primary documents and indexes, Congressional Universe also offers the thorough LEXIS-NEXIS bill tracking reports. These reports chronologically compile every action and document related to a bill or public law and provide hyperlinks to allow a user to connect to the full text of the documents referenced. These bill tracking reports are quite similar to the CQ.com on Congress bill tracking reports, and now include links to committee bill markup analysis from the National Journal Group. Congressional Universe bill tracking reports also include references to floor remarks made by individual members, something that CQ.com does not include in its bill tracking reports.

Further, Congressional Universe offers biographical, financial, and voting information about members of Congress, committee rosters and schedules, and its own publications that offer current congressional news and analysis, *National Journal* and *CongressDaily,* written in large part by former Legi-Slate reporters and editors recently hired by LEXIS-NEXIS.

In its archive of full-text materials, Congressional Universe offers bills and its bill tracking service from 1989, the transcripts of selected hearings from 1988, the text of most written testimony submitted by witnesses from 1993, committee markup analysis from late 1999, committee reports from 1990, selected committee prints from 1996, committee documents from 1995, the *Congressional Record* from 1985, public laws from 1988, and the *Federal Register* from 1980. Unlike CQ.com On Congress, which requires a separate search of its archive, the archival materials on Congressional Universe may be searched along with its current files.

As a supplement to its legislative history materials, Congressional Universe offers the current full-text *U.S. Code Service* and *Code of Federal Regulations* from LEXIS-NEXIS in addition to the *Federal Register* from 1980. CQ.com provides the *Federal Register* from 1997 (and from 1990 in its CQ Archives) but merely provides links to the U.S. House of Representatives web site for the more dated official *U.S. Code* and to GPOAccess for access to the *Code of Federal Regulations.*

Searching on Congressional Universe is simple and its search screens are clear and uncluttered. A user initially chooses the category of material sought, such as the *CIS Index,* publications, testimony, bills, laws, and regulations. From here, the user selects a specific type of document and receives a search screen tailored for that document.

The ambiguously-named "Publications" section allows a user to select a search screen for full-text committee reports, among other things. A user may search for a report by keyword, committee, and Congress but not by report number or associated bill number. The search screen offers search tips below the search template, although it is not immediately evident that these search tips are below. While CQ.com's search screens are too busy, its search tips are easier to find, with hyperlinks to relevant tips right next to each dialog box on the search screen.

Searching within the *"CIS Index"* section of Congressional Universe allows a user to retrieve legislative histories to public laws by keyword, subject heading, bill number, and public law number, with links to the abstracts or, in some cases, the full text of documents included. The information found in these legislative histories complements what Congressional Universe offers in its bill tracking reports, which track much more closely every action associated with a bill, whether it became a public law or not. Bill tracking reports also provide links to full-text documents related to the bill. While the CIS legislative histories do not track a bill's chronological progress, as a bill tracking report does, their abstracts to committee documents do provide a level of description that cannot be found in a bill tracking report.

A user within the *CIS Index* section may also search for abstracts of individual congressional committee documents by keyword or subject heading, publication title, public law, bill or document number, committee, or witness name. These abstracts may offer hyperlinks to the full text of the documents they describe depending on the date of the documents.

One major flaw in Congressional Universe is the inability to search within the "Testimony" or "Publications" sections for the full text of various committee publications by the document number, bill number, or public law number. A user must go, instead, to the *CIS Index* section, where she may search by bill number, public law number, or document number to retrieve only an abstract to a committee publication that may, depending on the date, contain a hypertext link to the full text. CQ.com's search screens always provide an option to search for committee publications by at least the bill number if not always by the public law or document number.

Another annoyance is the inability to search several related fields at the same time. Thus, in the *CIS Index* section, a user is unable to conduct one search by keyword, committee, and witness, for instance. Three separate searches must be done to search each of these fields. Similarly, in the Publications section a user cannot conduct one search of the *Congressional Record* by keyword and date. Congressional Universe forces a user to search each field separately, limiting the utility of combined field searching. CQ.com does allow searching across multiple fields.

Congressional Universe offers information about members of Congress, such as biographical, voting, and financial information. While most of this information is also available on CQ.com, only Congressional Universe offers the full text of the campaign finance reports that all candidates file with the Federal Elections Commission as well as information about the contributors to candidates' campaigns. However, CQ.com provides the ability to tailor a custom vote analysis to generate vote tracking reports while Congressional Universe does not. Both services also offer congressional committee roster and scheduling information.

CIS Congressional Universe is a useful tool for anyone who tracks current congressional activity as well as for those engaged in retrospective legislative history research. It is easy to use although it would benefit from more document number search options and the ability to combine related search fields.

CONCLUSION

LEXIS-NEXIS and Westlaw continue to provide legal research systems second to none but at a significant price. Many of the resources that researchers have counted on them to supply are now available from other, less expensive and more limited services. The rapidly-expanding materials on Loislaw. com and V. provide less costly alternatives for primary legal research that may be used instead of, or at least as a supplement to, LEXIS-NEXIS and Westlaw. Congressional Universe and, to a lesser degree, CQ.com On Congress are good alternatives for congressional research.

Move over, LEXIS-NEXIS and Westlaw. The new kids on the block are here to stay.

NOTES

1. The reviews that follow are based on analyses of these services in November and December 1999. It is possible that changes have occurred to some of these services in the meantime.

2. <loislaw.com>, (800) 364-2512 or (501) 471-5581. Prices vary; contact Loislaw. com for current prices; law school program provides access to law students and faculty at no charge; judicial program for full-time state and federal judges and judicial staff consists of free access to federal or state libraries covering judge's jurisdiction; CD version also available.

3. U.S. public laws are searchable on Loislaw.com only as part of the *U.S. Code.*

4. <versuslaw.com>, (888) 377-8752 or (425) 250-0142 M-F, 8:00 a.m.-5:00 p.m. (PST). Twenty-four-hour plan: $14.95/24-hour period "per attorney," monthly

plan: $6.95/month per attorney, annual plan: $83.40/annual per attorney; free to individual law students, law faculty and law school staff doing academic research or $1250/annual for access for all law school users (prices as of 01/03/00); CD version also available; contact VersusLaw, Inc., for current prices.

5. V. has recently begun to add full-text state statutes and regulations.

6. Not to be overlooked is the fact that many congressional documents may also be found at no cost on the Internet at Thomas <thomas.loc.gov> and GPOAccess <www.access.gpo.gov>.

7. <oncongress.cq.com>, (800) 432-2250, ext. 279 or (202) 887-6279. Prices vary; contact CQ, Inc., for current prices; introductory free trial.

8. <www.access.gpo.gov/nara/cfr/cfr-table-search.html>.

9. <uscode.house.gov/usc.htm>.

10. <www.lexis-nexis.com/cis>, (800) 638-8380. Prices vary; contact Congressional Information Service, Inc., for current prices; introductory free trial.

The Internet Alternative

Kristin B. Gerdy

SUMMARY. The author discusses the practical nature of Internet legal research by providing examples of actual research problems solved on the Internet and by providing a selective listing of Internet legal resources for judicial materials, federal legislative and administrative materials, and state materials. *[Article copies available for a fee from The Haworth Document Delivery Service: 1-800-342-9678. E-mail address: <getinfo@haworthpressinc.com> Website: <http://www.HaworthPress.com> © 2001 by The Haworth Press, Inc. All rights reserved.]*

INTRODUCTION

Scenario 1

Monday afternoon, the week following the Law Review Write-On Competition, the phone in my office rings. I answer it and connect with a very nervous law student. She has just finished her first year of law school, and it is her first day of a corporate internship out of state. During the interview

---

Kristin B. Gerdy is Visiting Assistant Professor of Law, Temple University Beasley School of Law, Philadelphia, PA, on leave from the Brigham Young University J. Reuben Clark Law School and Howard W. Hunter Law Library. She teaches first-year Legal Research and Writing, Advanced Legal Research, and Advanced Appellate Advocacy, and is the 1999-2000 Chair of the Research Instruction and Patron Services Special Interest Section of the American Association of Law Libraries.

[Haworth co-indexing entry note]: "The Internet Alternative." Gerdy, Kristin B. Co-published simultaneously in *Legal Reference Services Quarterly* (The Haworth Information Press, an imprint of The Haworth Press, Inc.) Vol. 19, No. 3/4, 2001, pp. 119-141; and: *Teaching Legal Research and Providing Access to Electronic Resources* (ed: Gary L. Hill, Dennis S. Sears, and Lovisa Lyman) The Haworth Information Press, an imprint of The Haworth Press, Inc., 2001, pp. 119-141. Single or multiple copies of this article are available for a fee from The Haworth Document Delivery Service [1-800-342-9678, 9:00 a.m. - 5:00 p.m. (EST). E-mail address: getinfo@haworthpressinc.com].

process, she was told the corporation had a small "law library," but when she arrived she found a copy of the *United States Code* and a few reference books, but that was about it–certainly no access to LEXIS or Westlaw. There is an academic law library downtown, but it is not close to the corporate offices. The first assignment she is given requires locating the text of an executive or-der–fairly simple. Remembering potential print sources from her legal research class, she heads for the office "library." Unfortunately, none of the sources she needs are there, and the trek across town to the academic law library is not an option because the answer is needed before she could complete the trip. She remembers, from attending a seminar on Internet Legal Research during Write-On Week, that many resources are available on the Internet, to which she does have access–unfortunately she had left the URL list from the class at home (who would have anticipated really using it!). So, frantically, she picks up the phone and calls the law school, desperate for help.

Both opening our browsers, we walk through the problem together. We choose the *United States House of Representatives Internet Law Library* as a potential source. Once there, we link into *Federal Laws by Source,* then *Presidential Documents,* and finally, *Executive Orders.* She has the Order's number so we easily construct a search and within a few seconds both of us are reading the Order online; she executes a print command and is off with the answer–much relieved and with greater confidence that the summer's experience will turn out all right.

Similar scenarios involving patrons searching for recent Supreme Court cases are becoming fairly routine. Feeling deprived by the lack of Westlaw and LEXIS access or having to deal with the consequences of a less than fully functional library, students and other patrons are thrilled to discover online opinions at sites like Cornell's *Legal Information Institute, FindLaw,* and InfoSynthesis's *USSC +.*

Scenario 2

It is 8:25 a.m. on Thursday of finals week. A second-year student ap-proaches the reference desk. She is obviously panicked and sleep-deprived. Dropping a load of books from her arms, and on the verge of tears, she explains her problem. Her last final exam is in five minutes; she is not fully prepared, has not slept in days, and to make things worse, as soon as she finishes the exam she has to go home, pack, get her children ready for a three-week stay with relatives, and be to the airport in the early afternoon. She is headed for Nairobi, part of a small NGO delegation from the law school, to attend a United Nations Conference. She is stressed, excited, and probably a bit nauseated, and to top it all off, the professor and head of the delegation has just given her the nebulous assignment to find a statement on the family given to the United States delegation to the United Nations Conference on Women in Beijing, China, sometime in 1995 by Congress–maybe the Senate, maybe the House, maybe official, maybe not, no one is really sure of the details, but they know that it exists! She doesn't have time to find it–but she must have it and she must have it NOW!

Persuaded that her exam should get priority at this point, she leaves vowing to come back the minute she is finished. I convince her we can find the material in time. There are several research options to solve this particular problem; I choose to see what I can find on the Internet. Linking directly to the Government Printing Office and searching the *Congressional Record* covering 1995 yields the results–an amendment to a Senate bill adopted specifically to guide the U.S. Beijing delegation. From the GPO site, I am able to print the applicable *Congressional Record* pages and the bill itself–the product looks better than any photocopy from the printed source would have. The student comes back two hours later, weary from her exam and hopeful that she will not have to spend the next hour researching when she really needs to be packing. I show her what I had found, give her the printouts–pointing out the URL for future reference–and send her on her way.

Admittedly, these same results could have been achieved by walking down to the *Congressional Record,* going through the indexes and pulling the appropriate daily publications. Either LEXIS or Westlaw also would have provided the desired material. It was not until later that I realized the importance of locating the source on the Internet. While in Nairobi the delegation would not have been able to access LEXIS or Westlaw, which had not yet launched their .com sites; they could not drive across town to the local law library and look up the United States' *Congressional Record* (and even if they could have, the $80 taxi ride would probably have prohibited it), but they could access GPO on the Internet.

Scenario 3

The first two scenarios illustrate patrons whose research problems were solved by turning to the Internet; this one, however, involves a situation where I wish I had thought of turning to it sooner–instead of after it was too late to help.

A desperate father calls the reference desk one morning. He has been in the law library the past three evenings trying to research his problem. His wife has left him and taken their one-year-old daughter to another state. Although a specific visitation schedule was yet to be drafted, an attorney advised him that the state's minimum/default visitation schedule would apply to the case. His immediate problem is that while his ex-wife had consented to visitation for part of the upcoming Memorial Day weekend; she now refuses to cooperate. He has researched the applicable state law and has found only a minimum visitation schedule for school-age children. No matter how hard he tries he cannot find anything applicable to his one-year-old because the current code is silent on younger children. He is at a loss as to what to do. We go through the sources he has researched and it appears he has been thorough, examining every pertinent available resource in the law library. Frustrated that we cannot find anything, I wish him good luck–maybe his ex-wife will have a change of heart–but as far as we can tell he is without remedy.

The very next day, while showing a colleague the *Utah State Legislature Bill Tracking* page on the Internet, I happen upon brand new legislation setting minimum visitation for children younger than five years old! The legislation has only been in effect for a month and the library had not yet received the session laws or legislative report, but there it is, the answer to the problem. Not anticipating such a find, I had not taken the discouraged father's name or phone number and had no way of contacting him. How I wish I had thought of the Internet sooner!

USING THE INTERNET FOR LEGAL RESEARCH

During the latter half of the 1990s, the Internet has exploded with law-based materials, particularly in the areas of federal case law, legislation, and administrative information. As more and more materials are placed on the Internet, its viability as a research option increases. However, in order to use the Internet effectively, legal researchers need training. Law librarians can help by providing tools to ease researchers into productive Internet strategies. To do so, they should focus on two central issues confronting novice Internet researchers. First, researchers need to recognize the potential concerns arising from Internet research. Second, they need a "game plan" including a manageable set of sources from which to begin their research.

Conducting legal research on the Internet raises at least three major concerns: accuracy/reliability, currency, and the potential for overload. Although these concerns face researchers dealing with any type of resource, they are exacerbated on the Internet. While an in-depth discussion of these concerns is beyond the scope of this article, a few cursory remarks are warranted. Because of its inherently anarchical nature, there are no universal standards assuring accuracy or reliability of information on the Internet. Cybercitizens are free to place whatever content they choose on their web sites. Lack of standards poses problems for novice researchers who have not learned or perfected their assessment skills. Beginners should be guided to sites that are maintained by recognized authorities such as law libraries and government organizations. They should be warned away from sites that either do not identify a sponsoring group or individual or whose sponsor is unknown to the researcher.

Currency also poses a risk for the researcher. Much of the information loaded onto Internet sites is never updated. "Dead" sites are as common as "live" ones. Internet researchers must get accustomed to checking the updating information on cites they reference.

Finally, researchers must realize the probability for information overload and devise methods to confront it. No researcher has the time to wade through 10,000 links generated by a search engine. Researchers must develop search skills, narrow their queries as much as possible, and determine when to stop looking.

As we do with print sources, law librarians can educate patrons about the importance of assessing information quality on the Internet. Many resources available online explore ensuring information accuracy, currency, and reliability. Among the best is the "Evaluating the Quality of Information on the Internet" located on *The Virtual Chase* at <http:www.virtualchase.com/quality/index.html.> Using the checklist and other resources compiled by webmaster Genie Tyburski, patrons can learn to evaluate the information they find on the Internet.

After recognizing the potential problems with Internet legal research, researchers must develop a "game plan"–a strategy for optimum research efficiency. The biggest problem with the Internet is knowing what is there, and what is not. There simply is not enough time to "surf" every time a question arises. Search engines are a good start, but they are not adequate. The best approach to productive Internet legal research is to identify and bookmark sites that have the type of information usually sought, that are updated frequently, and that receive good marks for accuracy. The bookmark list should be personally customized to fit the researcher's needs. Law librarians can also create link pages on their own library home pages to lead patrons to legal resources on the Internet.[1]

The remainder of this article provides law librarians and researchers with some "starting points" for bookmark lists or link pages. The sites are divided into categories: judicial sources, legislative and administrative sources, and state sources. All of the sites listed are free. Many other sites exist, some of which require subscriptions; however, I have used these sites to successfully assist students and other patrons. The source categories are organized with a general introduction to the scope of materials available, a tabular overview of the sources, and annotated bibliographies of some specific sources.

JUDICIAL SOURCES

United States Supreme Court Decisions

Internet availability of United States Supreme Court decisions is excellent. Particularly for current decisions and other ongoing information, the Internet is as good as any other source, and better than some. Several services have focused on providing Court cases to the public free of charge. While their features and coverage vary, each site has value for the legal researcher.

United States Supreme Court Decisions[2]

Service	URL	Coverage	Searching	Calendars	Other
Legal Information Institute: Hermes	<http://supct.law.cornell.edu/supct/>	since May 1990; more than 600 historical decisions	keyword, boolean, topic, 1st and 2nd party names, date, historical by opinion author	court calendar, oral argument calendar	background information on the court and its justices, Supreme Court rules, summary of questions presented in cases before the Court
USSC+	<http://www.usscplus.com/current/> AND <http://www.usscplus.com/topk/> AND <http://www.usscplus.com/ecase/>	more than 7,500 cases, selected leading cases from 1793-1945, complete coverage from 1945- Current court term is by date in a separate file	citation, party name, subject matter, docket number, keyword		requires a frames-supportable browser. Includes links to other federal court sites, supreme court news and information
FindLaw U.S. Supreme Court Decisions	<http://www.findlaw.com/casecode/supreme.html>	150 U.S.-present (1893 to the present)	browse by *U.S. Reports* volume number and year, search by citation, title, keyword, boolean	yes (located in Supreme Court Resources)	links to other federal court web sites and other documents
FLITE	<http://www.fedworld.gov/supcourt/index.htm>	*U.S. Reports* volumes 300-422 (1937 to 1975)	Case name, keyword	no	
Oyez Oyez Oyez: A Supreme Court WWW Resource	<http://oyez.nwu.edu>	audio cases: varied links to printed opinions in FindLaw	title, citation, subject, date choice of RealAudio or Written Opinions	no	biographies and portraits of justices, audio recordings of speeches by justices, virtual tour of the Supreme Court building

Legal Information Institute: Hermes
<http://supct.law.cornell.edu/supct/>

The Supreme Court division of the *Legal Information Institute,* maintained by Cornell Law School, contains all United States Supreme Court decisions issued since May 1990 in addition to an archive of more than 600 of the Court's most important historical (pre-1990) decisions.

Current Court materials include decisions reported by date, the Court calendar, and an oral argument schedule. Decisions from 1990 to the present and the prior year's major decisions are arranged by topic. Decisions from 1990 through 1997 are also indexed in annual segments by both first and second party name. The service also includes excellent background information about the Court and biographies of its justices.

The archive is keyword searchable, allowing searches of either syllabi or full opinion text. Boolean searches are supported using the operators AND, OR (also space), ANDNOT, and XOR (exclusive or-to find files containing either term but not both). Grouping operators with parentheses-nesting-allows more precise searching. Exact phrases must be enclosed in quotation marks. All terms are case insensitive and * may be used as a wildcard or root expander.

The Historic Decisions archive contains more than 600 opinions searchable by topic, party name, and opinion author.

When a case is retrieved, the researcher is given the option of viewing or downloading each opinion. Within the text of the case, any authorities available on the Internet (either in LII or other services) are hyperlinked for easy accessibility.

USSC+
<http://www.usscplus.com/current/> and
<http://www.usscplus.com/topk/> and
<http://www.usscplus.com/ecase/>

USSC+ was developed by InfoSynthesis to make the Court's decisions available in digital format for the general public and solo practitioners.[3] The service also attracts Internet users to InfoSynthesis' CD-ROM products and fee-based Internet services. However, the free version is sufficient for most research needs.

Using Folio search engine and requiring a frames-supportable browser, the Online division of *USSC+* provides access to more than 7,500 cases, including selected leading cases from 1793 to 1945 and complete coverage from 1945 through the present, with new cases added within a few days of decision. Opinions are searchable by citation, party name, subject matter, docket number, or keyword. Decisions are also listed in chronological and alphabetical order.

Current term decisions are arranged by date in the Current subdivision. The service also maintains links to other federal court sites, Supreme Court news, background information about the Court, and argument and session calendars.

Because it is based on a Folio search engine, users familiar with CD-ROM searching will have few problems adapting to *USSC+,* which employs the same boolean operators: quotation marks for phrases; space, & for AND; ctl-O, or for OR; not, ctl-6 for NOT; ~, xor for EXCLUSIVE OR; ? for a single character wildcard; and * for a multiple character wildcard. The system also allows searches involving ordered proximity using the "word word"/*n* command, similar to LEXIS and Westlaw but requiring the terms to appear in the given order. Unordered proximity searching is accomplished using "word word"@*n.*

Particularly useful to researchers using *USSC+* are the indications of hard-copy (*U.S. Reports*) page-breaks and links to cited authorities available on the Internet.

FindLaw U.S. Supreme Court Decisions
<http://www.findlaw.com/casecode/supreme.html>

The most comprehensive coverage of Supreme Court opinions on the Internet is found at *FindLaw,* which boasts an impressive collection beginning with the 1893 term (volume 150 of the *U.S. Reports*). The opinions are browseable by year or *U.S. Reports* volume number, and are searchable by citation, case title, and keyword. Consecutive search terms are treated as a phrase and queries are case-insensitive. *FindLaw* supports the Boolean operators AND, OR, and NOT, the proximity operator NEAR, as well as a wildcard (*) and stem operator (**). Parentheses may be used to nest query terms.

A different type of service than those discussed above provides RealAudio versions of the oral arguments in many Supreme Court cases as well as the announcements of Court opinions.

Oyez Oyez Oyez: A Supreme Court WWW Resource
<http://oyez.nwu.edu>

Oyez is maintained by Northwestern University with the support of the National Endowment for the Humanities' "Teaching with Technology" program. Digital recordings of many Court proceedings since 1961 as well as information about major constitutional cases are available at this site. Cases are indexed by subject, date, and party name. The service also contains biographies of all 108 justices, digital recordings of judicial speeches, a virtual tour of the Supreme Court Building, and links to written opinions since 1893 that are housed on *FindLaw.*

FedWorld/FLITE
<http://www.fedworld.gov/supcourt/index.htm>

In late September 1996, the Administrator of the Office of Information and Regulatory Affairs' Office of Management and Budget announced that the U.S. Air Force had released "a historic file of Supreme Court decisions from its FLITE ('Federal Legal Information Through Electronics') system."[4] FLITE contains more than 7,400 Supreme Court opinions, spanning volumes 300 through 422 of the *U.S. Reports* and dating from 1937 to 1975. Several sites provide access to the FLITE database, including FedWorld.

FedWorld's access to FLITE, maintained by the National Technical Information Service, uses a very simple search protocol involving fill-in-the-blank search term boxes and connectors pull-down menus. Case name searching is also possible; however, party names must be in the correct order. Search results may be viewed by relevance ranking, alphabetically, or reverse alphabetically.

Circuit Court Decisions

Unlike the Supreme Court, which is covered quite thoroughly, the Internet's coverage of United States Circuit Court opinions is more narrow. Although each circuit is represented and its cases are available to the researcher, the scope of coverage is generally limited to post-1995 decisions. Many decisions can be accessed by date, party name, or keyword search. Generally, keyword searching allows the use of Boolean operators and wildcards.

The majority of the circuit case databases are maintained by law schools in cooperation with the court; however, court-maintained sites are becoming more common.

Circuit Court Decision

Circuit	URL	Coverage	Searching
First Circuit	<http://www.law.emory.edu/1circuit/>	November 1995-	date, party name, keyword
Second Circuit	<http://www.law.pace.edu/lawlib/legal/us-legal/judiciary/second-circuit.html> and <http://www.tourolaw.edu/2ndCircuit/>	September 1995-	date, docket number, party name, keyword

Third Circuit	<http://vls.law.vill.edu/Locator/3/index.htm>	May 1994-	date, party name, keyword
Fourth Circuit	<http://www.law.emory.edu/4circuit/>	January 1995-	date, party name, keyword
Fifth Circuit	<http://www.law.utexas.edu/us5th/us5th.html> and <http://www.ca5.uscourts.gov/>	1991-	date, party name, docket number
Sixth Circuit	<http://www.law.emory.edu/6circuit/> and <http://www.ca6.uscourts.gov/>	January 1995-	date, party name, keyword
Seventh Circuit	<http://www.kentlaw.edu/7circuit/> and <http://www.ca7.uscourts.gov/>	January 1993-	1993-April 1995: browse by docket number only May 1995-present: date, party name, keyword The official court site also includes the court's rules
Eighth Circuit	<http://ls.wustl.edu/8th.cir/cindex.html>	1995-	date, party name, case number, keyword
Ninth Circuit	<http://www.ca9.uscourts.gov/>	June 1995-	date, party name, keyword, docket number
Tenth Circuit	<http://www.law.emory.edu/10circuit/> and <http://www.kscourts.org/ca10>	August 1995-October 1997 and October 1997-	date, party name, keyword and date, party name, docket number, filing date, keyword
Eleventh Circuit	<http://www.law.emory.edu/11circuit/> and <http://www.ca11.uscourts.gov/opinions.htm>	November 1994-	date, party name, keyword

| D.C. Circuit | <http://www.ll. georgetown.edu/ Fed-Ct/cadc.html> and <http://www.cadc. uscourts.gov/> | March 1995- | date, keyword |
| Federal Circuit | <http://www.ll. georgetown.edu/ Fed-Ct/cafed.html> and <http://www.law. emory.edu/fedcircuit/> and <http://www.fedcir. gov/> | August 1995- | date, party name, keyword |

Although having information to access the individual circuit courts can save a researcher a lot of time, for some it is not helpful. Law librarians constantly answer questions about which circuit a particular state is in (and most of us end up consulting a map at least part of the time). Other times the researcher requires information from many circuits during the course of one project and does not want the burden or time consumption involved with typing in (or looking up bookmarks for) URLs for each circuit. To assist with these problems and to quickly connect researchers to the information they seek, a number of circuit court "locator" services have been established.

Circuit Court Locators

Emory: U.S. Federal Courts Finder	<http://www.law.emory.edu/FEDCTS/>
Georgetown University Law Library: Federal Court Opinions	<http://www.ll.georgetown.edu:80/Fed-Ct/>
Villanova: The Federal Court Locator	<http://www.vls.law.vill.edu/Locator/fedcourt.html>
Findlaw Circuit Court Opinions	<http://www.findlaw.com/casecode/courts/index.html>

The first three sites, Emory, Georgetown, and Villanova, all provide maps of the United States with the federal circuits identified allowing the researcher to click on the circuit of interest and connect to online decisions–either within their own database or elsewhere on the Internet. The *Findlaw* site does not offer a map but does provide links to cases within all thirteen federal circuits.

To search online decisions of all federal circuits at once, go to the *LII: Search all U. S. Circuit Court of Appeals Opinions on the Internet* site at <http://www4.law.cornell.edu/cgi-bin/fx?DB=Circuits>.

District Court Decisions

Federal district courts are finding their way onto the Internet. While the majority of these courts still do not maintain such a presence, links for those that are established are available from both *Findlaw*[5] and *Villanova*.[6] The most common information available on district court sites includes court opinions, rules, and forms.

FEDERAL LEGISLATIVE AND ADMINISTRATIVE MATERIALS

The availability of federal legislative and administrative materials on the Internet is excellent. The federal government's efforts to make such information readily accessible to the public does not go unnoticed by the researcher surfing the Internet. A major advantage to most of the legislative and administrative information available on the Internet is that it is housed on services maintained by the government itself or by entities operative under governmental authority. This lessens concerns for accuracy and reliability that may be encountered in other arenas. Additionally, current materials are posted quite quickly, often daily while the legislature is in session.

Overview of Federal Legislative and Administrative Materials

Service	URL	Contents Overview
GPO Access	<http://www.access.gpo.gov/su_docs/aces/aaces002.html>	*Federal Register & Unified Agenda*, 1994- *The Budget of the United States Government*, FY 1997- Congressional Bills, 103rd Congress forward Congressional Calendars–House and Senate, 104th- Congressional Directory, 1995-1996 Congressional Documents, 104th Congress forward *Congressional Record*, 1994- Congressional Reports, 104th Congress forward *Congressional Record Index*, 1983-*Economic Report of the President* 1996-1998 *GAO Comptroller General Decisions*, October 1995- *General Accounting Office (GAO) Reports*, October *1994-* *United States Government Manual* History of Bills, 1983- *House Rules Manual* Public Laws, 104th Congress forward *Supreme Court Decisions* (1937-1975) *United States Code*

Library of Congress: United States Legislative Branch	<http://lcweb. loc.gov/global/ legislative/ congress .html>	Links to Congressional Mega Sites About the United States Congress Members of Congress Congressional Committees Congressional Schedules Floor Proceedings Bills and other Legislation *United States Code* House and Senate Rules *Congressional Record* Voting Records
Library of Congress: Official Federal Government Web Sites: Executive Branch	<http://lcweb. loc.gov/global/ executive/ fed.html>	Office of the President including sites for the Council of Economic Advisers; Council on Environmental Quality; National Security Council (NSC); Office of Management and Budget (OMB); Office of The First Lady; Office of National Drug Control Policy; Office of Science and Technology Policy; and United States Trade Representative (USTR) Executive Agencies Independent Agencies Boards and Committees
		Quasi-Official Agencies
THOMAS: Legislative Information on the Internet	<http://thomas. loc.gov/>	Bills: Major Legislation, Bill Summary & Status, Bill Text (coverage begins as early as 1973) *Congressional Record:* Text and Index 101st Congress- Committee Information: Reports and Home Pages House Floor This Week House Floor Now Senate Schedule House and Senate Directories Historical Documents: Chiefly from 1774-1789; Constitutional Convention and Continental Congress, *Declaration of Independence, Federalist Papers, Constitution*

Specific Federal Legislative and Administrative Sources

Source	Locations (Service and URL)
U.S. CODE	*GPO Access* <http://www.access.gpo.gov/congress/cong013.html> *House of Representatives* <http://uscode.house.gov/usc.htm> *Legal Information Institute* <http://www4.law.cornell.edu/uscode/>
Bills/Bill Tracking T	*GPO Access* <http://www.access.gpo.gov/congress/cong009.htm> *Library of Congress: U.S. Legislative Branch: Legislation: Bills, Amendments, and Laws* <http://lcweb.loc.gov/global/legislative/bill.html> *THOMAS* <http://thomas.loc.gov/>
CONGRESSIONAL RECORD	*GPO Access* <http://www.access.gpo.gov/su_docs/aces/aces150.html> *Library of Congress: U.S. Legislative Branch: Congressional Record* <http://lcweb.loc.gov/global/legislative/congrec.html> *THOMAS* <http://thomas.loc.gov/>
FEDERAL REGISTER	*GPO Access* <http://www.access.gpo.gov/su_docs/aces/aces140.html>
CODE of FEDERAL REGULATIONS	*GPO Access* <http://www.access.gpo.gov/nara/cfr/index.html> *Legal Information Institute* <http://www4.law.cornell.edu/cfr/>

GPO Access

<http://www.access.gpo.gov/su_docs/aces/aaces002.html>

GPO Access is an official site of the Government Printing Office, and is part of the implementation of Congress's effort to distribute U.S. government information to the public by electronic media.[7] The majority of the information in the databases on the GPO site is available in both ASCII text and Adobe Acrobat portable document format (PDF).

Each database uses the same search protocol supporting boolean operators, including AND, OR (also the default space), NOT, ADJ (to retrieve documents where the words follow one another by up to 20 characters), and * (to search for all words with a particular stem). Unlike many sites, at *GPO Access* the boolean operators must be capitalized or they are considered stopwords and ignored. Phrases may be searched using ADJ or quotation marks. Parentheses for nesting operators are also supported.

GPO Access contains nearly fifty databases; the following are of particular use to the legal researcher and are easily accessed from the Specialized Search Pages section of the GPO site.

Federal Register

GPO Access contains the *Federal Register* from 1995 (volume 60) to the present; however, each volume of the *Register* is a separate database. The archived databases contain all daily issues. The current database is updated each day the *Federal Register* is published. Each database contains the full text including notices, rules, proposed rules, presidential documents, tables of contents, preliminary information, list of the CFR parts affected, and other reader aids.

The Budget of the United States Government and Economic Reports of the President

Databases are online for fiscal years beginning in 1996. Each budget database includes the *President's Budget Message,* information on the president's budget proposals, descriptions of federal programs, and other secondary sources useful to budget researchers. The *Economic Report* database includes descriptions of trends on topics ranging from employment to production and real income, employment objectives for significant groups within the labor force, annual numeric goals, and a program for carrying out these objectives.

Congressional Bills

All published versions of bills from the 103rd Congresses forward are available in these databases. The current bills database is updated daily while Congress is in session.

Public Laws

The *Public Laws* databases contain all of the laws enacted beginning with the 104th Congress in full text as enrolled. The current database is updated each time the publication of a new slip law is authorized by the Office of the Federal Register.

Congressional Record

Individual *Congressional Record* databases beginning with the 103rd Congresses are available at *GPO Access*. The current database is updated daily while Congress is in session.

Congressional Documents, Reports, and Hearings

These databases contain select House, Senate and treaty documents, reports, and hearings beginning with the 104th Congresses.

GAO Comptroller General Decisions and *General Accounting Office (GAO) Reports*

These GPO databases are sponsored by the U.S. General Accounting Office (GAO). The Decisions database includes comptroller general opinions in federal law areas including appropriations, civilian or military personnel pay, and transportation rates. Coverage begins in October 1995. The *Reports* database contains GAO "blue book" reports to members of Congress or congressional committees beginning October, 1994. Both databases are updated daily with reports and decisions generally available within two business days after release.

United States Government Manual

The *Government Manual* database contains the *United States Government Manual,* 1995-1996, 1996-1997, 1997-1998, and 1998-1999 editions, prepared by the National Archives and Records Administration, Office of the Federal Register.

Weekly Compilation of Presidential Documents

Presidential Documents from 1995 forward are keyword searchable. GPO is currently working to create date-range and subject searches within this database.

Supreme Court Decisions

GPO Access is another supplier of the FLITE database.

United States Code

This database is another source of accessing the *United States Code*. The database contains the Code and three supplements, updating the 1994 code through January 1998.

Library of Congress: United States Legislative Branch

<http://lcweb.loc.gov/global/legislative/congress.html>

In addition to providing information about Congress (taken from the *United States Government Manual*), its members (directories by name, district, party and photograph), committees, organizations, and commissions, the site offers e-mail addresses for Congress, calendars and schedules, House and Senate rules, and voting records.

THOMAS: Legislative Information on the Internet

<http://thomas.loc.gov/>

Arguably, *THOMAS* provides the most comprehensive and current legislative information available on the Internet. Maintained by the Library of Congress in response to a 104th Congressional directive to make federal legislative information more readily accessible to the public, *THOMAS* went online in January 1995.[8] Usage figures maintained by its server show that *THOMAS* is becoming a popular choice for Internet researchers seeking legislative information. In fact, between January 1, 1999 and August 22, 1999, the server reported an average of 379,760 files transmitted daily.[9]

THOMAS is divided into several separate databases including *House Floor This Week, House Floor Now, Senate Schedule, Legislation, Congressional Record, Committee Information, Historical Documents,* and *The Legislative Process.* One of *THOMAS*'s greatest assets is its currency. Many of the databases are updated daily while Congress is in session. When new files are received from the Government Printing Office, they are immediately indexed and added to the database.[10]

LC plans to continue upgrading its services, including the addition of a feature allowing researchers to conduct searches of multiple databases simultaneously.

House Floor This Week, House Floor Now, and Senate Schedule

THOMAS's most current information is found in these databases, which include daily schedules and information on pending legislation. Also included are all bills that have received floor action or for which floor action is expected. Bills are accessible by number, title, and chamber of origin (House or Senate). From this database the researcher may link directly to the *THOMAS Bill Summary and Status* record for the legislation.

Legislation

There are five subcategories within the Legislation database: *Major Legislation, Bill Summary and Status, Bill Text, Public Laws,* and *Roll Call Votes.*

Major Legislation files, including bills beginning with the 104th Congress, were selected by the legislative analysts of the Congressional Research Service as "major legislation" because they were the subject of hearings, debate, media coverage, or floor action.

The *Bill Summary and Status* database includes all bills and resolutions dating back to the 93rd Congress. In addition to a link to the full text of the bill, entries provide information on a bill's sponsor(s) and cosponsor(s), official and popular names, any floor action taken, a detailed legislative history, references to pages in the *Congressional Record* where the bill is discussed, the committee or subcommittee to which the bill was referred, and descriptions and text of amendments. Also included in the database are browseable lists of public laws and vetoed bills. This database is updated continually. *Bill Summary and Status* files are updated the day after the information is entered into the system; however, during times of heavy legislative activity, inputting of the legislative status may be delayed. Bill digests are generally available on the database within forty-eight hours of the bill's introduction.

The *Bill Text* database includes the full text of all bills beginning with the 101st Congresses supplied by the Government Printing Office. This database is updated several times daily while Congress is in session.

All bills databases are searchable by word, phrase, subject, sponsor, committee, or bill number; queries can be limited to bills receiving floor action, enrolled bills, or to House or Senate bills. Many of the databases also include browseable lists of bills by type and number.

The *Public Laws by Law Number* database includes all Public Laws beginning with the 93rd Congress. Public Laws are not keyword searchable and can only be accessed by Public Law Number.

The *Roll Call Votes* database contain the records of House and Senate votes as tabulated by the electronic voting machine. Vote records are available from the 101st Congress forward.

Congressional Record

The *Congressional Record* database is divided into four sections: *Text, Index, Résumés of Congressional Activity,* and *Days in Session Calendars.*

Congressional Record Text contains the full-text of each daily edition beginning with the 101st Congress. The database is searchable by keyword or phrase, by member of Congress, and by date or date range. Searches can be limited to any of the three text sections of the Record (House, Senate, and Extensions of Remarks). A list of daily issues, divided by section and including table of contents links, is also available. *The Congressional Record* database is updated daily while Congress is in session.

The *Congressional Record Index* database includes the biweekly indexes beginning with the 103rd Congress. Access to the indexes is by index term, which may be searched as a word or phrase. A browseable, alphabetical list of major index terms is provided. Index page references are directly linked to the *THOMAS Congressional Record Text* database. References to bills also include links to the *Bill Text* database. The *Index* database is updated biweekly when the current edition of the *Index* is received. To update information during the intervening period, a link to the daily, unedited Government Printing Office version of the *Congressional Record Index* is provided.

The *Résumé of Congressional Activity* database includes the *Résumé* sections of the *Congressional Record* beginning with the 91st Congress. The *Résumés* contain summary information about each Congressional session including the number of days and hours Congress was in session; the total number of bills and resolutions introduced, passed, reported, and enacted into law; the number of conference reports; the number of quorum calls and votes; and the number of bills vetoed and the number of vetoes overridden.[11] The *Résumés* also contain summaries of executive nominations during the Congressional year.

Committee Information

The *Committee Information* database consists of three sections: *Committee Reports, Committee Home Pages, House Committees,* and *Senate Committees.*

The *Committee Reports* database includes the full text of all Committee reports printed by the Government Printing Office beginning with the 104th Congress. Reports are searchable by keyword or phrase, report number, bill number, and committee. Additionally, a sequential list of reports is provided for both the Senate and the House.

Beginning in 1996, many congressional committees established Internet home pages. The *Committee Home Pages* database provides links to those home pages located on the House and Senate servers. A typical committee home page would include such information as the committee's jurisdiction, its chair and full membership, descriptions and membership of subcommittees, committee schedules, press releases, hearing witness lists, and committee publications.

The *House Committees* division includes Schedules and Oversight Plans and Hearing Transcripts. The *Senate Committees* division includes information on committee meetings and hearings scheduled.

Historical Documents

This database contains historical documents primarily dating from 1774 to 1789, including broadsides from the Constitutional Convention and Continental Congress, the *Declaration of Independence,* the *Federalist Papers,* and the *Constitution.* In addition to the documents themselves, commentary on their origin and impact is provided. The documents in the database are keyword searchable, collectively as well as individually.

The Legislative Process

A small database, *Legislative Process* contains two publications useful to students and others interested in the basics of the United States' legislative process: *How Our Laws Are Made,* revised and updated by Charles W. Johnson, House Parliamentarian, and *Enactment of a Law* by Robert B. Dove, Senate Parliamentarian. These materials were updated in December 1997 to reflect legislative process changes including the introduction of the line-item veto.

Library of Congress: Official Federal Government Web Sites: Executive Branch

<http://lcweb.loc.gov/global/executive/fed.html>

This site from the Library of Congress provides access to nearly every federal administrative resource imaginable. Arranged in categories by Office of the President, Executive Agencies, Independent Agencies, Boards, Commissions and Committees, and Quasi-Official Agencies, the resources are presented in a logical and user-friendly fashion. From this site the researcher can access materials ranging from the Department of Housing and Urban Development and the National Security Council to the Central Intelligence Agency and Smithsonian Institution.

The Federal Web Navigator

<http://lawnt.law.vill.edu/fedweb>

The *Federal Web Navigator,* part of Villanova system, contains an impressive list of links to federal administrative offices and agencies. Researchers may access the White House, Office of Management and Budget, and the

United States Departments of Agriculture, Commerce, Defense, Education, Energy, Health and Human Services, Housing and Urban Development, Interior, Justice, Labor, State, Transportation, and Veterans Affairs. Many departmental listings include numerous links to specific divisions. Recent additions to the site include links to Internal Revenue Service, National Park Service, Federal Bureau of Investigation, Immigration and Naturalization Service, United States Copyright Office, and the National Labor Relations Board.

In addition to agency listings, researchers may search the *Federal Web Navigator* by keyword using boolean operators.

STATE RESOURCES

Unlike federal materials that are generally consistent in their coverage, availability of state materials on the Internet runs across the full spectrum, from online versions of state court opinions and legislative codes to gubernatorial messages and agency home pages. Many states are beginning to sponsor official Internet presences including home pages for legislatures and courts.[12] Others, however, have not. Researchers concentrating on particular jurisdictions would be wise to bookmark those sites that contain information applicable to their states, but for more general coverage, the sites that follow provide excellent starting points.

State Resources

Service	URL	Features
American Law Sources On-Line	<http://www.lawsource.com/also/>	all fifty states, U.S. territories and tribal governments, dates vary with emphasis on post-1995 materials
Practicing Attorneys Home Page–State Subdivision	<http://www.legalethics.com/pa/ states/states.htm>	all fifty states, dates vary with emphasis on post-1995 materials
StateLaw: State and Local Government Information–Washlaw	<http://www.washlaw.edu/uslaw/ statelaw.html>	allows keyword full text searching of state case law available on the Internet
State and Local Government on the Net–Piper Resources	<http://www.piperinfo.com/state/ states.html>	includes additional links to state boards and commissions, counties and cities
State Court Locator– Villanova	<http://vls.law.vill.edu/Locator/ statecourt/>	provides links to state court home pages and opinions
Municipal Codes Online	<http://www.spl.org/govpubs/ municode.html>	currently 47 states with more than 200 codes are included

American Law Sources On-Line

<http://www.lawsource.com/also/>

American Law Sources On-Line, or *ALSO!*, is a public service of LAW-SOURCE, INC. The site includes links to legal information for the United States, Canada, and Mexico. The state section includes all fifty states, the District of Columbia, American Samoa, Guam, the Northern Mariana Islands, Puerto Rico, and the Virgin Islands. Each state page contains an extensive compilation of links to legal resources of that state. The links are listed in the following order (however, the particular sources listed on each page depend on online availability): (1) state appellate courts; (2) U.S. district; (3) other courts for which decisions are available on the Internet; (4) Constitution; (5) bills from the current and prior legislative sessions; (6) session laws; (7) codes; (8) rules of practice and procedure; (9) administrative law sources (regulations, orders, decisions, and opinions); and (10) local law sources (municipal codes, ordinances).[13] The site also includes links to uniform and model laws that may be useful for the state law researcher.

Practicing Attorneys Home Page

<http://www.legalethics.com/pa/states/states.htm>

Established in 1995, the *Practicing Attorney's Home Page* is a compilation of nearly 4,500 links to legal resources. In addition to business and federal legal information, the site includes a useful collection of state legal resource links. The links are arranged by state, each state page providing links to resources including (when available) state agencies, state bar associations, state case law, state home pages, state constitutions, state courts and court rules, state legislation, state statutes, and states attorney generals' offices.

The *State Ethics Resources* portion of the site includes links to state bar associations, rules of conduct/ethics, ethics opinions, and updates on what the states may be doing to regulate attorneys' use of the Internet.

StateLaw: State and Local Government Information

<http://www.washlaw.edu/uslaw/statelaw.html>

A part of Washburn University's *Washlaw* service, *StateLaw* provides links to state information including state home pages, legislative information, court opinions, statutes, and regulations. The *StateLaw Search Page* allows the researcher to search by subject matter–state home pages, legislative information sites, judicial information sites, state statute sites, miscellaneous sites including agencies, local governments, constitutions, etc. *A Keyword Search For State Case Law* feature, accessed from the *StateLaw Search Page,* allows full text searching of state case law available on the Internet.

State and Local Government on the Net

<http://www.piperinfo.com/state/states.html>

Piper Resources' *State and Local Government on the Net* includes state-by-state links to home pages, statewide offices (governor and attorney general, etc.), legislative and judicial branches, executive branch agencies, boards and commissions, counties, and cities. Several multi-state links, including the Interstate Oil and Gas Compact Commission and the Delaware Valley Regional Planning Commission, are also provided. Other links of interest to the researcher include those of national organizations such as the Council of State Government WWW, National Association of Counties, National Associations of Towns and Townships, the National Civic League, and the Western Governors Conference.

State Court Locator

<http://vls.law.vill.edu/Locator.statecourt/>

This Villanova site is "intended to be the home page for state court systems on the Internet."[14] The links from this site include state court opinions and other court information.

Municipal Codes Online

<http://www.spl.org/govpubs/municode.html>

Of interest to researchers seeking legal information on the local level, this site, maintained by the Seattle Public Library, includes links to more than eighty city and county codes in more than thirty states.

NOTES

1. Examples of link pages from law libraries around the country include: Baltimore County Circuit Court Law Library, <http://www.co.ba.md.us/bacoweb/circuit/html/lawlib2.htm>; Maricopa County Law Library, <http://www.superiorcourt.maricopa.gov/lawlibrary/>; University of San Francisco Law Library,<http://www.usfca.edu/

law_library/lawlinks.html>; University of Nevada Las Vegas Law Library, <http://www.law.unlv.edu/library/genlinks.html>; Ballard Spahr Andrews & Ingersoll, LLP, <http://www.virtualchase.com/resources/index.shtml>; and Brown, Pinnisi & Michaels PC, <http://www.bpmlegal.com/research.html>.

2. Since the completion of this article the United States Supreme Court has launched its own "official" web site at <http://www.supremecourtus.gov/>.

3. *See* <http://www.usscplus.com/> (visited Jan. 19, 2000).

4. *Historic File of Supreme Court Decisions Available On-line*, (visited Jan. 19, 2000) <http://vls.vill.edu/Locator/fedcourt.html>.

5. <http://www.findlaw. com/casecode/district.html>.

6. <http://vls.vill.edu/Locator/fedcourt.html>; scroll past the circuit court information to the district court section.

7. *See* The Government Printing Office Electronic Information Access Enhancement Act of 1993, 44 U.C.S. 4101-04 (1997).

8. The search engine that powers *THOMAS* uses the InQuery information retrieval system, which was developed by the University of Massachusetts at Amherst's Center for Intelligent Information Retrieval.

9. *See* <http://thomas.loc.gov/stats/stats.html>.

10. *See* <http://thomas.loc.gov/home/abt_thom.html#updates>.

11. <http://thomas.loc.gov/home/resume/resume.html>.

12. For examples of state-sponsored sites *see* the *Utah State Home Page* <http://www.state.ut.us/> and the *California State Home Page* <http://www.ca.gov/>.

13. <http://www.lawsource.com/also/alsouser.htm>.

14. <http://vls.law.vill.edu//> (visited Jan. 19, 2000).

Developing an Electronic Collection: The University of Minnesota Human Rights Library

Marci Hoffman

SUMMARY. The Internet has had a profound impact on the way people access and use information, especially in the area of monitoring and protecting human rights. This article reviews the development of the University of Minnesota Human Rights Library, one of the largest collections of human rights documents available on the web. The focus is on how the collection was built, how it is used to support research and teaching, and how it is maintained. Many of the issues examined in this article are relevant to the development, maintenance, and use of any electronic collection. *[Article copies available for a fee from The Haworth Document Delivery Service: 1-800-342-9678. E-mail address: <getinfo@ haworthpressinc.com> Website: <http://www.HaworthPress.com> © 2001 by The Haworth Press, Inc. All rights reserved.]*

HUMAN RIGHTS AND THE INTERNET

While the Internet was once considered an elite tool available only to the few, it has quickly become a principal medium for human rights research and

Marci Hoffman is Co-Director/Web Coordinator of the University of Minnesota Human Rights Library <http://www1.umm.edu/humanrts>. She is also International and Foreign Law Librarian at the Georgetown University Law Library. Ms. Hoffman continues to work on this project even though she has moved to Washington DC.

[Haworth co-indexing entry note]: "Developing an Electronic Collection: The University of Minnesota Human Rights Library." Hoffman, Marci. Co-published simultaneously in *Legal Reference Services Quarterly* (The Haworth Information Press, an imprint of The Haworth Press, Inc.) Vol. 19, No. 3/4, 2001, pp. 143-155; and: *Teaching Legal Research and Providing Access to Electronic Resources* (ed: Gary L. Hill, Dennis S. Sears, and Lovisa Lyman) The Haworth Information Press, an imprint of The Haworth Press, Inc., 2001, pp. 143-155. Single or multiple copies of this article are available for a fee from The Haworth Document Delivery Service [1-800-342-9678, 9:00 a.m. - 5:00 p.m. (EST). E-mail address: getinfo@haworthpressinc. com].

143

activism around the world. The Internet is now an integral part of information technology infrastructure, insuring that almost anyone with access to a computer, a telephone line, and a modem can exchange information with colleagues both within and across national boundaries. As a result of its widespread availability, the Internet has had a profound impact on the way human rights advocates and educators communicate and work. For instance, the human rights community quickly adopted e-mail as a major tool for communication and action. Human rights advocates can now respond within hours to crises that previously might have required days or weeks of preparation. In addition, individuals, including those in countries where there are limitations on the free flow of information, can use the Internet to gain access to a wide range of human rights documents, reports, and norms that are being published on the Internet. Even in regions of the world where access is limited, the Internet has had considerable impact because those who do have access can download and print information and make it available to people who do not have direct access themselves.

As its availability has grown more widespread, groups in both the developing and developed world have used the web to compensate for the shortcomings of traditional print-based document collections. Researchers in most developing countries previously did not have the resources to obtain even the most fundamental printed materials, including relevant treaties, jurisprudence, and other important standards. They were also deprived of current information about the activities of aid-giving agencies, international institutions, governments, and nongovernmental organizations (NGOs). A good deal of this information is now available on the web. Similarly, in developed countries, human rights workers found it difficult to keep abreast of the vast and quickly expanding volume of human rights law and related commentaries. Often large research libraries, and even smaller human rights documentation centers, were nearly drowning in materials that were not cataloged or otherwise indexed. The improved search capabilities available on the web and other electronic media have allowed researchers to identify, locate, and obtain the basic materials necessary for their work.

As the web has expanded, however, it has exhibited some problems similar to those faced by print-based document collections. In particular, it has become increasingly difficult to handle and organize the growing volume of information available on the web. For a lawyer trying to locate important treaties or case law, a researcher looking for a specific report by a human rights treaty monitoring body, or an educator hoping to find human rights curricula, sorting through the results of an Internet search is often frustrating and time-consuming. This frustration is compounded by repetitive and self-referential links between sites that may only point to more links. These problems are felt most intensely by human rights researchers and advocates in developing countries, where costly local phone connections and slow modem speeds make searching the web for relevant documents prohibitively expensive.

THE HUMAN RIGHTS LIBRARY ON THE WEB

The University of Minnesota Human Rights Library ("the Library") was launched in the early days of the web in response to the needs of researchers, activists, educators, and students for access to primary human rights documents. Since its establishment, the Library has become a core resource for the entire human rights community. It is now one of the largest electronic human rights documentation sites on the web, providing a single location from which users can access more than 6,500 documents in various languages. These materials include the principal human rights treaties, declarations, adjudicative decisions, official documents, and reports of the United Nations and regional bodies that monitor and protect human rights. In addition to resolutions, decisions, general comments, country conclusions, and other documents from the UN's Charter and treaty-based human rights bodies, the Library maintains a collection of materials from the Inter-American Court of and Commission on Human Rights, the Organization for Security and Cooperation in Europe, and the African Commission on Human and Peoples' Rights. The Library also contains human rights bibliographies and educational materials, as well as an extensive collection of links to intergovernmental (IGO) and nongovernmental organizations dedicated to human rights and related topics.

In 1994, Professor David Weissbrodt[1] and I began talking about creating a broadly-accessible collection of core human rights treaties, instruments, documents, and other materials relating to human rights for use by scholars, advocates, government personnel, NGOs, and others. We both recognized a critical need for access to key human rights documents for those who lacked access to print-based collections. The Internet was beginning to be used as a means to access and transfer information via e-mail, electronic bulletin boards, gopher files, ftp-data, telnet, and the like. At the time, we were considering making documents available via a gopher site or an electronic bulletin board.

At the same time, the DIANA[2] advisory board was formed. Project Diana, named in the memory of Diana Vincent-Daviss, was established by the Schell Center for International Human Rights at Yale Law School. The goal of DIANA was to "promote the creation, organization, dissemination and preservation of primary and secondary electronic materials critical to human rights research."[3] Professor Weissbrodt and I were asked to join the consortium of law librarians, human rights scholars and NGOs, and to start discussing the development of this project. For a variety of reasons, the consortium never really got off the ground, although a few sites, including the University of Minnesota Human Rights Library, are still referred to as DIANA sites.

BUILDING THE COLLECTION

I would like to say that we had a coherent, well-laid-out plan for building the Human Rights Library on the web. Unlike the developers of many other digital collections, however, we did not sit down and formulate a collection development plan–nor any kind of formal plan. But even when a library has a written collection development policy, these policies are constantly being reviewed and revised. Written or unwritten, the mission of a law library and its collection development policy is usually to support the teaching and re-search mission of the law school and to respond to the ever-changing research needs of the faculty and students. The mission of the Human Rights Library is quite similar–to support the research and educational needs of the human rights community, including scholars, activists, educators, and students, and to respond to the changing and growing needs of this community of users. Even though we had no concrete plan, we did have some primary goals, including: (1) provide a core collection of instruments; (2) obtain documents from primary sources; (3) make materials available at no cost; (4) make materials easy to access, download, and print; (5) supply reliable citations for the primary instruments; and (6) provide access to other relevant web sites in a coherent framework.

Since this was during the early days of the web, we really had no idea where this medium would go or how this electronic collection would be received by the human rights and online communities. What we did have was Professor Weissbrodt's dedication to the project and his ability to obtain the necessary documents and funding. His participation was absolutely crucial.

We started development in 1994 with the ASCII text versions of ninety of the most important UN treaties and instruments. These ninety documents formed the nucleus of what we call our "core collection." The first thing we had to do was to decide how best to make these documents available. As I mentioned earlier, our first idea was to make them available on the Internet via a gopher site or through an electronic bulletin board. We also explored making the materials available on Westlaw, but we were concerned about how people without access to this commercial database would obtain the documents. As we began to explore these options, a better mechanism for distributing information was becoming available on the Internet–the World Wide Web. Another professor on the University of Minnesota Law School faculty was experimenting with creating a personal web page. He provided us with a copy of his page and we started by looking at the document as a text file and changing the words on the page without really understanding the HTML coding or anything else about the web. There was a good deal of trial and error. After playing around with the code, learning some HTML basics, and looking at a few of the web pages that existed at the time, we developed a very rudimentary homepage. We hired a talented law student who learned to create HTML documents and he really got the project going.[4] Then we began to convert each of the ninety instruments into HTML. This was in the early days of the web and no HTML editors were available, so the conversion process was no easy task. The HTML code was added to each document using a text editor and every document was then compared to the print text for accuracy. We also decided that it was important to provide reliable citations. Thus, a great deal of time was spent researching the proper citations for each instrument using the resources from the print collection at the University of Minnesota Law Library. We then decided to create a basic subject list for organizing and accessing the documents in a coherent, well-organized fashion. We worked on many versions of this list before deciding on the final one. Although this was a painstaking process, it was well worth the effort because this basic organizational scheme is still being used today. In 1995, the Human Rights Library went live on the World Wide Web.

As we were building our collection, other web sites were appearing online. We looked closely at the work of these sites and learned from them as well. These sites included the Multilaterals Project at the Fletcher School of Law and Diplomacy,[5] Wiretap,[6] and the House of Representative's Internet Law Library.[7] We also had many conversations with people who were starting to host sites on the web. The emergence of these new sites prompted us to add a collection of annotated links in order to add more value to our core collection. Again, we developed a framework for organizing the links and, consequently, our collection was starting to act as a catalog of other relevant sites. The idea was to provide access to information, whether from our site or from another site.

Since there is so much information that may be of use to the human rights community, it can cause overload for the researcher or activist. To this end, we had to decide how to limit what we would make available on the web site. Early on, we decided that since we are not an organization that monitors human rights conditions, such as Amnesty International or Human Rights Watch, we would leave the collection and dissemination of these important sources to those who produce that kind of information. We would focus first on providing the primary materials necessary for researching international human rights law. Deciding what would go into the collection was based upon what documents we could obtain from authoritative sources in electronic form, our knowledge of human rights documentation and print resources, our understanding of the research needs of the user community, and application of a standard set of criteria for adding documents and resources to the collection.

A standard set of criteria is something that selectors and bibliographers use every day when evaluating materials to add to any collection. Some of the factors we considered included: user need and interest, authority of source, accuracy and quality of information, subject content and scope, type of information (full-text or abstract), and language. In selecting which sites to add to our links collection, we considered the above criteria as well as clarity of presentation, ease of use and navigation, and frequency of updating.

As our collection grew over the years, we decided to add other documents (bibliographies, INS materials, U.S. human rights documents), but our focus has always been on the primary sources of human rights law. While we have a good collection of basic treaties and instruments, we want to provide more complete access to human rights documents and jurisprudence from the bodies charged with monitoring and protecting human rights. We are constantly trying to make contacts with individuals and organizations around the globe in order to obtain important documents that are lacking on the web generally. This is becoming more difficult as issuing bodies and organizations want to provide documents on their own sites and are not willing to give us the documents. However, posting of documents is often slow and in some cases is influenced by political pressures. Sometimes the documents are just not available in electronic form. Therefore, adjudicative decisions and other primary documents from important regional bodies, such as the African Commission on Human and Peoples' Rights, are still, for the most part, unavailable on the web. These documents can be difficult to locate in print, let alone in electronic form. By contacting other organizations that may have access to these documents and offering to make these documents available, we are working on building our collection of regional documents.

Another way we intend to improve our collection is by providing better access to the documents that exist on other web sites. Since not all sites are easy to access and navigate, we have provided more detailed links and access to information available through other valuable collections. For example, the UN High Commissioner for Human Rights (UNHCHR) site has a very good collection of documents from the UN Commission on Human Rights. Since this collection can be a bit difficult to navigate, we have provided the user with not only a link to the collection, but also an explanation of how to access the documents available on the UNHCHR site. To aid the user even further, we are also adding parallel links to individual documents within the UNHCHR collection as well as our version of the document.

USING THE COLLECTION

The primary goal of the Library is to provide easy access to primary sources and information related to human rights. I can honestly say that I use the Library every week to provide someone with the text of a document, a citation for a needed UN treaty, or as a quick way to locate a relevant web site. From my conversations with my colleagues, they too use the Library frequently for the same purposes.

When we built the Library, we carefully considered how users would navigate through our site and locate needed documents. There are four prima-ry ways by which to access the Library: (1) by monitoring body or regional system (UN, Council of Europe, Inter-American system), (2) by type of materials (bibliographies, links), (3) by subject access (treaties and instru-ments), or (4) by using one of the search mechanisms. Our primary method of access has always been the list of instruments by subject.[8] By browsing the subject list, the user can easily locate the desired group of documents. These topics should be recognizable to the veteran human rights researcher and the novice alike. These are the same basic subject headings we established early on in the project, and we continue to use this same structure for our growing collection of instruments.

Unlike many other web sites, we have tried to provide some value-added components to the documents in the collection. For instance, the Library provides authoritative citations for many of the documents it contains, thus allowing the researcher to use the documents with confidence. In addition, the Library adds value to its documents by providing access to ratification information. By linking to specific information, such as the ratification infor-mation from treaty secretariats and depositories, we endeavor to provide more information for the user and not duplicate the work of other sites. For example, from the instruments page,[9] we link to ratification information provided by other sites that we feel provide authoritative information, such as the United Nations High Commissioner for Human Rights,[10] the Council of Europe European Treaties Chart of Signatures and Ratifications,[11] and the Signatures and Current Status of Ratifications from the Basic Documents of the Inter-American Commission on Human Rights.[12] This enables the re-searcher to obtain the text of the document as well as the ratification informa-tion from the same page. We also provide access to other research tools, like bibliographies and research guides, to assist users in furthering their research.

Generally, a collection on the web expands accessibility by offering re-mote, twenty-four-hour access. The Human Rights Library expands accessi-bility and usefulness even further by providing mirror sites for easier and more cost-effective access to people around the world.[13] Currently, we have mirror sites in Geneva and South Africa, and we are considering relationships with institutions in Asia and Latin America. Another way we provide more access is by providing a multilingual collection. Non-English speaking hu-man rights advocates, researchers, and educators would agree that the web is still an English-language dominated medium and they are hampered by the lack of official documents in their own languages available online. The Library has started to provide some of the primary instruments in French and Spanish and we are continuing to build our multilingual collection by translating the pages and documents into French, Spanish and Russian. This means we will offer the basic pages in these languages, offer as many documents in these languages as possible, and begin building collections of links in these languages. While the English-language pages are the most comprehensive, we are committed to providing more multilingual access to a wider community. This requires a good deal of time and effort since each time we add a language we need to find someone with good language expertise to create and maintain the foreign language pages, and we need to obtain the necessary multilingual documents in electronic form.

A primary goal in keeping the Library accessible is to keep the navigation and design basic. We decided to stay away from frames and keep graphics and complicated tool bars to a minimum, and we have not rushed to adopt high-end Internet technologies. Recently we changed our basic navigational structure in order to make our collection easier to use. However, some of our users were so comfortable with the old style that they complained. As a result, for a short period of time, we decided to offer a link to the old navigational design to help our users transition to the new format.

Judging from our usage statistics,[14] the site is heavily used with over 500,000 hits logged each month. Visitors come to the Library from more than one hundred countries, including Argentina, Australia, Canada, China, Israel, Italy, Japan, The Netherlands, the United Arab Emirates, and Nepal, to name a few. Our most heavily used pages, other than the homepage, are the search device page, the treaties and instruments page, the collection of links, and, most recently, our meta-search device.

Our site has also become an electronic reference desk of sorts and the questions and comments come from lawyers, students, educators, and advocates from around the globe. We have received approximately 1,000 substantive questions. These questions vary from basic things like looking for a particular document to more complicated queries. We are very careful to frame our answers so as never to offer legal analysis or advice. We provide direction for research and recommend other sites or resources (sometimes even print resources). Some recent examples of these questions include: requests for information on the philosophical foundations of human rights; materials on human rights in a particular country; examination of freedom of religion articles of the UN Covenant on Civil and Political Rights; recommendations on relevant listservs for human rights current awareness; general information on the Inter-American Commission on Human Rights; information on humanitarian law for a class presentation; and information on human rights programs at U.S. law schools. Some of the questions require pointing users to specific pages within the Human Rights Library whereas others require referring them to other sites or resources. Since some of the questions can be time consuming and can require a great deal of research, we try to offer basic advice on how to get started and then refer them to their local library, if possible. When asked to provide assistance for specific cases or asylum proceedings, we try to direct them to relevant organizations or individuals who can provide the proper assistance. When it is impossible for us to provide any assistance, we let the user know that as well.

In addition to its role as a reference resource, the Human Rights Library can be used as a teaching tool in the classroom. Professor Weissbrodt uses the collection to teach the substance of human rights, and I use it for teaching human rights documentation and research methodology. By providing information on human rights education, including curriculum, lessons, and teaching materials, we endeavor to assist the human rights educator at various educational levels.[15]

MANAGING THE COLLECTION

Collection management is one of the issues that I get queried on the most from other librarians charged with developing collections on the web. There are three areas to consider: general maintenance of the collection, staffing, and continued funding.

General Maintenance

We maintain the collection in much the same way a library maintains any collection. We are constantly evaluating and considering new materials and sources to add, trying to improve the design and use of the site, looking at what researchers need from the collection, and looking for ways to support and pay for it all. Not only do we have to maintain the quality of the information, especially if we decide to scan materials, but we must maintain the electronic environment. We are continually looking at the overall structure and design of the pages because maintaining a fresh look is important. Within that, we must check the consistency and style of each page.

As anyone who has created a page of links knows, checking the validity of the links, both internal and external, is a major challenge. This is especially true when the links are embedded deep within a web site or in a web database. Even though there are automated link checkers, these tools only provide half of the solution. These programs may help identify broken links, but a person must then be employed to locate the new links and change the URLs on the pages themselves. Since our links collection contains over 2,000 sites, this has become a very time-consuming task. Initially we provided brief annotations about the content for every site we added to our links collection. However, because the number of links in our collection has grown so much over the past few years, we recently decided to forego the annotations in favor of getting our links into better shape. We have now developed a database to better manage this growing and ever-changing collection, and this has helped tremendously. We hope to be able to add back the annotations in the future, but this will be another labor-intensive task.

Since we started building the Library during the early days of the web, we have made a few mistakes along the way. First, we developed the collection using absolute links rather than relative links.[16] Hence, the collection could not be easily reorganized, moved, mirrored, or otherwise manipulated. It has taken us a good deal of time to remedy this problem. Second, our documents need more enhanced meta-data in order to better utilize current search devices more effectively. This process will involve adding descriptive tags to the documents that already exist in the collection. Third, since our resources have fluctuated over the years, we have not always been able to keep up-to-date with the constant flow of new materials. New treaties, protocols, interpretive materials, and adjudicative decisions are continuously being issued and it is not always possible to keep up.

Staffing

It may be surprising to know that we have created this unique collection with a very small staff. Basically, we have two co-directors, Professor Weissbrodt and myself, and four to six part-time research assistants who handle the technical and foreign language work. We also utilize other students for particular projects or use outside contractors for the technical work we cannot handle ourselves. Our meta-search device is an example of when we decided to use an outside contractor. This contractor was interested in designing this search tool and also wanted some exposure for his services. By allowing him to put a small advertisement on the search page, we were able to keep our cost down without sacrificing the integrity of the page with an obstructive logo.

We hire and train students with different skills to work on the site, such as technical skills, language skills, and good research skills. Since we have limited physical space in the Law School, our students do most of their work at home and are supervised virtually. Nonetheless, we are in constant communication via e-mail and the students send us documents and files electronically for review and comment. Each semester, I prepare detailed lists of priorities and tasks for each student. For the most part, this has been a successful strategy. However, our reliance on part-time students, even with their valuable skills, is time consuming and not always efficient in an ongoing project like this one. Inevitably, there are lag times when hiring, during the training process, and at certain times of the year when students are just unavailable to work. The cost of recruiting, hiring, and training takes its toll—not to mention the fact that they graduate!

Funding

Funding is crucial for any collection, especially one that is not formally part of any print collection budget. The Human Rights Library is not directly supported through the library or the law school budgets. From the beginning, it has been supported through grant money and indirectly by the library and law school budgets by the use of our time. We are fortunate to be able to utilize many standard mechanisms in the law school for support, including posting jobs through career services, using some supplies of the law school or the Human Rights Center, and sometimes using secretarial or technical support services. Nevertheless, we still have to pay for staff, equipment, software, supplies, contractual services, storage, and ongoing maintenance. Being part of a larger institution with superior web access and support has helped our budgetary situation. The University of Minnesota was home of the gopher and was at the forefront of offering web space to faculty, staff, and organizations. Consequently, we are able to host our site on the University's server and take advantage of backup systems and high-speed connections. Therefore, server space is much less expensive than if we had to seek an outside Internet service provider. Also, since server space has not yet become an issue, we have not had to archive or weed any of the documents in our collection.

While many of our expenses are offset by being part of an academic institution, we are constantly on the lookout for new sources of funding. Any new projects, like converting our documents into a web database or adding enhanced meta-data, would require more funding. We were fortunate to get onto the web early and many of our grants were obtained by being the first to offer a unique electronic collection. As the web continues to develop and more collections are coming online, we must compete with many other organizations seeking the same share of the funding pie. Thus, we have to focus our grant proposals on things that we can do that other sites cannot provide. Since we are not an institution that develops original content (for the most part), we must consider ways in which to organize and offer the content. The number of human rights IGOs and NGOs providing their documents on the web are ever increasing. Many of these sites are not well organized, making them slow and difficult to navigate, and they tend to have weak search tools. In addition, the establishment of separate web sites by different human rights bodies requires users to visit several locations on the web to track down materials and information. Add to this, the fact that web search engines are just wholly inadequate. A recent report stated that no general search engine (i.e., Yahoo! or AltaVista) indexes more than approximately 16% of the publicly available web sites.[17] Therefore, in order to take advantage of the growing collection of documents on other web sites, the Human Rights Library sought funding to develop a cross-site search device. Our goal was to provide a mechanism that would allow visitors to our site to conduct searches across a range of human rights sites from one convenient form.[18] For example, if the researcher wants to locate the country reports from Amnesty International, the UN High Commissioner for Human Rights, and the UN High Commissioner for Refugees, they can use the Library's meta-search device to locate them all with one search versus visiting each site individually and conducting three or more separate searches. This search device is now functional on the web site. In addition to adding a cross-site search device, we have recently added an improved local search engine.[19] This device allows the user to search the entire Human Rights Library as well as selected collections.

CONCLUSION

The impact of the Human Rights Library has been tremendous. The site has won numerous awards and is even cited in law review articles. A recent note in the *Harvard Human Rights Journal* says "[t]he University of Minnesota Human Rights Library, with its well-organized, diverse, and user-friendly collection of human rights documents, is a particular favorite of students and researchers."[20] In addition, in a recent issue of the *Internet Law Researcher*, the Human Rights Library was listed as a leading subject-oriented academic site.[21] A quick search on the web reveals that approximately 900 sites link to the Library's homepage, and there are probably hundreds of other links to other pages and individual documents within our collection– another illustration of the site's popularity.

Although this collection has enjoyed much success, we realize that we have much more to do. As more institutions and governments provide primary sources of information on their own sites, perhaps the focus of our collection will shift to commentary and analysis, a source of information that is absent on the web for the most part. No matter the future of our collection, this experience has provided me with a unique opportunity as a librarian. I take great pride in being part of a project and a technology that has had a profound impact on the way people access and use information.

NOTES

1. Professor David Weissbrodt is the Briggs and Morgan Professor of Law at the University of Minnesota Law School and the Co-Director of the University of Minnesota Human Rights Library.

2. DIANA is an acronym for Direct Information Access Network Association. The site is available at <http://diana.law.yale.edu>. For more information about the

DIANA consortium, *see* Nicholas D. Finke et al., *DIANA: A Human Rights Database,* 16 Hum. Rts. Q. 753 (1994).

   3. *Id.*

   4. Many thanks to Brian T. Pierce (JD, University of Minnesota, 1997) for all of his help and dedication to the Human Rights Library. Brian continues to work on the Internet; his Center for Rational Correctional Policy web page is available at <http://www.correctionalpolicy.com>.

   5. Multilaterals Project, Fletcher School of Law and Diplomacy <http://fletcher.tufts.edu/multilaterals.html>.

   6. Unfortunately, this site is no longer available on the Internet.

   7. Effective May 28, 1999, the House Internet Law Library was discontinued. The collection of treaties and documents is available at other institutions and firms on the Internet, such as <http://www.lectlaw.com/inll/89.htm>, <http://www.austlii.edu.au/links/hrill/>, and <http://www.priweb.com/internetlawlib/89.htm>.

   8. University of Minnesota Human Rights Library, Instruments by Topic <http://www1.umn.edu/humanrts/ainstls2.htm>.

   9. University of Minnesota Human Rights Library, Instruments page <http://www1.umn.edu/humanrts/ainstls1.htm>.

   10. United Nations High Commissioner for Human Rights, Status of Ratifications of the Principal International Human Rights Treaties <http://www.unhchr.ch/pdf/report. pdf>.

   11. Council of Europe, Chart of Signatures and Ratifications <http://conventions.coe.int/treaty/EN/cadreprincipal.htm>.

   12. Inter-American Commission on Human Rights, Signatures and Ratifications <http://www.cidh.oas.org/basic.htm>.

   13. A mirror site is a replica of a web site and resides on a different server. In the case of the Human Rights Library, these servers are located in other parts of the world. Mirror sites increase the speed with which information and documents can be accessed since users can download files more quickly from a server that is located geographically closer to them.

   14. University of Minnesota Human Rights Library, Usage Statistics <http://www1.umn.edu/humanrts/info/statistics.htm>.

   15. University of Minnesota Human Rights Resource Center <http://160.94.193.60/>.

   16. An absolute link provides the complete http address in the form of a full URL, including the server name and the full path of the desired document, whereas a relative link provides a partial http address in the form of partial directory pathname and file name.

   17. Steve Lawrence & C. Lee Giles, *Accessibility of Information on the Web*, Nature, July 8, 1999, at 107. See also <http://www.wwwmetrics.com/> for a summary of this report.

   18. University of Minnesota Human Rights Library, Meta Search Device <http://www1.umn.edu/humanrts/lawform.html>.

   19. University of Minnesota Human Rights Library, Local Search Engine <http://www1.umn.edu/humanrts/localsearch.html>.

   20. Susan Heintz, Book Notes, *An Introduction to Human Rights Resources on the Internet,* 12 Harv. Hum. Rts. J. 407, 409 (1999).

   21. *Leading Subject-Oriented Academic Sites,* Internet L. Researcher, Sept. 1999 at 8.

Building the Global Legal
Information Network (GLIN)

Janice S. Hyde

SUMMARY. Although the quantity of sources of foreign and international law available on the World Wide Web is rapidly growing, users quickly discover that everything is *not* available, and the quality of much of what exists is suspect. Driven by its mission to collect, preserve and provide access to reliable legal information from around the world, the Law Library of Congress is developing the Global Legal Information Network (GLIN), a database containing statutes, regulations and related legal materials from countries in Africa, Asia, Europe and the Americas. This article describes the history of this effort; the future plans for development; standards for quality, and the organizational structure of the GLIN network. The article concludes that although the creation of a comprehensive digital law library is a mammoth undertaking, the need for GLIN is obvious. *[Article copies available for a fee from The Haworth Document Delivery Service: 1-800-342-9678. E-mail address: <getinfo@haworthpressinc.com> Website: <http://www.HaworthPress.com> © 2001 by The Haworth Press, Inc. All rights reserved.]*

Janice S. Hyde is Program Officer of the Law Library of Congress and is responsible for programming and administering the Global Legal Information Network (GLIN). Since 1989, she has served in various capacities at the Library of Congress, and since 1992, all of these positions have required increasing levels of responsibility for GLIN. Ms. Hyde has a PhD in anthropology and has authored and edited works on women and development in South Asia.

[Haworth co-indexing entry note]: "Building the Global Legal Information Network (GLIN)." Hyde, Janice S. Co-published simultaneously in *Legal Reference Services Quarterly* (The Haworth Information Press, an imprint of The Haworth Press, Inc.) Vol. 19, No. 3/4, 2001, pp. 157-173; and: *Teaching Legal Research and Providing Access to Electronic Resources* (ed: Gary L. Hill, Dennis S. Sears, and Lovisa Lyman) The Haworth Information Press, an imprint of The Haworth Press, Inc., 2001, pp. 157-173. Single or multiple copies of this article are available for a fee from The Haworth Document Delivery Service [1-800-342-9678, 9:00 a.m. - 5:00 p.m. (EST). E-mail address: getinfo@haworthpressinc.com].

INTRODUCTION

The explosion of information available on the World Wide Web includes a rapidly growing number of sources of foreign and international law. National legislation from many countries is available through web sites hosted by legislatures throughout the world. Treaties and international agreements are offered online by the United Nations (http://www.un.org/Depts/Treaty/collection/series/search.htm) and the Organization of American States (http://www.oas.org/en/prog/juridico/english/treaties.html) to name just two sources. Although the quantity of information available through the Internet is astounding, users quickly discover that everything is *not* available, and the quality of much of what exists is suspect.

The Law Library of the Library of Congress (hereafter LLC) has a long-standing interest in foreign, comparative, and international law. Since its founding in 1832, LLC has assumed the daunting responsibility of collecting legal material from all over the world to carry out its mission.

> The mission of the Law Library is to provide high quality, timely and innovative research, analysis and reference services to the United States Congress, as well as to the Supreme Court, other courts, executive agencies, the legal profession, academic community and the general public, based on the strength of the world's largest and most complete collection of international, foreign and national legal resources.[1]

Because of its unique mission to collect, preserve, and provide access to legal information from around the world, LLC embarked upon the development of the Global Legal Information Network (GLIN), a database containing statutes, regulations and related legal materials from countries in Africa, Asia, Europe and the Americas. It has joined other interested legislative information centers from around the world with the goal of providing electronic access to primary sources of the law of all nations. This article will describe the history of this effort, which is critical to understanding the current content of the database, the future plans for development, standards for quality, and the organizational structure of GLIN.

HISTORY OF GLIN

The Law Library of Congress has always relied on primary sources of law wherever possible to respond to requests from the U.S. Congress, the courts and executive agencies. For foreign countries, the fundamental source of law is generally the "official gazette." In general, "an official gazette is the official legal newspaper of a jurisdiction in which, usually, the texts of new laws are published. The contents are not limited to major laws, but may also include various types of related decrees, regulations, treaties, legal notices, and texts of court decisions."[2] Many nations statutorily declare the gazette as *the* official source of law.[3] Starting in 1858, with the acquisition of the official gazette of Mexico, the Law Library of Congress has endeavored to collect official gazettes from as many nations of the world as possible. For federal jurisdictions, it collects gazettes from the subnational level as well. One can easily imagine how much paper this has amounted to in one-and-a-half centuries. For preservation purposes, LLC microfilms gazettes from the countries of Latin America and Northern Africa and has partnered with other institutions, primarily New York Public Library, to film other regions of the world.[4]

While committed to the use of the official sources, there have been two major problems: difficulty in acquiring these sources in a timely fashion and a general lack of indexing for these sources. The latter is a particular problem for the foreign law specialists in the Law Library of Congress who handle numerous jurisdictions. LLC currently employs two attorneys to handle over 26 Spanish- and Portuguese-speaking nations. Requests for the laws of multiple jurisdictions are common as are immediate deadlines. Consequently, an obvious task was the creation of an index for the gazettes.

In 1950, in what was then the Hispanic Law Division of the Law Library of Congress, the foreign law specialists began to create an index for the official gazettes of Spanish- and Portuguese-speaking nations. Using $3'' \times 5''$ index cards, the attorneys drafted short summaries of legal instruments published in the gazettes, and they included basic bibliographic information about the source of publication. To access the information quickly, the attorneys began to assign subject terms to the cards–initially only one term was used for each instrument.

The cards were accumulated into folios published in eight volumes as the *Index to Latin American Legislation,* covering the period from 1950-1975. LLC has not yet digitized this information, and it is in the process of determining the size and potential cost of the task. These volumes remain the primary source for locating pre-1976 laws from Spanish- and Portuguese-speaking nations.[5]

In 1976, LLC decided to take advantage of the prevailing technology of the time, the mainframe computer system. The Library of Congress's proprietary SCORPIO system was adopted for the Law Library's legal indexing system, and the LAWL system was born. LLC attorneys began keying indexing information into the LAWL system, providing an online index that could be searched by country and subject. To locate the law itself, however, a researcher still needed to locate the paper or microfilm.

Although the LAWL system helped speed access to the information that the Law Library of Congress had acquired, timely receipt of official gazettes remained, and continues to be, a major problem. In the best cases, the Law Library might receive material in as little as two weeks (from Mexico, for example), in the worst cases, it may take as long as two to three years (certain African nations, for example). The importance of currency in legal information will not be belabored here, but an institution cannot claim to be a reliable source of information if its source material is out of date. The Law Library used whatever means it could, including acquisitions trips to various nations and contact with the Library of Congress's field offices (Cairo, New Delhi, Jakarta, Karachi, Nairobi, Rio de Janeiro) to minimize the lag time between publication of laws and their receipt at LLC.

In the early 1990s, the Law Library convened three meetings of librarians and staff of legislative research services from around the world to share information about the development of a number of online systems of legal information and to discuss possible cooperative efforts. For its part, the LLC coordinated the creation of a union list of gazette holdings for a number of institutions in the U.S. and Europe. The two publications stemming from these meetings[6] describe efforts of the time to define and create the International Legal Information Network (ILIN) as it was then called. The premise of ILIN was that different institutions around the world would develop legal databases that would somehow be linked together. In the days before the World Wide Web, this notion seemed fanciful, and the working metaphor was a patchwork quilt–the "stitching together" of disparate databases into a "seamless" blanket.[7]

In 1992, the Law Library of Congress began an experiment with Mexico and Brazil in which these nations transmitted scanned images of the texts of their laws electronically to LLC. The process was painfully slow but proved the concept that LLC could acquire texts of laws electronically. Moreover, the LLC's partners in both Mexico and Brazil expressed an interest in receiving texts in the same manner. The idea of an electronic exchange of laws between nations thus became the foundation for the Global Legal Information Network (GLIN). Today, GLIN member nations contribute official texts of laws and related legal materials to a common database housed at the Library of Congress; and in exchange, each member has access to the contributions of all other members.

CURRENT STATUS OF GLIN

GLIN is a cooperative, not-for-profit federation of government agencies or their designees that contribute national legal information to the GLIN database (http://www.loc.gov/glin). It is an automated database of statutes, regulations and related material that originate from countries in the Americas, Europe, Africa and Asia. The data are in a central server at the Library of Congress in Washington, DC. Access is equally shared by all participating national GLIN stations. Anyone with Internet connections can access summaries of and citations to over 75,000 laws from forty-six nations, although copyright and distribution-rights issues currently preclude public access to full texts. A distributed network is envisioned, and the database will reside on servers in other member nations as well as the Law Library of Congress.

Elements of GLIN

One important element of GLIN is its global focus. All countries are invited and encouraged to participate in the network as the usefulness of the database increases and membership expands. Since there is no subject that is not of potential interest to LLCs clients, there is global subject coverage as well. Finally, the aim of GLIN is to be chronologically complete. As nations join GLIN, they are expected first to maintain the currency of their files, while LLC works with partner nations on a plan for the inclusion of retrospective material to insure a complete record.

GLIN is currently a non-commercial venture. There are no fees for joining GLIN and no portion of the database is sold or presently available for subscription. The entire database, including the full-text of laws, is available to contributing members for free, or more precisely, in exchange for their contribution of legal information. Membership in GLIN does not in any way preclude a country from doing whatever else it may wish with its own laws, including selling its laws in electronic or other formats.

One of the features that distinguishes GLIN from most other legal databases of foreign law is that the database is being built cooperatively. No one country owns the database, and all members are responsible for making decisions related to the network. GLIN member nations are encouraged to participate in further research and development activities. Building a network cooperatively requires agreement on a set of standards. There are both technical standards and content standards for GLIN that members have agreed to follow. The standards for selecting the texts, analyzing them, producing summaries, assigning index terms, and the testing and selection of applicable hardware and software were developed originally at the initiative and as the contribution of LLC.

Reliability of GLIN

GLIN does not seek to replace existing legal databases developed by nations around the world. However, navigating the World Wide Web to find and use these databases is far from seamless. The need to understand different search engines, the difficulty of locating information in different languages, and retrieving and displaying this information can frustrate anyone trying to locate legal texts from different nations. Moreover, the quality of much of the information found on the Internet is questionable.

> On the World Wide Web, straight facts can be hard to find. After plowing through dense and recalcitrant search engines that offer more sites than you can point a mouse at, after enduring delays, lost links and dead ends and arriving at a site that looks just right, Web surfers must deal with uncertainty: Is the information true, unbiased and free of hidden sales pitches?[8]

The development of GLIN was driven largely by the LLC's need for reliable legal information.

Given that the attorneys at the Law Library have always relied on primary sources of law, it is imperative, when developing an electronic law library, that the information be as reliable as published paper sources. Authenticity of the texts in GLIN is critical. GLIN does not accept re-keyed texts of laws, commercial publications, or other versions that are not from the official sources. Users should be able to verify quickly, by sight, that the legal instrument is from the official publication of the nation. GLIN should be an authoritative source for foreign law. Consequently, texts remain in the vernacular.

The current content of the GLIN database very much reflects its origins. As of December 1999, there were over 75,000 records in the database. Of these, approximately 50,000 are summary records only from the LAWL file, covering the period of 1975-1995; and a preponderance of these records are for Spanish and Portuguese speaking nations. As an outgrowth of a project initiated to index instruments found in official gazettes, GLIN contains primarily statutory material. Plans exist to expand the database to include other categories of legal information and these will be discussed below.

GLIN Summaries and Thesaurus

The indexing tools used in the early 1950s have been retained in the GLIN system. The full texts of legal instruments in the vernacular are accessible through English-language summaries and English-language subject terms derived from the GLIN thesaurus. The summaries are not meant to be provision-by-provision digests of the law, but the goal is to reflect, where possible, the "anatomy" of the law: subject, enforcement agency, procedure, penalties, and transitory provisions. As the bulk of laws enacted are amendatory, not all of these elements may be present in every summary.

The GLIN thesaurus has been developed specifically as a finding aid. The terms first assigned by attorneys in the 1950s form the base of the thesaurus, and terms are added as needed to index specific pieces of legislation. There are, therefore, no "blind entries" in the thesaurus, so every term in the GLIN thesaurus will be assigned to at least one record in the database. The GLIN thesaurus uses a multi-national, multi-system approach, using legal concepts from various legal systems. Legislation from civil law nations can be located by using legal terms specifically appropriate for this system, but can also be located in the database through terms unique to common law systems.[9]

A great deal of thought is given to the adoption of terms for inclusion in the thesaurus. A GLIN thesaurus committee comprising some ten attorneys representing different jurisdictions and legal cultures meets weekly to consider candidate terms. There are often lively debates about how best to render complex legal concepts with a term or phrase. Indeed, there are "culture-bound" terms that defy the designation of an equivalent term or phrase in English. These terms must be maintained in the vernacular in the GLIN thesaurus. Examples of two such terms from the GLIN thesaurus include the Spanish term, "amparo," and "kafala" from Arabic-speaking jurisdictions.

Familiarizing oneself with the GLIN thesaurus is vital to conducting successful searches of the GLIN database. Although free text searching is a common search method, and one that makes users comfortable because they feel they can get instant results–type in a word, get back a list of "hits," the resulting list is often excessively large. Some systems allow refinements of the initial search, and provide hints on how to do this, but these are the exceptions rather than the rule. The option of conducting free text searches on texts across a comprehensive, multilingual database such as GLIN is not yet technically viable, although UNICODE and XML are promising developments.

Even if it were available, there is great value in descriptive metadata, such as that found in the GLIN summaries, and in the use of a controlled vocabulary as found in the GLIN thesaurus. The attorneys who compose GLIN summaries and assign subject terms are trained to follow specific standards for format, style, content, and representation of legal concepts with specific GLIN thesaurus terms. A few minutes of browsing through the GLIN thesaurus in advance will enable a targeted search that is more likely to yield desired results more quickly than sorting through a lengthy list of hits. In anticipation of the future when full text searching of multilingual texts becomes common, GLIN will nonetheless insist on offering summaries and a controlled vocabulary method of searching.

Standards for Full Texts

In developing GLIN, LLC very early confronted the need to store, retrieve, and display texts in multiple languages. The need for authenticity led to the adoption of images of texts that were transmitted to the database in the early experiments with Mexico and Brazil. The size of images resulted in slow transmission as well as storage issues. Additionally, there was no single standard for creating or viewing images, and as a result, a digital image might look very different when viewed on computer running different operating systems (e.g., Windows, UNIX, Macintosh).

In searching for the solution to some of the problems GLIN encountered in its earliest tests, the usefulness of Adobe's Portable Document Format (PDF) was immediately apparent, and the current standard for full texts in GLIN is PDF. The fact that there is a single standard for creation and display of PDF texts, coupled with the need to display all languages, made this format an obvious choice for GLIN.

Quality Control and Maintenance

Insuring compliance with GLIN standards for quality of information (both metadata and texts), currency, and completeness is an important and time-consuming responsibility. Attorneys at the Law Library are often asked to review the quality of the material being sent to the database by countries for which they are responsible. As users of the information, the attorneys are indeed interested in the quality of the data. Over the last decade, however, LLC has lost foreign law specialists for some jurisdictions that are currently contributing to GLIN. The contribution of laws from these "orphan" jurisdictions, with the corresponding English-language summaries, has been an important benefit for the LLC; but it means that LLC must rely heavily upon contributing partner nations to maintain GLIN standards of quality, currency, and completeness–with mixed results.

Members and Partners

Building the Global Legal Information Network cannot be done alone, although this was not immediately apparent to the Law Library of Congress. Accustomed to acquiring material from all over the world for its paper collections, the early tests of GLIN were predicated on the concept of doing essentially the same thing in a new medium. When LLC's early test partners in Brazil and Mexico noted their interest in the same material from other countries, the idea of a cooperative, international network was born.

At present, twelve nations contribute their legal information directly to the GLIN database: Argentina, Brazil, Guatemala, the Republic of Korea, Kuwait, Lithuania, Mexico, Romania, Tunisia, Ukraine, Uruguay, and the United States. LLC continues to abstract and scan texts for Spanish- and Portuguese-speaking nations, although for these nations, the original problems of lack of currency and completeness remain.

GLIN members represent a nation's information unit, governmental agency in charge of printing the official version of that nation's laws, or other governmental, quasi-governmental, or government-designated agency responsible for generating, collecting, publishing, or disseminating official publications of that country's laws, regulations, or court decisions. The most successful partnerships tend to be with those institutions that are eager to participate in GLIN for the same reason as the Law Library, i.e., because they need the information. It is suggested that new GLIN directors consider making GLIN the center of a robust legal information delivery service for their legislatures. In Uruguay, for example, GLIN served as the centerpiece for the development of a comparative legislative research department for the legislature.

Recruiting new member nations to contribute information to GLIN is an ongoing task. GLIN has been adding new member nations at the rate of two to three new countries per year and ultimately aims for a core of forty to fifty member countries. The most frequently asked question about GLIN is about the current membership content–why certain countries are members and not others. In fact, the Law Library of Congress has not had the luxury of being proactive in the area of recruitment. Rather, it has reacted to interest as it has been expressed by individual nations or sponsoring institutions (about which more will be said below).

It is clear that the membership of GLIN needs to be expanded to include both the economically powerful nations and the less economically well-off countries, but for different reasons. While there is certainly interest in laws of nations that have similar economic standing to the U.S. (including G8 nations), LLC has the most difficulty obtaining current legal material from the least developed countries. To make their laws available through GLIN would be enormously useful and would fill obvious gaps in existing online sources of foreign law.

Joining GLIN can be extremely useful for those countries that are considering some form of digitization but have not the time nor resources to invest in the development of a tailor-made system. For the majority of nations that already have legal databases, GLIN is meant as a complement, not a replacement. Countries should consider contributing to an international effort for international consumption. There is great value in making the laws of nations available in one place where comparative searching is possible.

In addition to the contributing member nations, another important group of GLIN partners includes supporting institutions. The World Bank and the Inter-American Development Bank have provided start-up costs that enabled several GLIN member nations to fully participate in the network. The strategy of the banks is simple: knowledge of laws related to business establishment, financial institutions, and commercial transactions is needed to spur investment, economic growth, and loan repayment.

Technical assistance to GLIN has been provided by another institutional partner, the National Aeronautics and Space Administration (NASA). Advice in the area of telecommunications has been particularly important as GLIN seeks ways to involve all nations, including those with undeveloped terrestrial communications links. Plans for testing a high-speed intranet for GLIN members are almost complete and will be outlined below.

Current Network Organization

The current GLIN organization might best be described as a federation of contributing members and institutional partners. The Law Library of Congress has developed a set of standards for the digitization and exchange of legal information that it thinks is reasonable at this time. Members of the network agree to adhere to these standards, although there is no way to enforce adherence, and much is left to the good will of the members.

Upon joining the GLIN network, designated representatives of member nations are asked to sign the *GLIN: Guiding Principles* document (Appendix). This document outlines the fundamental rights and obligations of members, and it has served, to date, as a general agreement on the goals of GLIN and has set the framework for how the members would work together. Although there is no way to enforce member adherence to the principles, nor to expel them if they do not comply, a cooperatively built database cannot succeed unless there is a commitment to a shared set of goals and standards.

FUTURE PLANS FOR GLIN

The Global Legal Information Network is far from complete. Over the next few years, the Law Library plans to introduce several new features and types of content.

Expanded Content

Although GLIN is essentially an outgrowth of an in-house effort to index statutes and regulations found in official gazettes, the Law Library is well aware that legal information encompasses much more. In March 1999, a new category of legal information, legal writings, was added to the database. Intended to include law review articles, opinions, and commentaries from legal scholars and national and international organizations, this portion of the GLIN database now houses the opinions of the Office of Legal Affairs of the United Nations.

An input form for entering information on judicial decisions or cases has been drafted and is being circulated to GLIN members for comment in preparation for inclusion of this category of legal information, which is particularly critical for common law jurisdictions. The goal was to incorporate this information into the database in the year 2000. The debate leading to the enactment of laws is extremely useful information, and the future GLIN database will contain legislative records or parliamentary debates as they pertain to particular statutes that are in the GLIN database. Handling the information in this category may present different challenges because some countries are moving in the direction of adopting different media (e.g., video) as the official records of their parliamentary proceedings.

The statutory material remains at the center of the database, and although each category of legal information can be searched independently through the common GLIN thesaurus, they are meant to be linked together. A user of GLIN who has retrieved the summary of a law may now see a reference to "related legal writings." In the future, this user will also see references to related judicial decisions and related legislative debates.

Distributed Network

In addition to expansion of the content of the database through the addition of both new countries and new categories of legal information, the GLIN network architecture will move from the centralized structure that currently exists to a truly distributed network. The first step toward this move is the creation of GLIN "regional centers." Regional centers will first be located in GLIN member nations that have proved to be in compliance with all GLIN standards for the quality of English-language summaries and original language full texts in PDF format, timeliness of data entry, and currency of the national file. They would also have the requisite hardware and software needed to first house GLIN data from neighboring countries (a loosely defined "region"), and ultimately to become a mirror site for the entire GLIN database. The establishment of a truly distributed network with multiple mirror sites that could be refreshed in real time is technically complex but remains the aim of GLIN.

Inclusion of Retrospective Material

Work needs to be done to digitize the texts of laws that correspond to approximately 50,000 summaries that are in the GLIN database for the period of 1975 to 1995. Since most of this material is now on microfilm, the Law Library has been dealing with a number of issues related to the digitization of that material. A small pilot project was started in 1999 to selectively digitize laws from Brazil, Mexico, and Uruguay in the area of environmental law. The

Law Library has discovered that the quality of the microfilm may not be high enough to render clear digital images. Whether this is due to the poor quality of the original gazettes, the microfilming standards for preservation, or some combination of both is not clear; but the result is a labor-intensive conversion process that may, in some cases, never yield acceptable results.

One of the biggest issues related to this conversion from microfilm has been the lack of standards for long-term preservation and archiving of digital images. Many institutions have collectively spent billions of dollars to create digital items, whether "born digital" or converted from paper. The future of these items is in question. The Law Librarian of Congress has convened two meetings of stakeholders within the federal government and law library community to attempt to establish a set of fundamental, functional requirements, and convey these to the industry so that a set of standards might be developed for archiving digitized legal records. Just as LLC has been committed to preserving print information, it remains committed to continued preservation and access to GLIN information while, at the same time, acknowledging that it will not be able to invest in multiple formats (paper, microfilm, and digital) indefinitely.

As noted earlier, the eight-volume *Index to Latin American Legislation* is an invaluable resource that is not currently available in digital form. Efforts have just begun within the Law Library to determine the scope of work needed to input approximately 96,000 card entries into the GLIN database–and to digitize the corresponding texts. The cost and magnitude of the effort preclude a good estimation of a target date for completion.

Developing a GLIN Intranet

The development of a high-speed GLIN intranet to better serve GLIN members is also being planned. Two satellite antennae were recently installed at Goddard Space Flight Center in Greenbelt, Maryland, and tests were set to begin in early 2000 to determine the feasibility of using satellites to transmit and receive GLIN data. The hope is that a GLIN intranet might attract the participation in GLIN of additional countries that still have problems with traditional, terrestrial communications links.

Future Network Organization

The current, informal cooperative arrangement has worked fairly well, but the need for a more formal organizational structure is being driven by two major factors. The first is growth of the network. The current membership of twelve nations may be managed by an ad hoc Advisory Council and the GLIN staff of the Law Library of Congress, but additional members will require an agreed upon set of rules with firmly defined rights and obligations.

Not surprisingly, the second factor propelling the need for a more formal organization is the need for revenue. Although initiated by the Law Library of Congress, GLIN is not "owned" by the Library. The need for current, complete, reliable legal information to carry out its mission justifies the staff time spent working on GLIN. However, there are a number of administrative activities that require resources above and beyond what the Law Library is able to commit. For the past two years, members of the network have discussed the possibility of incorporating as a not-for-profit organization as the first step toward the creation of an entity that could enter into contracts and raise funds through various means. It is not hard to imagine that the members have not yet agreed to take this step.

Some membership organizations request dues or membership fees; however, GLIN members already provide a valuable contribution to the network in the form of legal information and the concomitant commitment of resources (primarily staff time) needed to provide this information to the database. Through annual meetings, GLIN Directors have a say in the way that the network is administered but do not yet feel the sense of responsibility for its continued sustenance.

Access to GLIN

The question of expanding access to the GLIN database remains an open one. Currently, only GLIN members are allowed unrestricted access to the complete contents of the database while "guests" are entitled to view only the summaries. This difference is due, in part, to restrictions of copyright and/or distribution that some countries have placed on their laws. One option is to identify everything in the GLIN database that is clearly in the public domain and offer it freely to anyone. Given the increasingly urgent need to recover the costs of developing and operating the network, some kind of fee-based system of distribution is currently a more attractive option.

CONCLUSION

The Law Library of Congress has a mandate to provide reference services to the public in the area of foreign, comparative, and international law. GLIN remains its most important reference tool in this area. When the Law Library collected its first official gazette from Mexico, it is not likely that anyone would have been able to guess the magnitude of its holdings a century and a half later. Collecting this information electronically through the Global Legal Information Network should, theoretically, be easier than collecting paper, and the need for GLIN should be obvious.

NOTES

1. Library of Congress Regulation § 216-1.
2. Amber Lee Smith, For. & Intl. L. Libr., L.A. County L. Lib., Presentation, *Official Gazettes* (A.A.L.L. July 20, 1999).
3. Two examples are Panama (Decree 26, 19 February 1990, *Gaceta Oficial,* art. 1, p. 2) and Peru (Unnumbered regulation, 6 March 1998, *El Peruano,* art 80, § 3, p. 160318).
4. For a description of efforts to preserve and make accessible retrospective backfiles of official gazettes, *see* Robert L. Buckwalter, Assoc. Libr. Collection Servs., Har. L. Sch. Lib., Presentation, *The Foreign Official Gazettes Task Force of the Center for Research Libraries* (A.A.L.L. July 20, 1999).
5. 1 *Index to Latin American Legislation,* 1950-1960, Argentina-Cuba (Comp. Hispanic L. Div., L. Lib., Library of Congress, G.K. Hale & Co. 1960); *Index to Latin American Legislation,* 1st Supp. 1961-1965, Argentina-Cuba (Comp. Hispanic L. Div., L. Lib., Library of Congress, G.K. Hale & Co. 1970); *Index to Latin American Legislation,* 2d Supp. 1966-1970, Argentina-Cuba (Comp. Hispanic L. Div., L. Lib., Library of Congress, G.K. Hale & Co. 1973); *Index to Latin American Legislation,* 3d Supp. 1971-1975, Argentina-Cuba (Comp. Hispanic L. Div., L. Lib., Library of Congress, G.K. Hale & Co. 1978); 2 *Index to Latin American Legislation,* 1950-1960, Dominican Republic-Venezuela (Comp. Hispanic L. Div., L. Lib., Library of Congress, G.K. Hale & Co. 1961); *Index to Latin American Legislation,* 1st Supp. 1961-1965, Dominican Republic-Venezuela (Comp. Hispanic L. Div., L. Lib., Library of Congress, G.K. Hale & Co. 1970); *Index to Latin American Legislation,* 2d Supp. 1966-1970, Dominican Republic-Venezuela (Comp. Hispanic L. Div., L. Lib., Library of Congress, G.K. Hale & Co. 1973); *Index to Latin American Legislation,* 3d Supp. 1971-1975, Dominican Republic-Venezuela (Comp. Hispanic L. Div., L. Lib., Library of Congress, G.K. Hale & Co. 1978).
6. *International Access to Legislative Information: A Preliminary Investigation* (Win-shin S. Chiang & Kathleen Price eds. (1992); *International Access to Legislative Information: Collection, Storage, Retrieval and Delivery of Public Information* (Thomas J. Blumer et al. eds., 1994).
7. For a more detailed description of this early phase, see Lovisa Lyman, *Electronic Access to the Laws of Foreign and International Jurisdictions: An Overview,* A.A.L.L. Newsletter, May 1996, at 12.
8. Tina Kelley, *Whales in the Minnesota River? Only on the Web, Where Skepticism Is a Required Navigational Aid,* N. Y. Times, Mar. 4, 1999, at E 1.
9. Glenn L. Reitze, Presentation, *The GLIN Central Thesaurus: An Introduction* (5th Annual GLIN Directors' Meeting, Sept. 17, 1998).

APPENDIX
The Global Legal Information Network (GLIN): Guiding Principles

We the Project Directors of the Global Legal Information Network (here-inafter GLIN), desiring to promote the orderly development of laws, under-standing the need for ready access to the laws of other nations, and believing that a current database of national laws shared by member nations will assist these ends, do hereby adopt the basic tenets that will guide our cooperative endeavor.

Chapter 1: Definition and Purpose

GLIN is a non-commercial database established to enable the exchange of full-text primary legal materials via the Internet. GLIN is also the name used to designate the partnership that has been established to make possible the database.

The purpose of GLIN is to share the benefits and burdens of acquiring, processing, and making retrievable the text of national laws in the vernacular and in English. After the texts are captured and processed, the partners are responsible for creating a summary of each statute and/or regulation selected for inclusion in the database and assigning subject headings from a controlled vocabulary approved by the partners for use with GLIN. The partners con-tribute to an electronic central file of legal texts.

Chapter 2: Membership

The charter members of GLIN are those countries who sent a representa-tive to the preliminary organizational meeting held at the Law Library of Congress on November 28-30, 1994: Argentina, Kuwait, Paraguay, Poland, and Ukraine. Brazil, which also sent a representative to that November meet-ing, and Mexico, which did not, are also charter members that have earned a special status in the project by virtue of their role as pilot partners in the first GLIN experiments.

All nations are welcome to become a GLIN member country. There are no special legal requirements for a country's membership in GLIN other than they have a sincere willingness to be a complete participant and partners in the project be sponsored by their governments as official representatives. This is necessary to ensure the authenticity of the sources as well as continu-ing access to the full legal texts. To initiate participation, partners must be willing to establish a GLIN Project Team, to permit a feasibility determina-tion to be made, and to obtain their own funding for the project.

Chapter 3: Project Teams

Each GLIN member country is represented by a Project Team consisting of a Project Director, a Lawyer Analyst, and a Technical Information Specialist.

The Project Director is responsible for implementing the policies, standards, and procedures adopted by the GLIN partnership. Each Project Director has one vote and decisions are made for the partnership by the Project Directors.

The Lawyer Analyst is responsible for analyzing the legislative and regulatory enactments, preparing a summary/abstract, and assigning subject terms from a controlled vocabulary.

The Technical Information Specialist is responsible for providing technical support to build the national database of abstracts and full texts and for providing quality control for the contents of the database.

The Project Team is responsible for ensuring that their national data is analyzed and added to the database on a current basis.

The Project Team members must be able to understand and communicate in English because among GLIN partners the common language used is English. Training and periodic meetings held for the partners require that they use and understand English.

The Lawyer Analyst and Technical Information Specialist members of the Project Team must be prepared to engage in intensive training at the Law Library of the Library of Congress and must be willing to take follow-up training as needed.

Chapter 4: GLIN Central

The central coordinator of the GLIN project is the Project Team at the Law Library of the Library of Congress (hereinafter GLIN Central). GLIN Central holds this position by virtue of its development of the GLIN prototype and procedures over a long period of time. GLIN began in the 1950s as an in-house, working card catalog of legal abstracts filed by subject that helped the staff of legal specialists retrieve the laws of thirty nations. In 1976, the file was automated and the Law Library continued to experiment with varied technology to find the best way to combine the GLIN thesaurus and the full text of the legal materials.

GLIN Central has devised a training program for GLIN Project Teams that is given at the Law Library of the Library of Congress. At present, GLIN Central absorbs the cost of providing this program as well as the cost of experimenting with new technology to make GLIN more efficient and effective for the partners.

GLIN Central also may provide suggestions about possible funding sources for potential partners, but cannot provide any funds for another Project Team.

GLIN Central currently will store the central data contributed by each Project Team and will continue to test new technology as it becomes available with a view toward improving the GLIN database.

Chapter 5: Access to GLIN

At present, access to all abstracts/summaries prepared by the legal analysts will be available to all. Access to the complete file of legal texts is available only to GLIN partners. Redistribution rights for a national file remain with the partner who creates the national file, and a partner may not redistribute the data and records of another partner without the express written permission of the partner whose data is to be redistributed.

Any other access or redistribution of data not provided for in these Guiding Principles is to be agreed upon by all of the partners concerned, including GLIN Central.

Chapter 6: Access to GLIN for Special Affiliates

Access to GLIN may be given to special affiliated organizations who are helping to fund the GLIN project in foreign countries or who make other contributions to the goals of the project. These currently include the Inter-American Development Bank, the National Aeronautics and Space Administration (Goddard Space Flight Center), and the World Bank. These affiliates are given access to GLIN for the use of the affiliate staff who are involved in projects to assist one or more member countries or in some other agreed upon, limited manner; they are not permitted to redistribute the data to others.

Chapter 7: Miscellaneous Provisions

This is a basic agreement subject to correction, amendment, or other necessary changes that the participants may adopt by simple majority vote or by unanimous consent. Country representatives also may make reservations to any policy adopted by the majority.

J

Copyright
and Electronic Library Resources:
An Overview of How the Law
Is Affecting Traditional Library Services

Anne Klinefelter

SUMMARY. As electronic resources represent a larger percentage of libraries' purchases and services, copyright law, licensing, and other information laws are changing some traditional library functions. This article reviews the law of electronic resources through an outline of affected library services, including acquisitions and collection development; gifts, exchanges, and sales; archiving and preservation; circulation; interlibrary loan and document delivery; reserve; and research, reference, and instructional services. Legal issues considered include copyright, licensing, and database protection. *[Article copies available for a fee from The Haworth Document Delivery Service: 1-800-342-9678. E-mail address: <getinfo@ haworthpressinc.com> Website: <http://www.HaworthPress.com> © 2001 by The Haworth Press, Inc. All rights reserved.]*

INTRODUCTION

Libraries and their patrons are embracing electronic resources that often improve upon print publications in their currency, remote access, indexing,

Anne Klinefelter is Associate Director for Research, Instruction, and Access Services and Clinical Associate Professor of Law at the Kathrine R. Everett Law Library, the University of North Carolina at Chapel Hill. She received her BA, MLS and JD degrees from the University of Alabama.

[Haworth co-indexing entry note]: "Copyright and Electronic Library Resources: An Overview of How the Law Is Affecting Traditional Library Services." Klinefelter, Anne. Co-published simultaneously in *Legal Reference Services Quarterly* (The Haworth Information Press, an imprint of The Haworth Press, Inc.) Vol. 19, No. 3/4, 2001, pp. 175-193; and: *Teaching Legal Research and Providing Access to Electronic Resources* (ed: Gary L. Hill, Dennis S. Sears, and Lovisa Lyman) The Haworth Information Press, an imprint of The Haworth Press, Inc., 2001, pp. 175-193. Single or multiple copies of this article are available for a fee from The Haworth Document Delivery Service [1-800-342-9678, 9:00 a.m. - 5:00 p.m. (EST). E-mail address: getinfo@haworthpressinc.com].

cross-referencing, and space saving. Not only are librarians purchasing and accessing free electronic products but we continue to create some of our own, building on our experience with online catalogs. At the same time, the copyright and related law of electronic resources is complicating and even compromising some traditional library services. This article provides an overview of traditional library services and how copyright, licensing and other information laws are changing those services.

ACQUISITIONS AND COLLECTION DEVELOPMENT

Once identified as a potential purchase for the library, an electronic resource may become immediately available or may take months to become a part of the library resources because the licensing process can become quite burdensome and can involve entities normally outside of the print material purchasing process. The process of reviewing licenses is changing the way libraries structure staff and organize collection building. Librarians have no choice but to redirect staff energies to licensing because what happens at the contract level affects almost all library support efforts and services to patrons.

To aid in this crucial endeavor, library associations have worked together to produce guidelines and resources, such as the liblicense listserv, to help acquisitions librarians and other library negotiators obtain agreements that give up as few as possible of the user rights set out under copyright law.[1] In addition, licensing workshops and conference programs have become popular forms of educational support.[2]

It almost goes without saying that with each product having different terms of use, the participation of many library staff members previously less involved in selection and acquisition is called upon. Librarians now organize licensing teams that include representatives from collection development, acquisitions, cataloging, systems, interlibrary loan, reference and other areas as needed.[3] In a corporate library or in a smaller library setting, the director might spend increasing amounts of her time negotiating and renegotiating licenses.[4]

The cost in staff time was one of the objections five major library associations presented in a July 1999 letter to the National Conference of Commissioner on Uniform State Laws (NCCUSL), the organization authoring a proposed uniform state law validating many forms of licenses. Because a significant number of the proponents of NCCUSL's Uniform Computer Information Transactions Act (UCITA) argue the economic necessity of licensing for growth in electronic publishing, the library associations countered that licensing will cost libraries inordinate amounts in staffing, threatening their annual expenditures for information resources. The library associations' letter notes that "under the terms of UCITA, increased licensing means that more time will be needed to educate library staff, to negotiate licenses, to track use of materials, and to investigate the status of materials donated to libraries."[5]

Enactment of UCITA by a state would change the state's contract law to better support the type of licensing publishers have been using for their electronic products.[6] Under the current Uniform Commercial Code, widely respected and enacted in the states, contracts in which the terms are not evident to the purchaser until after purchase may not be valid.[7] Many mass-marketed software packages are sold with these sorts of licenses, often called shrinkwrap licenses because the breaking of the plastic wrap enclosing the product has been designated in some contracts as the purchaser's manifestation of assent to the terms contained within. Similar to the shrinkwrap license, some software is simply included as a diskette or CD-ROM supplement to a book purchased by the library. This material may arrive with a license outlining the publishers' terms for its use. Shrinkwrap contracts have been criticized as one-sided contracts of adhesion and as an attempt to work an end-run around federal copyright laws that afford publishers less control over use of their publications.[8]

UCITA proposes that purchasers who discover such licenses after purchase would have only the option of returning the material for a refund if the terms are unacceptable. The legitimacy of shrinkwrap licenses remains hotly debated as a smattering of court decisions split on the issue and as UCITA is introduced to state legislatures.[9] If UCITA is enacted by the states, these one-sided contracts will gain legitimacy, though some argue that federal copyright law could preempt terms that are contrary to articulated federal copyright law balances.[10] Acquisitions staff members opening the mail must be taught to look for all licenses as they unbox and unwrap packages, and the librarians must read and react to each license.

Librarians are dealing with an array of electronic products that have different types of licensing in addition to the shrinkwrap variety. Some electronic products are major investments in CD-ROMs that run on a local network or in a remote access Internet resource. Publishers of these products usually have standard licensing contracts but may be open to negotiation. Collection development/acquisitions librarians have to know what they should seek from a license and what rights they bring to the bargain. Fortunately, librarians are providing each other with support and guidance in this process.[11]

With electronic publications governed more by contract than by copyright, not only is the library acquisitions process made much more complex, but the whole concept of collection development is altered. No longer is the library becoming an owner of the material. The publisher instead is selling certain rights to use its product, generally for a specified period of time. Librarians now necessarily speak more about library "resources" than of the library "collection."

Licensing and copyright issues upstream from the library are also affecting the collection management process. These developments may have an effect on the reliability of licensed access to specific electronic resources. A 1999 Second Circuit case found that publishers must secure specific rights from free-lance writers to place their print materials in an electronic database.[12] This decision may require publishers and database providers to drop materials currently included in their databases unless they retroactively secure permission to publish them in this format. Strict attention to this process could lead to electronic materials being less complete and useful than their print counterparts. And, as licensing between providers reflects the competitive market trends for publishers developing their own web products, libraries are seeing less on-the-web versions of conglomerate resources like LEXIS and Westlaw. Librarians making cautious decisions to cancel print materials in favor of electronic ones must keep watch to make sure the product continues to provide the necessary materials.

Another recent copyright decision may have additional upstream effects on law collection managers. In 1999 the Second Circuit denied West Publishing's claim to copyright in its page numbers, in contrast with an earlier Eighth Circuit decision.[13] Many librarians hope this decision will open up the market to other publishers to provide court-required West page numbering citations in their databases. Others, however, fear this decision will only weaken one of the country's best sources for legal materials.[14]

GIFTS, EXCHANGES, AND SALES

The idea of the "resource" becomes particularly important to libraries that have engaged in gifts, exchanges, and sales of material from their collections. The licensed resource, once added to the collection, provides few of the traditional opportunities for efficiencies achieved by building collections from gifts or through library exchange. Libraries also are unable to support services by selling weeded materials at a library "book sale." The point of licensing is to allow software providers to sell copies of their information products without the attachment of the first sale doctrine.[15] Section 106 of the copyright code provides that when a lawful purchase of a copy of a copyrighted item takes place, the owner of that copy may dispose of the copy by lending, reselling, or giving it away.[16] Licensing avoids the first sale doctrine by characterizing the exchange as a purchase of rights to use the electronic product in certain ways rather than as a sale of a copy. The language of the copyright law provides first sale rights only to an owner of a copy. So, if there is no sale, there is no owner; and if there is no owner, there are no first sale rights. UCITA legislation goes so far as to provide that a contract term prohibiting transfers is enforceable, protecting the purchaser only by requiring that a non-negotiated, mass-market license makes this term "conspicuous."[17]

Various types of law libraries have participated in gifts and exchange programs. Academic libraries seeking growth space may withdraw an unused set of materials no longer important to the mission of the school. Another school, interested in building a collection on the topic, may wish to purchase the material or receive it as a gift. This type of acquisition, whether by sale, trade, or gift, is sometimes the only way to acquire material no longer published nor generally available.[18] Law firms also have participated in these cooperative collection development efforts, particularly when opening new branch offices or when accommodating a split or merger. Gifts collections, in fact, are very important to prison libraries, as they attempt to meet court mandates to provide meaningful access to the law.[19] Licenses that restrict these activities create new responsibilities for librarians who must try to determine the legal status of gift material and also limit libraries' long-term opportunities for return on their investment.

ARCHIVING AND PRESERVATION

Some libraries consider it their mission to collect and preserve certain materials. This archiving function has been an important traditional role of libraries. When the library is merely the purchaser of certain uses of a product for a limited time, that library is in no position to fulfill its archiving role for that product. Licensed information products present great challenges to the library's role in archiving and preserving the human record. As the electronic medium of choice shifts from CD-ROMs to remote access web sites, libraries no longer even have a tangible item representing the information.[20] Even if licenses would allow it, unless the library has some control over the material, the library cannot provide preservation of that material. Although it does not appear in their license, Congressional Information Service has responded to this concern by marketing its web-based Congressional Universe with promises to maintain ongoing access to its historical legislative materials collections.[21] JSTOR has also responded to this concern in developing a service to provide an electronic archive of core scholarly journals. JSTOR provides scanned copies of journals in various disciplines with a "moving wall" of several years prior to the current date so that libraries with space constraints can maintain access, perhaps even improved access, to older materials.[22] But, overall, publishers have not been interested in taking over the archiving role that libraries have traditionally assumed.[23]

At the Second International Virtual Libraries Conference in the summer of

1999, publishers and librarians discussed options for preserving and archiving electronic material. One publisher suggested that there might be a "transitional point" where publishers find their profit on a publication is dwindling, and they would then allow libraries to distribute their product. German publishers and libraries reported that some agreements there allowed libraries to pay to load electronic resources on a local network for a certain period after which the library could retain the material and provide access to it for free.[24] Assuming that contracts between publishers and libraries in the United States are the controlling legal model, libraries must work to negotiate this kind of arrangement with each purchase.

However, publishers and other intermediaries may discover that technology provides them with tracking mechanisms to open up a new market for publications traditionally found through libraries that would archive and preserve materials. Researchers may not be using libraries at all because they can go directly to the provider now selling a download of a single article or "out-of-print" resource for a discounted fee. The Copyright Clearance Center is currently adding publishers to its roster of copyright owners allowing the CCC to collect fees and give permission for copying and other use of their material. A new company called iCopyright is further developing this model by working with publishers such as Dow Jones & Company and Washington-post.Newsweek Interactive to provide instant reuse or reprinting of content. The iCopyright business is based on the concept that publishers could make more money on a popular single article than the original publication if licensed separately and made easily downloadable.[25]

While some have predicted that licensing and electronic resources would require the library with walls in order to restrict and manage access to large groups,[26] the advances in single-use tracking software may prove this prediction untrue. If contract supplants copyright in controlling sale of access to publications, archiving and preservation may cover only those materials found to be so low in use that they are not worth adding to a fee-based tracking system.[27] The ease of simply adding all materials without further editorial participation would argue, though, against a large margin of materials to be omitted from such systems. This combination of factors means libraries seeking to negotiate some archival control over electronic materials may have an uphill battle once tracking and fee collection systems mature.

Librarians seeking to negotiate any license to include archiving or preservation options should also make sure that the electronic material is not programmed to turn into a pumpkin at the end of the standard license period. UCITA sections 605 and 816 would allow the seller to include electronic restraints on contractually prohibited uses of the software. Often called "self-help," these processes allow sellers to recover their data or block use of their software at the end of the contracted use period or when the seller believes use is otherwise in violation of the license.[28]

At the federal level, Congress has enacted copyright provisions that could thwart archiving or preservation efforts if the material to be preserved has been electronically protected from access. The Digital Millennium Copyright Act (DMCA) adds a new "anti-circumvention" section to prohibit circumvention of technological measures that effectively control access to a copyrighted work.[29] Opponents of this law have warned that it is overbroad and does not anticipate legitimate, even if technologically blocked, uses of materials.[30] Much of this prohibition was scheduled to go into effect on October 28, 2000, two years after the enactment of the DMCA. During this period, rule-making proceedings were conducted so that educators, librarians and others concerned about restrictions of legitimate uses could demonstrate classes of copyrighted works that should be exempted from the application of this provision.[31] The difficulty in producing a response to this call for an exception is that electronic publications and technological locks are still immature, especially in terms of library archiving efforts. Fortunately, this review is scheduled to be repeated every three years thereafter as well.[32]

The DMCA also made changes to copyright law specifically targeting libraries and archive copying. The act opened up the opportunity for libraries to make certain archival copies of materials–not just one copy in facsimile form but three copies in digital form, presumably a longer-lasting medium than most facsimile copies.[33] The tradeoff, though, left libraries with digital copies they could not loan to other libraries or to patrons outside of the library.[34]

The Sonny Bono Copyright Term Extension Act extended the duration of United States copyrights by twenty years, diminishing in the process the public domain.[35] The Act made a concession to libraries in allowing, during the last twenty years of any term of copyright of a published work, a library or archives to reproduce, distribute, display, or perform in facsimile or digital form a copy of phonorecord of such work for purposes of preservation, scholarship, or research under specified circumstances. The new copyright code section 108(h) sets out the conditions libraries must meet before taking advantage of this special exception. The library must first determine by a reasonable investigation that the work is not commercially available nor subject to normal commercial exploitation. Large academic libraries with significant archiving and preservation resources may find this exception helpful for providing access to older materials and for allowing them to provide their own digital resource for patrons to use.[36]

CIRCULATION

Loaning or circulating an electronic resource is fraught with complications both technical and copyright related. With a book, the first sale doctrine protects a library's right to allow the patron to take the material outside of the library, presumably to use it elsewhere. With electronic products, licensing terms may outline whether the library can provide off-site access or check-out disks or CD-ROMs to a patron to use elsewhere.

Some libraries have developed policies and procedures to allow patrons to check out the disks or CD-ROMs containing software.[37] Law libraries may circulate the electronic components that sometimes accompany books, usually forms or cited documents that accompany a practice guide or treatise. Nonprofit libraries may circulate software under the protection of the first sale doctrine, even though that section of the copyright code was amended in 1990 to prevent rental or lending that publishers feared led to illegal copying of the software.[38] Nonprofit libraries taking advantage of this exemption must have no reason to believe the borrowing serves a for-profit purpose and must affix the warning designated by the Copyright Office.[39]

If someone in the library negotiates a license for the electronic product, then the terms of that negotiated contract, or license, govern how the library may use the product. If the license indicates the resource is to be loaded onto a network accessible only within the library, then the federal copyright law allowances have been contracted away, possibly traded for other access, such as multiple concurrent users of one copy.

The difficulty comes in knowing what is the lawful approach when the copyright law allows lending and the shrinkwrap license prohibits it. Courts have provided differing opinions about the validity of shrinkwrap-style licenses.[40] The Register of Copyright, in March of 1994, when last reporting to Congress on the nonprofit library exception to the Software Rental Amendments Act of 1990, noted concern among librarians about restrictive shrink-wrap license terms. In that report, the Register noted that representatives of the software industry had "no interest in asserting that shrink wrap licenses override the capability of nonprofit libraries under section 109(b) to lend copies of computer programs for nonprofit purposes."[41]

Shrinkwrap licenses may become even more pervasive as states begin adopting UCITA. This controversial uniform law grew out of the joint effort of the American Law Institute (ALI) and NCCUSL and was originally structured as a new section of the Uniform Commercial Code.[42] ALI withdrew its support after many of its members expressed concern about compromising consumer rights, but NCCUSL continued the drafting effort, offering the text as a free-standing uniform law, rather than as a component of the highly influential Uniform Commercial Code.

UCITA covers a range of issues including support for the non-negotiated license. These take-it-or-leave-it agreements include shrinkwrap or clickwrap licenses in which the purchasing party agrees to the terms by opening shrink-wrap or clicking through contract text on the Internet. For consumers such as libraries, UCITA offers the reassurance that courts could find invalid license terms that are "unconscionable."[43] Opponents of UCITA argue that federal copyright law preempts contracts overstepping the bounds of copyright and that publishers offering these contracts may be liable under a theory termed "copyright misuse."[44] None of these defenses, though, is widely tested, and risk-adverse libraries are unlikely to blithely challenge such licenses.

The practical result of the loss of the first sale doctrine is that librarians must keep up with separate rules for the on-site and off-site use of each piece of licensed material.[45]

INTERLIBRARY LOAN AND DOCUMENT DELIVERY

Interlibrary loan and document delivery are similarly affected by licensing trends. Sometimes licenses specifically prohibit interlibrary loan of electronic materials or omit interlibrary loan from a list of the permitted uses.[46] Interlibrary loan is a right often sought by librarians who negotiate licenses, and some publishers are allowing this service, looking to the copyright law, sections 108 and 109 for limitations that have served the print world.[47]

Section 108 of the copyright code specifically provides for limited interlibrary loan photocopying independent of photocopying permissible as fair use under section 107. The National Commission on New Technological Uses of Copyrighted Works (CONTU) Guidelines have offered libraries a safe harbor for judging how many copies from recent journal publications may be obtained.[48] While the statute is generally technologically neutral, publishers and librarians have disagreed about the permissibility of scanning materials for interlibrary loan.[49]

Fair use photocopying and ILL photocopying allowed under copyright law might be permissibly restricted under UCITA section 502. Robert Oakley, Director of the Georgetown Law Library, suggests that the language of this section leaves room for restrictions of all photocopying, not just that exceeding fair use and other federal copyright limitations.[50]

Librarians seeking to negotiate interlibrary loan rights may face some resistance from publishers as resale systems develop. The opportunity for publishers to create or participate in tracking and fee collecting programs, such as the Copyright Clearance Center and iCopyright, may cast interlibrary loan as an unattractive compromise of the publisher's market.[51] Section 108 of the copyright code does limit borrowing libraries from receiving copies "in such aggregate quantities as to substitute for a subscription to or purchase of such work."[52] If publishers provide purchase options for single journal articles of any publication date, section 108, interlibrary loan copying, might be defined as violating the copyright owner's rights. The CCC, in fact, has mounted an aggressive campaign seeking broad investments from law firms and academic libraries, saying that this type of copyright management will allow them to avoid the cost of internal tracking and the risk of violating the vague confines of fair use.[53] Of course, librarians can still try to gain interlibrary loan rights by negotiating for them in the license.

As the technology develops for single use, single article sales, librarians could find themselves shifting to the "just-in-time" model of document delivery and dropping the "just-in-case" model of collection development in larger and larger parts of their collections.[54] Certainly, newer libraries and libraries in for-profit institutions have been looking to document delivery services for a significant part of their service since they do not have the collection to lend nor all of the protections for fair use and Section 108 nonprofit copying. If research libraries move in this direction, they will have less of a collection to lend, and interlibrary loan would decrease. Of course, this shift would mean those libraries with archiving and preservation goals would be shifting this responsibility to publishers and the intermediary vendors.

Interlibrary loan copying of some works has been permissible because they are not covered by copyright. Such works are referred to as being in the public domain. Works with expired copyright terms,[55] works created by the federal government and arguably state governments,[56] and works lacking the modicum of creativity to allow them to qualify for copyright are generally considered unprotected and in the public domain.[57] A number of recent legal developments have shrunk the public domain. The Sonny Bono Copyright Term Extension Act of 1998, as mentioned above, added twenty years to the copyright term.[58] Even materials in the public domain may have restricted uses if they are only available through licensed products. Publishers are also looking to database protection legislation to secure more control over the use of their products than copyright provides. If courts allow such terms in licenses, and if database legislation covers public domain materials, interlibrary loan rights could be further compromised.

These same issues are part of the battle surrounding the anti-circumvention provisions enacted as part of the DMCA. Technological blocks incorporated into the electronic product could prevent not only legitimate fair use and section 108 copying but also legitimate uses of public domain material. Any anti-circumvention measures to achieve the legitimate use would be illegal under this federal law.

Most large publishers are viewing the public domain not as a resource for new publications but as a threat to their own profits, and they are seeking legislation that would provide the protection that copyright will not. Several versions of federal database legislation have been designed strictly for protection of electronic material and have been based on a return on investment. This kind of law would offer non-copyrightable material as well as copyrightable material more protection than copyright as long as it is in electronic form.[59] Certainly, this legislation would have serious implications for interlibrary loan and other library services as publications increasingly move from print to digital formats.

If the material is increasingly held in only licensed electronic form, and those licenses prohibit interlibrary loan copying, libraries with the rare research need cannot depend on the kindness of other libraries to meet these unusual patron requests. The library seeking delivery might try to secure a one-time, specific material request directly from the publisher, but most publishers are not yet prepared to meet that sort of need. The CCC is gaining greater publisher participation, though, and this clearinghouse or a commercial document delivery source may be the library's best option. Almost always, however, these sources involve fees not paid through interlibrary loan arrangements.

Interlibrary loan in some academic libraries has actually been growing as a result of their institution's offering of distance education programs.[60] While many of these requests are probably now met by the shipment of books allowed under the first sale doctrine or of photocopies of journal articles allowed under fair use or section 108, future requests may more and more require satisfaction through access to electronic resources. As long as the resource license permits an enrolled but remote user to gain access, by password or by some other relatively secure means, the goal of interlibrary loan is met. Educators and librarians have asked Congress to amend the copyright law to better support distance education, but the changes sought are mostly remote display rights to resemble those allowed for in-classroom teaching.[61] Congress has responded by including in the DMCA a call for the Register of Copyrights to collect information and report back with recommendations.[62] While a display-right amendment could have some indirect ameliorative effect on interlibrary loan services, its main advantage for academic libraries would be to improve their ability to offer instructional technology support, a responsibility increasingly assigned to law school libraries and some other discipline-specific academic libraries.

RESERVE SERVICES

In many ways, the addition of locally networked or remote access databases offers a sort of reserve service. If the license allows for enough multiple users that access is generally open, the purpose of reserving material for frequent use is achieved. If the network is available in a variety of locations, such as attorneys' or law professors' offices, the material has become more conveniently accessible. In this way, technology and licensing provide for improvements in the service.

When libraries attempt to create their own electronic resources, though, by scanning materials, copyright laws govern the limits on what is permissible. If libraries seek to do more than is allowed under copyright, they must seek permission from the copyright holder. An attempt to develop safe harbor guidelines for fair use scanning for electronic reserve ended without agreement when representatives from libraries, educators, and publishers refused to endorse the resulting document.[63] Nonetheless, some libraries are using these guidelines as a "fair" compromise since both sides of the effort found them too restrictive of their respective rights.[64]

RESEARCH, REFERENCE, AND INSTRUCTIONAL SERVICES

The fundamental purpose of the library in providing research support is met through unmediated use of the library as well as with the direct assistance of the reference librarian or with guidance from instructional materials prepared by the reference librarian. All of the legal issues of electronic resources that affect the other library services find their final impact at the point where patrons are trying to use the materials and, perhaps, trying to get help from the reference librarian. Sometimes reference librarians must explain, if not defend, licenses that restrict access to certain groups of patrons. These librarians may respond by trying to perform short searches on behalf of the unlicensed patron or may try to refer the patron to another, comparable source. This type of restriction can frustrate attorneys seeking the occasional use of their library's web product purchased for a different section of the firm and can cause friction when a graduate student in a non-law field seeks use of the law school's Westlaw subscription.

One of the most important copyright provisions for researchers is the fair use provision, and libraries are concerned that licenses the library signs or accepts may curtail the patron's right to fair use of copyrighted materials. The Association of Research Libraries, in conjunction with the Association of Law Libraries and other major library associations, has published a working document outlining expectations of fair use for patrons and for libraries in the electronic environment.[65] Fair use provisions of federal copyright law protect the consumer's right to make uses of a copyrighted work that would otherwise be infringing. Copying for purposes such as criticism, comment, news reporting, teaching, scholarship, or research are listed in the statute as uses that might be fair judging by factors also listed in the statute.[66] Fair use, unlike the first sale doctrine, is not predicated on ownership of a copy of the work. Access is the assumed predicate, and with restricted license terms that limit access and use, the publisher is able to curtail the patron's ability to exercise fair use of the material. Library associations have objected to UCITA's view of the license contact as a binary transaction because it can mean the signing away of the third party's rights.[67] Another important aspect of the basic research service offered by libraries is the protection of patrons' privacy. The licenses for some electronic products ask for individual accounts that can provide tracking of each participating patron's research habits. In law libraries, LEXIS and Westlaw passwords may be assigned to individuals whose research patterns these publishers could study and conceivably share with others. Even without individual passwords, publishers are asking for personal contact information of each potential user.[68] Unless the library negotiates to protect the privacy of its patrons' research patterns, this information might become personalized marketing data.

To offer researchers assistance beyond the personal exchange, librarians have created instructional and research guides. The digital age allows librarians to create these guides as electronic resources for patrons on-site and off-site. The law of these electronic resources includes the library's copyright claim to its own creations, online service provider liability, and a possible obligation not to compromise other providers' copyright through framing techniques or by linking to unpermitted postings of copyrighted material.

The law of linking to materials and framing those materials through one's own site is new territory and, arguably, a way of creating a derivative work that violates the rights of the copyright owners of the framed material. Simply linking to copyrighted material, even without framing, may or may not require permission. Some point out that the purpose of the World Wide Web is to be able to click on text or a URL and quickly move to another site, and that posting material on the web implicitly includes permission for others to create links to that material. Others assert that linking violates the owner's rights to display and copy the material and therefore requires permission from the copyright owner.[69]

As libraries create web pages, they must take care to avoid posting any copyrighted material without permission. Libraries taking the extra precaution of seeking permission to link to copyrighted material may find the industry is ill prepared to respond to such requests.[70]

The DMCA added section 512 to the Copyright Code and provided some limitations on such liability as long as the online provider followed certain procedures. Basically, if the library provides access to the Internet or to any network, it might be able to participate in the limited liability procedures. To complete the qualification, the library has to designate a web site agent who must register with the Copyright Office, and the library must rapidly respond to notifications of infringement. The statute details further the requirements for this limited liability. Libraries are now trying to decide whether qualification and compliance are worthwhile. An adviser to the Association of Research Libraries has suggested that registration with the Copyright Office might increase defensive activities since copyright owners could seek to contact all registered providers as soon as they identify any unpermitted posting of or linking to their material anywhere on the Internet.[71]

CONCLUSION

The traditional values of librarianship and even the value of libraries are being tested by changing legal structures designed for the electronic environment. As familiar forms of information access and use are restricted, core professional values and activities are becoming unattainable or are shifting to other groups.[72] Measuring the benefits and losses in copyright rights to electronic resources by looking at some of the library's traditional services may seem unimaginative. Such a review, however, can supply the impetus to consciously adapt to meet the transcending goals, understanding that new models may achieve those goals through very different means.

NOTES

1. Jean O'Grady, *Checklist for the Negotiation of Internet Subscriptions,* The CRIV Sheet, Nov. 1999, at 9, insert in AALL Spectrum, Nov. 1999; Trisha L. Davis, Licensing in Lieu of Acquiring in *Understanding the Business of Library Acquisitions* (Karen A. Schmidt ed., 1999); *Managing the Licensing of Electronic Products: a SPEC Kit* (George J. Soete comp., 1999); Patricia Brennan et al., *Licensing Electronic Resources: Strategic and Practical Consideration for Signing Electronic Information Delivery Agreements* (1997); Yale maintains web resources to assist librarians in negotiating and managing licenses, Yale University Library Liblicense: Licensing Digital Information: A Resource for Librarians <http://www.library.yale.edu/~llicense/>. The Association of Research Libraries also provides licensing negotiation information on their web site: Licensing Electronic Resources <http://www.arl.org/>.

2. The Association of Research Libraries has provided a number of two-day workshops on licensing for librarians in research libraries. Current offerings are listed at <http://www.arl.org/>.

3. John Webb, *Managing Licensed Networked Electronic Resources in a University Library,* 17 Infor. Tech. Libr. 198 (1998).

4. Linda Will, *A Day in the Life of A Mad Cybrarian,* Legal Info. Alert, Feb. 1999, at 1.

5. Letter from Duana E. Webster, Executive Director of the Association of Research Libraries, to Gene N. Lebrun, President, National Conference of Commissioners on Uniform State Laws, July 12, 1999 <http://www.ll.georgetown.edu/aallwash/lt071299.html>.

6. *Arizona Retail Sys., Inc. v. Software Link, Inc.*, 831 F. Supp. 759 (D. Ariz. 1993); *Step-Saver Data Sys., Inc. v. Wyse Tech.*, 939 F. 2d 91 (3d Cir. 1991) (not finding a valid contract in shrinkwrap licenses); *ProCD, Inc. v. Zeidenberg*, 86 F.3d 1447 (7th Cir. 1996) (finding a shrinkwrap license valid).

7. U.C.C. § 2-207. *See, Step Saver Data Sys., Inc. v. Wyse Tech.*, 939 F.2d 91 (3d Cir. 1991).

8. J.H. Reichman & Jonathan Franklin, *Privately Legislated Intellectual Property Rights: Reconciling Freedom of Contract with Public Good Uses of Information*, 147 U. Pa. L. Rev. 875 (1999); Mark A. Lemley, *Beyond Preemption: The Law and Policy of Intellectual Property Licensing*, 87 Cal. L. Rev. 111 (1999); Dennis S. Karjala, *Federal Preemption of Shrinkwrap and On-Line Licenses*, 22 U. Dayton L. Rev. 511 (1997) ; Mark A. Lemley, *Intellectual Property and Shrinkwrap Licenses*, 68 S. Cal. L. Rev. 1239 (1995).

9. *Supra* note 6.

10. *See supra* note 8.

11. *See supra* note 1.

12. *Tasini v. New York Times Co.*, 206 F.3d 161 (2d Cir. 2000).

13. *Matthew Bender & Co. v. West Publishing Co.*, 158 F.3d 693 (2d Cir. 1998), *cert. denied*, 119 S. Ct. 2039 (1999); *Matthew Bender & Co. v. West Publishing Co.*, 158 F.3d 674 (2d Cir. 1998), *cert. denied*, 119 S. Ct. 2039 (1999).

14. Robert Berring, *On Not Throwing Out the Baby: Planning the Future of Legal Information*, 83 Cal. L. Rev. 615 (1995); Kelly Browne, *Does the Law Governing Public Access to Judicial Options Mandate Citation Reform? It Depends*, 17 Legal Reference Services Q. Nos. 1/2 1999 at 75.

15. As two attorneys wrote before the validating authority of the *ProCD* decision, "though of doubtful enforceability in many circumstances, traditional shrinkwrap licenses are nonetheless universally included in mass-market software. They are basically costless and if enforced they offer valuable protection to software vendors. If not enforceable, they at least have some residual deterrent effect." Gary H. Moore & J. David Hadden, *On-Line Software Distribution: New Life for "Shrinkwrap" Licenses?* 13 Computer L. 1, 1-3 (1996).

16. 17 U.S.C. § 106 (1996).

17. *Uniform Computer Information Transactions Act (UCITA)* § 503 (2) enforces terms prohibiting transfer. Section 503(4) requires that a term prohibiting transfer of a mass market license be conspicuous.

18. Thomas W. Leonhardt, *The Gifts and Exchange Function in ARL Libraries: Now and Tomorrow*, 21 Libr. Acquisitions: Practi. Theory 141 (1997).

19. Arturo A. Flores, *Manual for Prison Law Libraries* (2d ed. 1989) (AALL Publication Series no. 36); Jay M. Ihrig, *Providing Legal Access, in Libraries Inside: A Practical Guide for Prison Librarians*, 195 (1995); Ryan, Wayne, *Access to the Courts: Prisoners' Right to a Law Library*, 26 How. L. J. 91 (1983); Karen Westwood, *Meaningful Access to the Courts' and Law Libraries: Where Are We Now?* 90 L. Libr. J. 193 (1998).

20. Abby Smith, *Preservation in the Digital Age: What Is to Be Done?*, Am. Libr., Mar. 1999, at 36.

21. The Congressional Universe online license links to the general license for their parent company, LEXIS-NEXIS, Terms and Conditions <http://www.lexis-nexis.com/cispubs/catalog/universe/terms.html>.

22. JSTOR's mission and license information are available though their web site. JSTOR, JSTOR Mission and Goals <http://www.jstor.org/about/mission/html>; JSTOR, Terms and Conditions of Use of the JSTOR Database <http://www.jstor.org/about/terms.html>.

23. Michael Rogers, Conference Report: *Librarians & Publishers Ponder Preservation and Archiving,* Libr. J., Jul. 1999, at 29.

24. *Id.*

25. Paula J. Hane, *IT Interview: iCopyright CEO Discusses a New Model for Rights and Permissions,* Info. Today, Nov. 1999, at 1, 774, 76. For a recent description of a law firm librarian's experience joining the CCC *see* Joanne Dugan, *True Confessions of a Copyright Wimp,* AALL Spectrum, Feb. 2000, at 4.

26. Thomas Mann, *Reference Service, Human Nature, Copyright, and Offsite Service–in a "Digital Age?"* 38 Reference & User Services Q. 55 (1998).

27. Jane C. Ginsburg, *Copyright Without Walls?: Speculations on Literary Property in the Library of the Future,* Representations, Spring 1993, at 53, 63-65 (noting that books could be licensed, legally, but the technology did not offer the tracing opportunities).

28. *UCITA* § 605 allows electronic devices to terminate functionality of the product at the end of the license term. Section 816 allows electronic self-help to disable use of the product 15 days after the licensor notifies that licensee that it has determined the licensee has breached the contract.

29. Digital Millennium Copyright Act, Pub. L. No. 105-304, § 103, 112 Stat. 2860, 2863-72 (1998) (adding 17 U.S.C. § 1201).

30. Even with a lawfully acquired copy of the work, bypassing a technical protection system to make fair use of that copy would appear to be unlawful under 17 U.S.C. § 1201(a)(1) and (c)(1)(Supp. IV 1998). Pamela Samuelson, *Intellectual Property and the Digital Economy: Why the Anti-Circumvention Regulations Need to Be Revised,* 14 Berkeley Tech. L. J. 519 (1999) . American Association of Law Libraries' Washington Representative Professor Robert L. Oakley provided testimony that the anti-circumvention legislation left no protection for fair use. *Commerce Hearing, WIPO Copyright Treaties Implementation Act and Online Copyright Liability Limitation Act: Hearing on H.R. 2280 and H.R. 2281 before the Subcommittee on Courts and Intellectual Property of the House Committee on the Judiciary,* 105th Cong 64-66 (1997).

31. 17 U.S.C. § 1201(a)(1)(C) (Supp. IV 1998).

32. 17 U.S.C. § 1201(a)(1)(D) (Supp. IV 1998).

33. Digital Millennium Copyright Act, Pub. L. No. 105-304, § 404, 112 Stat. 2860, 2889-90 (1998) (amending 17 U.S.C. § 108 and expanding the right of libraries to make certain facsimile copies to include digital copies).

34. Laura N. Gasaway, *Library Preservation and Recent Copyright Act Amendments,* Info. Outlook, Apr. 1999, at 38.

35. Sonny Bono Copyright Term Extension Act, Pub. L. No. 105-298, 112 Stat. 2827 (1998).

36. *See supra* note 34.

37. Anne Klinefelter, *The Circulation of Software by Libraries, in Growing Pains: Adapting Copyright for Libraries, Education, and Society* 215, 221-22 (Laura N. Gasaway ed., 1997).

38. Judicial Improvements Act of 1990, Pub. L. No. 101-650, 104 Stat. 5089, 5134-37 (1990).

39. 17 U.S.C. § 109(b)(2) (1994). The warning is found at 37 C.F.R. 201.24 (1999).

40. *ProCD Inc. v. Zeidenberg,* 86 F.3d 1447 (7th Cir. 1996) (most often cited as authority for the validity of shrinkwrap licenses. The court refused to find preemption of a mass-market contract restricting use of presumably non-copyrightable factual information and found valid the assent to the agreement even though the terms were not available until after the software was purchased). *Hotmail Corp. v. Vans Money Pie, Inc.,* 47 U.S.P.Q. 2d (BNA) 1020 (N.D. Cal. 1998) (also provided support for shrinkwrap licenses). On the other hand, *Step-Saver Data Sys., Inc. v. Wyse Technology,* 939 F.2d 91 (3rd Cir. 1991) (held previous oral agreement could not be displaced by the arrival of the product with differing shrinkwrap). *Arizona Retail Sys., Inc., v. Software Link, Inc.,* 831 F. Supp. 759 (D. Ariz. 1993) (a shrinkwrap contract valid when no prior agreement existed but proposal for modification ineffectual when it followed a telephone order and agreement). *Vault Corp. v. Quaid Software Ltd.,* 847 F. 2d 255 (5th Cir. 1988) (Louisiana statute validating shrinkwrap license terms preempted by federal copyright law).

41. The Register refers to a roundtable discussion at which representatives from the Business Software Alliance and the Software Publishers Association provided these assurances. Acting Register of Copyrights, U.S. Copyright Office, *The Computer Software Rental Amendments Act of 1990: The Nonprofit Library Lending Exemption to the "Rental Right"* 90 (1994).

42. NCCUSL posts drafts and revisions to UCITA at <http://www.nccusl.org/>.

43. UCITA § 111 allows a court to find as a matter of law that a contract or a term in a contract is unconscionable and therefore enforceable or to limit a term to avoid an unconscionable result.

44. *See supra* note 8.

45. Yale University Library, *supra* note 1; *see supra* note 2.

46. LEXIS licenses, for example, do not specifically mention interlibrary loan as a permitted use. Some specific databases on LEXIS list "internal use only"–Dun & Bradstreet, Inc. Newsweek Magazine: "You may not publish, broadcast, sell or otherwise redistribute these materials for commercial purposes." *See* <http://www.lexis-nexis.com/lncc/about/terms.html>.

47. 17 U.S.C. §§ 108-09 (1994).

48. *Id.* The National Commission on New Technological Uses of Copyrighted Works (CONTU) developed guidelines offering some definition to the term "systematic." These are sometimes awarded quasi-authoritative status because they were included in the legislative history of the 1976 Copyright Act, H.R. Conf. Rep. No. 94-1733, at 72-73 (1976), reprinted in 1976 U.S.C.C.A.N. 5810, 5812-15.

49. James Heller, *The Impact of Recent Litigation on Interlibrary Loan and Document Delivery,* in *Growing Pains: Adapting Copyright for Libraries, Education, and Society* 189 (Laura N. Gasaway ed., 1997).

50. Robert L.Oakley, Speech, The Uniform Computer Information Transactions Act: An Update (Annual Meeting of the Association of Research Libraries, Washington, Oct. 13, 1999), available at <http://www.ll.georgetown.edu/aallwash/so101399. html>.

51. *See supra* note 25.

52. 17 U.S.C. § 108(g)(2) (1994).

53. *See supra* note 25.

54. Kent Mulliner, *E-Commerce–A Collection Development Perspective–Parts 2 & 3, Against the Grain,* Dec. 1999-Jan. 2000.

55. Melville B. Nimmer & David Nimmer, Nimmer on Copyright § 2.03 (2000).

56. *Id.* § 5.06.

57. *Id.* § 2.01.

58. *See supra* note 35.

59. J. H. Reichman & Paul F. Uhlir, *Database Protection at the Crossroads: Recent Developments and Their Impact on Science and Technology,* 14 Berkeley Tech. L. J. 793 (1999).

60. Arturo Lopez Torres & W. Clinton Sterling, *Will Law Schools Go the Distance? An Annotated Bibliography on Distance Education in Law,* 91 L. Libr. J. 665 (1999).

61. *Hearings on the Copyright Office Report on Distance Education Before the House Judiciary Committee Subcommittee on Court and Intellectual Property,* 106th Cong. (1999) (statement of Laura N. Gasaway, Director of the Law Library and Professor of Law at the University of North Carolina at Chapel Hill, representing various higher education associations).

62. Digitial Millennium Copyright Act, Section 403 (a), Limitations on Exclusive Rights; Distance Education, Pub. L. No. 105-304, 112 Stat. 2860, 2888-89 (1998): 2860 (provides for recommendations by the Register of Copyrights to be submitted to Congress after consultation with representatives of copyright owners, nonprofit educational institutions, and nonprofit libraries and archives. *See* Register of Copyrights, U.S. Copyright Office, *Report on Copyright and Digital Distance Education* (1999).

63. Bruce A. Lehman, Working Group on Intellectual Property Rights of the Information Infrastructure Task Force, *The Conference on Fair Use, Final Report to the Commissioner on the Conclusion of the Conference on Fair Use* 15-16 (1998). Also available on the Web at <http://www.uspto.gov/web/offices/dcom/olia/confu/> Gregory K. Klingsporn, *The Conference on Fair Use (CONFU) and the Future of Fair Use Guidelines* 23 Colum.-VLA J. L. & Arts 101 (1999).

64. Steven J. Melamut et al., *Fair Use or Not Fair Use: That is the Question,* J. Interlibrary Loan, Document Delivery & Info. Supply (forthcoming).

65. *Fair Use in the Electronic Age: Serving the Public Interest, in Copyright, Public Policy, and the Scholarly Community,* 53 (Michael Matthews & Patricia Brennan eds., 1995).

66. 17 U.S.C. 107 (1994).

67. *See supra* note 3.

68. RIA asked for individual attorneys' names and addresses of potential users of their product in a law firm. *See* Will, *supra* note 5.

69. Dan L. Burk, *Muddy Rules for Cyberspace,* 21 Cardozo L. R. 121, 123-124 (1999).

70. Carol Ebbinghouse, *Terms and Conditions and Permissions: By Jove! I Think They've Got It!–Not!* Searcher: A Magazine on Database Profs., Apr. 1999, at 61.

71. Arnold P. Lutzker, *Primer on the Digital Millennium: What the Digital Millennium Copyright Act and the Copyright Term Extension Act Mean for the Library Community* <http://www.arl.org/info/frn/copy/primer.html> (accessed Feb. 6, 2000).

72. Richard A. Danner, *Redefining a Profession,* 90 L. Libr. J. 315 (1998).

The New Reference Librarian: Using Technology to Deliver Reference Services

James E. Duggan

SUMMARY. This article will explore the world of the "new reference librarian" and examine how advances in technology have changed forever the way reference librarians interact with both patrons and reference sources. Special attention will be paid to the current uses that reference librarians make of technology to deliver reference assistance to remote users, along with a section on whom a reference librarian is expected to serve today. Finally, predictions for the future of reference librarians will be provided, including suggestions for new librarians entering the field. *[Article copies available for a fee from The Haworth Document Delivery Service: 1-800-342-9678. E-mail address: <getinfo@haworthpressinc. com> Website: <http://www.HaworthPress.com> © 2001 by The Haworth Press, Inc. All rights reserved.]*

INTRODUCTION

Stardate 5943.7. The Planet Sarpeden is about to blow up into a super-nova. Captain Kirk, Mr. Spock, and Dr. Kelly materialize on the planet,

---

James E. Duggan is Professor and Director of Information Technology at Southern Illinois University School of Law Library, 1150 Douglas Drive, Carbondale, IL 62901-6803 (E-mail: duggan@siu.edu). He received his BA from Virginia Tech; his JD from the University of Mississippi; and his MLIS from Louisiana State University.

[Haworth co-indexing entry note]: "The New Reference Librarian: Using Technology to Deliver Reference Services." Duggan, James E. Co-published simultaneously in *Legal Reference Services Quarterly* (The Haworth Information Press, an imprint of The Haworth Press, Inc.) Vol. 19, No. 3/4, 2001, pp. 195-202; and: *Teaching Legal Research and Providing Access to Electronic Resources* (ed: Gary L. Hill, Dennis S. Sears, and Lovisa Lyman) The Haworth Information Press, an imprint of The Haworth Press, Inc., 2001, pp. 195-202. Single or multiple copies of this article are available for a fee from The Haworth Document Delivery Service [1-800-342-9678, 9:00 a.m. - 5:00 p.m. (EST). E-mail address: getinfo@haworthpressinc.com].

and discover that they are in a building that appears to be "a library or archive of some kind." Although no intelligent life is expected to remain on the planet, the intrepid star trekkers encounter Mr. Atoz, a crotchety old man, who greets the visitors with that familiar library inquiry, "May I help you? I am the librarian."

The trio inform Mr. Atoz that they are interested in "recent history, specifically what happened to the population of the planet." The librarian, although initially appearing to be helpful ("A library serves no purpose unless someone is using it"), deliberately misunderstands the question, and directs them to a bank of drawers containing metallic disks (presaging the CD-ROM!), which, when viewed, display video of past history. After fumbling around for a while in "the stacks," Captain Kirk confronts Mr. Atoz and again asks for guidance concerning the library. "Reference service is available at the desk," Mr. Atoz replies. Rolling his eyes, Captain Kirk turns back towards the desk, and is surprised to see Mr. Atoz yet again, this time sitting at the reference desk. "You're a very agile man, Mr. Atoz!" Kirk exclaims![1]

In my favorite episode of Star Trek, Captain Kirk discovers that Mr. Atoz, the librarian, actually cannot run the library single-handedly, and must rely on android "replicas" to staff all departments, including cataloging, circulation, and reference. Late 1960s viewers must have wondered if this was the "library of the future," a question shared by contemporary viewers today. Certainly, media formats have changed over the subsequent years, and the advent of the personal computer has presupposed a sea change in library operations. What hasn't changed, however, is the need for reference service. Today's reference librarians still face a barrage of reference assistance requests. Only now, thanks to the explosion of the Internet via the World Wide Web and electronic mail, reference questions may come from anywhere in the world.

This article will explore the world of the "new reference librarian," and examine how advances in technology have changed forever the way reference librarians interact with both patrons and reference sources. Special attention will be paid to the current uses that reference librarians make of technology to deliver reference assistance to remote users, along with a section on whom a reference librarian is expected to serve today. Finally, predictions for the future of reference librarians will be provided, including suggestions for new librarians entering the field.

THE CHANGING ROLE OF THE REFERENCE LIBRARIAN

Nearly twenty years ago, Dick Danner posed the question, "What happens to the legal reference librarian if at some point his or her traditional clientele–

the law faculty, students and other patrons–all have direct and economical access to legal and other information at terminals in their homes or offices?"[2] Although Danner suggested that "direct access may alter the forms of law library service," he predicted that intermediaries (such as reference librarians) would continue to be needed and, indeed, calls for "new services at higher levels of skill and competence."[3]

As Danner prophesied, much has happened in the past two decades, including the development of the personal computer, individual access to LEXIS and Westlaw via the desktop, and the explosion of available information on the Internet. Never before have researchers been bombarded with so much information,[4] and from so many different sources. The traditional formats, such as manuscripts, books (bound or looseleaf), and audio tapes, have been supplemented by a wide variety of electronic formats, including disks and CD-ROMs, CALR databases, and Internet web pages. Who can make sense of it all, much less provide organizational talents to help classify and retrieve the information so that researchers are not left wandering the crowded electronic portals, hopelessly grasping byte after byte, in a vain search for relevant material? The reference librarian is the obvious answer.

But all this technical savvy has come at a price–often at the expense of traditional reference services (such as compiling bibliographies, becoming subject experts, and providing extended one-on-one assistance). Twenty years ago reference librarians had the luxury of learning their library's collection content in order to steer patrons in the right direction. What was not available locally could be verified via union lists and printed catalogs and requested via interlibrary loan. In addition, reference staff mastered the intricacies of the library's various print indexes and finding aids, and could thus instruct library users as needed.

Today, the almost exponential increase in the availability of electronic information means that the biggest concern of reference librarians is having enough time to properly learn to identify emerging sources on the Internet, analyze search engine capabilities, and instruct patrons (wherever they might be) about utilizing all information sources. To quote the popular Peace Corps recruiting slogan, "It's the toughest job you'll ever love."

DELIVERING REFERENCE TO THE MASSES: TECHNOLOGY AND THE REFERENCE LIBRARIAN

The classic reference situation involves a librarian, a patron, a library, and most importantly, a reference desk. The patron approaches the librarian at the reference desk and asks questions or seeks information on a specific subject. The librarian then may ask the patron a series of questions attempting to refine the patron's request (also called the "reference interview"), and then either points the patron to the specific area of the library containing appropriate information sources or consults various reference materials and indexes to ascertain an acceptable answer for the patron. The ultimate goal is to send the patron away happy (or at least satisfied that the reference librarian has provided enough assistance to guide the patron in the right direction). The reference desk serves as a focal point for those with questions and is a familiar icon in libraries nationwide.

However, advances in technology are changing the way reference is delivered to patrons on a global basis. Questions now come from a variety of sources, including telefax, e-mail, and the library's web site, and reference librarians are increasingly responding in kind. A look at the various technologies both in existence now and on the horizon will help to define the reference librarian's job during this first decade of the twenty-first century.

Telefax

The 1980s saw the growing popularity of the telefax, a machine that allows any text and graphics to be transmitted via telephone lines. Although first printed on rolled paper with ink that perpetually rubbed-off on anyone who handled the "fax," telefax transmissions eventually were printed on "plain" paper and now can even be received by library computers. The telefax meant that documents no longer had to be mailed (or expedited using delivery services), and reference requests that resulted in identifying materials owned by the requested library often could be answered by simply "faxing" the document directly to the requestor.

Many libraries upgraded their document delivery services with the telefax and often "advertised" telefax availability as an enhanced reference service. Today, requests for documents, many requiring reference intervention, often come by telefax, and the telefax machine remains one of the most used mechanisms in libraries for document delivery.

Personal Computer

Although the computer is utilized in every aspect of technology described herein, it is described in this section chiefly as the mechanism for document transmission via software such as the Research Library Group's Ariel[5] and Adobe Acrobat.[6] Each of these applications has neatly revolutionized document delivery by making electronic versions of documents available without the constant copying and scanning of materials. As with the telefax, the provision of reference services has been greatly enhanced by the ability to provide documents electronically.

Electronic Mail

E-mail has emerged as the new standard of reference communication, both as the vehicle for reference requests from patrons and delivery of reference assistance by librarians. Ease of use, coupled with almost instantaneous reception despite the lack of physical proximity, contributes to the near-universal popularity of this medium for all aspects of reference work.

Most libraries have established at least one e-mail address for reference questions[7] and use e-mail in a variety of ways. The University of Virginia Law Library offers "refdesk," an e-mail service directed to its faculty that provides everything from "involved research query[s]" to requests for photocopies.[8] The Cleveland Law Library Association invites members to e-mail reference/research questions and promises that the "professional staff will respond as soon as possible."[9]

In addition to reference e-mail addresses, various electronic listservs are utilized to post reference questions and answers.[10] LAWLIB, hosted by Judy Janes at the University of California-Davis, averages over 600 postings per month.[11]

The Web

The web is the "new frontier" in reference service. In addition to providing links to various research sources, library web pages also feature pathfinders,[12] electronic databases,[13] and research guides.[14]

Reference services are also featured. Members of the Jenkins Law Library can submit reference questions during regular library hours via the library's web page.[15] The *Jurist Virtual Reference Librarian*[16] offers answers to reference questions from anyone; reference assistance is provided courtesy of the University of Pittsburgh's Barco Law Library staff.

A general library reference service is featured at the Internet Public Library (<http://www.ipl.org/ref/QUE>). Hosted by the University of Michigan School of Information, the IPL Reference Center is staffed by many volunteer librarians and library students who are "willing to contribute their time to answering questions for people whom they never see or meet in person."[17] Because of the volunteer nature of the service, users are strongly cautioned that reference questions may not receive an answer if needed in less than three days.

Distance Learning/Interactive Databases

Although apparently not in operation yet in any law library, the future holds out the possibility of the using either distance learning equipment or interactive databases to augment or refine the reference experience. In perhaps a retro return to the face-to-face reference interview, distance learning equipment can link up patrons to live reference librarians (either via video/telephone lines or the Internet) and enable both the questioner and librarian to see and hear the audio and visual clues that are frequently missing in computer-generated reference requests.

Similarly, library interactive databases are on the horizon that will provide computer-generated reference assistance to a user when the user selects or types a search query.[18]

The Reference Desk

Finally, even the reference desk may be a thing of the past. Barbara Gontrum suggests that librarians today are "expected to perform many other duties besides answering basic reference questions."[19] In order to accommodate these new duty expectations, some structural changes might be made, including "eliminat[ing] the reference desk as a physical location."[20] Because the information world continues to change so fast, reference librarians must also change and take on new roles. Removing the reference desk may help librarians achieve those new functions.

THE REFERENCE PATRON IN THE VIRTUAL LIBRARY

Reference librarians today are faced with a myriad of demands on their time, not only from patrons inside the library but from potential "patrons" throughout the world. Web-based library catalogs open the collection globally, and patrons may search remotely from their computers without ever having to leave the comfort of their homes or offices. Electronic mail has opened the doors of the library to that most casual category of "library" patrons, those who never even physically enter the facility. Libraries that have established general reference e-mail addresses often receive requests for reference assistance from patrons "outside" the traditional group of library users (i.e., patrons who live beyond the geographic vicinity of the library service population). Does the reference librarian have a duty to serve all patrons?

The answer, as one might expect, depends on a number of considerations, including library policy, librarian service orientation, time constraints, and the practicalities of conducting a "reference interview" via electronic communication. Reference librarians working in "public" libraries (such as state-supported law school libraries, and state, court, and county libraries) may feel more of an obligation to assist online users (in the same way they assist anyone physically coming into the library) than their private librarian counterparts (private law school libraries, and corporate and law firms).

Of course, levels of service to "virtual" reference patrons may differ just as they do in-house. E-mail requests from non-primary patrons may result in a quick reference to a web site of interest, whereas primary patrons who request information electronically might receive actual documents and citation lists. The library's reference policy should spell out what categories of patrons exist and the degree of service extended to each category. However, given the way most patrons interact with libraries today, the method of request (whether in person, telephone, telefax, e-mail, or via the web) should make little difference as to how much effort the reference librarian puts into answering the reference question.

THE FUTURE OF REFERENCE LIBRARIANS

The survival of the reference librarian profession depends on how well librarians adapt to the changing realities of patron access. Technological advances dictate new methods of document delivery and provide innovative means of access to patrons of libraries, both physical and virtual. Although the explosion of internet-available materials could potentially cut the librarian out of the information equation, that same "explosion" practically ensures that someone is needed to help organize, categorize, and "master" the information sources. The reference librarian is favorably poised to be that "someone." The future is in very strong hands.

To ensure that these "strong hands" continue to embrace the future, new librarians who enter the field must have a healthy interest in the internet, computer technology, and emerging document delivery options. The time has passed when reference librarians could rely on their knowledge of print-only sources. New librarians must be enthusiastic about imaginative ways to provide reference services and realize that unless they stay "ahead" of the curve, they, like Mr. Atoz,[21] will ultimately be lost.

NOTES

1. From the 1969 Star Trek episode "All Our Yesterdays." For a plot summary, *see* <http://home.mira.net/~marcop/StarTrek.htm#yesterdays>.

2. Richard A. Danner, *Reference Theory and the Future of Legal Reference Service*, 76 L. Libr. J. 217, 231 (1983).

3. *Id.* at 232.

4. A search for the word "law" using the search engine Altavista, <http://www.altavista.com>, resulted in over seven million web pages.

5. *See* <http://www.rlg.org/ariel/index.html>.

6. *See* <http://www.adobe.com>.

7. The e-mail address for reference requests at Southern Illinois University School of Law Library is *lawlib@siu.edu*.

8. Barbara Selby, *Refdesk: UVa Law Library's Approach to E-mail Reference*, 12 Va. Librs. 12 (1999). Selby indicates that *Refdesk* is the faculty's point of contact with the library.

9. *See* <http://clelaw.lib.oh.us/Reference/Reference.htm>. Document delivery fees are charged. Non-members may also take advantage of the service, but are charged fees for reference/research assistance as well as document delivery fees.

10. Examples include LAW-LIB@UCDAVIS.EDU (for law librarians); LAWLIBREF-L@LAWLIB.WUACC.EDU (for law library reference queries); and STUMPERS-L@CRF.CUIS.EDU (for difficult reference questions). For a comprehensive list, *see Library-Oriented Lists & Electronic Serials* at <http://www.wrlc.org/liblists//liblists.htm>.

11. *See*, <http://lawlibrary.ucdavis.edu/LAWLIB/lawlib.html>.

12. *See, e.g.*, University of Minnesota Law Library's web site at <http://www.law.umn.edu/library/tools/pathfinders/pathfinders.html>.

13. *See, e.g.*, Vanderbilt Law School's Alyne Queener Massey Law Library web site at <http://www.vanderbilt.edu/Law/library/resource.html>.

14. *See, e.g.*, University of Nebraska's Schmid Law Library web site at <http://www.unl.edu/lawcoll/library/guides.html>.

15. *See* <http://www.jenkinslaw.org/services/reference.shtml>.

16. *See* <http://jurist.law.pitt.edu/ref_desk.htm>.

17. Nettie Lagace and Michael McClennen, *Questions and Quirks: Managing an Internet-based Distributed Reference Service,* Computers in Libr., Feb. 1998, at 24.

18. For a non-library example, *see* the Vermont *Children's Well-Being Online* mapping system at <http://geo-vt.uvm.edu/ahsdoe>.

19. Barbara Gontrum, *Redefining Reference: Is the Reference Desk a Thing of the Past?* AALL Spectrum, Nov. 1998, at 12.

20. *Id.*

21. Mr. Atoz turned out to be rather evil and thus not the best example of a "good" librarian image.

Access Services:
Linking Patrons
to Electronic Legal Research

David Armond

SUMMARY. Managing patron entitlements to law library resources is an increasing need. In the past, collection access has been shaped by material culture, i.e., social rules of conduct and technology. At the beginning of the twentieth century, circulation librarians efficiently adopted existing commercial technology to meet patron demands. The development of centralized access services departments and the evolution of library automation provide a foundation for managing patron access to digital collections. In the future, access services librarians must integrate technology with library service models to maintain efficient patron access. *[Article copies available for a fee from The Haworth Document Delivery Service: 1-800-342-9678. E-mail address: <getinfo@haworthpressinc. com> Website: <http://www.HaworthPress.com> © 2001 by The Haworth Press, Inc. All rights reserved.]*

In hindsight it was a simple suggestion. Really. The proposal was to script through all remote databases so once a patron logged on to the campus online

David Armond is Information Technology and Database Librarian at the Howard W. Hunter Law Library, J. Reuben Clark Law School, Brigham Young University (BYU). He was formerly Associate Director for Public Access Services. He received a MLIS and BA from BYU and is completing his JD.

[Haworth co-indexing entry note]: "Access Services: Linking Patrons to Electronic Legal Research." Armond, David. Co-published simultaneously in *Legal Reference Services Quarterly* (The Haworth Information Press, an imprint of The Haworth Press, Inc.) Vol. 19, No. 3/4, 2001, pp. 203-217; and: *Teaching Legal Research and Providing Access to Electronic Resources* (ed: Gary L. Hill, Dennis S. Sears, and Lovisa Lyman) The Haworth Information Press, an imprint of The Haworth Press, Inc., 2001, pp. 203-217. Single or multiple copies of this article are available for a fee from The Haworth Document Delivery Service [1-800-342-9678, 9:00 a.m. - 5:00 p.m. (EST). E-mail address: getinfo@haworthpressinc.com].

public access catalog (OPAC), he or she would never have to enter another password. The integrated library system's (ILS) patron file would track users' rights to resources and provide the accountability that information vendors wanted before they included off-campus access in their standard licensing agreements. The controversial aspect of this approach was that it required patrons to have active, nondelinquent/nonoverdue status. Patrons are routinely restricted from certain types of materials based on their patron classification and record status. In this case, blocked patrons could still access the online resources; they would just be prompted for user IDs and pins. I never really gave the finer policy implications much thought until seconds after my immodest proposal at a combined meeting of campus libraries. I was just verbally brainstorming an efficient way to keep track of electronic patron privileges for law library patrons using the patron record of our campus ILS.

The controversy my suggestion fomented forced me to reconsider how law librarians manage the access to electronic resources. Managing the access to print materials has been clearly assigned to circulation librarians. There has been less enthusiasm to recognize access services librarians as specialists who can balance the need for consistent patron accessibility with the need to preserve the integrity of the library's collections, both digital and print. The predisposition to focus on the object being used by the patron–book, database, web page–without realizing that there are inherent access management issues in every aspect of library use has been part of the problem. In the past, librarians who were responsible for collection access developed systems to deal with increasing patron demands. In the future, access services librarians should be prepared to adapt existing technology to solve the emerging problems of digital access to library collections. This specialization will leave reference librarians free to master the use of ever-increasing digital sources without getting bogged down by the management of access.

There are some major conceptual challenges in selling access services as a solution for managing digital access. This article is organized in eight sections in an attempt to overcome some of the traditional obstacles that arise when librarians discuss access. The first three sections deal with the challenges that stem from library access and with pitching access services as a potential solution. The fourth and fifth sections deal with how cultural and, more specifically, commercial practices influence library access models. After this broad historical treatment, the sixth section examines the development of modern circulation practices, which lays the foundation for managing the use of new formats. The seventh, eighth, and ninth sections deal with possible futures for developing access services.

ACCESS: A PERSISTENT CHALLENGE

It is widely recognized that libraries store information, but less frequently reflected that wherever there is a library, there are librarians who manage access to that library's collections. This may be one of the reasons that the concept of "access services" within academic law libraries, and in academia in general, has received a mixed reception. For many who read this article, the concept of a department that predominantly focuses on providing access to legal resources and communicating with patrons about how that access is structured may seem artificial and unnecessary. Methods for circulating print material have been consistent for close to a century. In my own library, there are senior librarians who have a hard time conceptualizing access as something more than a clerical task–one that has persistently been labeled circulation.

The current system of book circulation was not spontaneously generated. For centuries the rules that govern the lending of materials developed along with popular perceptions of the net worth of literacy. Ultimately, librarians adapted existing technology, including tools and practices of the business community, to solve the problems caused by increased patron demand for books.

In 1900, the number of books housed in libraries was rapidly increasing. In 2000, the number of online sources increased almost as fast as patron demand for them. Few law libraries can deal with the new material as efficiently as they can print sources. Among the pressing needs are standardized ways to authenticate users of remote databases, to track use of copyright-restricted materials to students in a specific class, and to monitor class members' use of interactive media to fulfill royalty agreements.

As the number of digital resources increases, the traditional balance between the preservation of collections and the provision of access is complicated by the intricacies of licensing law and the often-complex methods of electronic delivery. Over the past decade, reference librarians have been forced to increase the amount of time they devote to electronic sources. To the extent that my library is representative of others, most reference librarians have struggled to keep up with the use of new sources, with little if any time devoted to managing various patrons' access to those sources. Where sources are simple web pages, managing access is relatively straightforward. However, sources that require patron authentication, metering, or multiple layers of user access demand greater managerial efforts.

Batch loading and JavaScripting can only go so far to make access integral to patrons' library use. Moreover, dissatisfied patrons have rapidly expanding options for acquiring information. System administrators do not have time to deal with individual patron problems in the above scenarios. Nor is it cost effective to have a systems librarian, if a law library is fortunate enough to have one, deal with each patron on a one-on-one basis. Whoever deals with patrons' ability to access digital sources, it must be someone readily available–like reference or access services personnel. Password management is not a highly coveted library skill. Most reference librarians focus on teaching and research. Their customer service skills are honed on solving problems of use, not access. Access service librarians, on the other hand, have been well trained to explain access limitations and restrictions. Expanding their patron management activities to include digital resources appears to be an obvious extension of their traditional duties.

ACCESS SERVICES DEFINED

Access service librarians have suffered from what one author has called an "identity crisis." Evidence of this crisis is the dearth of literature devoted to access services. True, in 1992, an entire issue of Collection Management was devoted to access services. In the concluding editorial essay of that issue, the editors speculated that the essays might "open the gate for a flood of articles that describe how access services operations function and are managed." However, their expectations were sized by noting that "[t]o date . . . the literature shows few articles or monographs that attempt to holistically describe access services departments."[1]

Eight years later, little has changed. Part of the problem is that the specific term "access services" has not been universally adopted for combined patron service departments. Even in the above-mentioned volume, only one-fifth of the contributing authors had "access services" in their professional title. The remaining four-fifths came from various levels of library administration, most commonly "public" services. A quick scan of the 1989-1999 volumes of AALL Directory reveals the same ratio of access service librarians to public services and circulation librarians, with less than one-fifth of academic law libraries listing access services positions.[2] The lack of universally adopted administrative vocabulary to describe patron-centered services has meant that access services librarians must consult the established literature of several specific functions, e.g,. circulation, ILL, or reserve, to find a literary treatment of their discipline. And largely, these segmented departments are more widely cognizable for the majority of academic law librarians who live within the public/technical services distinction.

The schizophrenic trend in literature can be, and at times is, mirrored by library administrative practice. It is not uncommon for the mix of services included in access services to change seasonally as public or technical services redefine their responsibilities. Even where an access services department has been established, a certain amount of friction often exists with other higher pedigreed departments. Access services is frequently viewed as the illegitimate child of technical services or the wayward younger brother to reference services. There is some foundation for this hostility. With the advent of automated systems, catalogers have had to fight the phantoms conjured by untrained circulation clerks creating dirty, though usually brief, bibliographic records. And reference librarians have legitimate concerns about circulation desk employees dispensing legal misinformation or, worse, starting their own legal consulting firms specializing in malpractice jurisprudence.

From the vantage point of the prosperous economy that characterized the close of the twentieth century, it is ironic that the most articulated sense of identity came in the late 1980s and early 1990s. A sour economy forced reductions in most academic library budgets. Reorganization and consolidation were celebrated ways to cut personnel costs. What emerged was the combination of several departments into a single patron-centered service entity. This mix of services in an access services department could range from a combined circulation and reserve department to a more complex mixture of circulation, stacks maintenance, reserve, ILL, document delivery, physical facilities management, building security, microforms, serials, government documents, and copy center. No specific rules governed the creation of these departments. The only common thread was that the departments attempted to provide service to patrons. The malleability of the service mix in an access services department is probably the most commonly shared identifying element across library types.

A bad economy led to consolidation and flexibility. A good economy has led to increasing digital resources, which in turn will stretch the traditional services that are provided at the circulation desk. Expanding the services that are provided by access services departments will help patrons, but it will make it difficult to articulate exactly what access services librarians do. The quest for mission statements aside, the main difficulty in explaining access services lies in the common misperception that access is a priori once a format is established. The typical Anglo-American treatment of access services history starts at the circulation desk of a late nineteenth and early twentieth century library. This history is unquestionably significant, but it is so mentally familiar that it can obscure the changes that have taken place in libraries over the course of human existence. Libraries have not always looked like well-landscaped warehouses, nor have circulation desks always resembled bar tops. Instead, librarians from ancient times to modern have adapted to the changing nature of their respective cultures and employed various technologies for storing and retrieving data. The management of access has been shaped first by the surrounding cultural attitudes about information and then by the technology available from commercial sources to manage the level of access that is socially acceptable.

ACCESS INHERENT IN LIBRARY USE

Digital access problems are not insurmountable; in fact, they may not even be unprecedented. Since libraries and library services have evolved over centuries, examining the history of access sheds light on how similar challenges have been handled. Pulitzer Prize winning historian Michael Kammen gives a three-part answer to the "rhetorical question" of "what is the good of history?"

> First, history helps us to achieve self-knowledge and thereby a clearer sense of identity. Second, it helps us to acquire moral knowledge and thereby enables us to make sensibly informed value judgments. Third, it improves our understanding of the actual relationship between past and present, as well as the potential relationship between the present and future.[3]

A "clearer sense" of access services' "identity" may be found in the history of material culture that has shaped how access is managed. The preservation of humans' inner thoughts is well recognized as the foundation of the modern library. "Examining the genesis of the library–the birth of the idea or conception of a library in its simplest form–it is found that the real beginning was when man first attempted to preserve in some permanent form, on a surface external to himself, the contents of his inner thoughts."[4] By extension, cave paintings may represent the first library collections. This seemingly simple example illustrates the complexity of access methods in the most rudimentary of library models. At the most basic level, the cave/library included an informational resource/collection, the painting, and a patron. At least on the surface, it rarely gets less complicated than this.

Quickly, however, things start to get more complex when the choices that plague the person charged with managing access to a painting are considered. First, should all members of the group or only selected members access the painting? Should the area around the painting be considered sacred or profane? If it is in a restricted area of the cave, what determines the times it can be viewed? If it is placed in a public area, what type of behavior is acceptable when appreciating the painting–howling, grunting, salivating? In any case, how are these rules communicated to the rest of the group? Who is responsible for administering discipline if someone misbehaves?

In the context of circulation, the primitive cave painting illustrates the myriad of cultural value judgments and rules that implicitly govern what behavior is appropriate when patrons access library resources. As societies become more complex, so do the rules that govern social behavior. Librarians have adopted these rules as they create access methods for library resources. Rarely do librarians create new service models ex nihilo. Instead, they apply elements of traditional material culture, including social rules and technology, to their individual problems. In this respect, access services librarians have existed as long as collections and libraries have existed. The distinguishing characteristic of access services is the focus on how to deliver materials to patrons.

ACCESS SHAPED BY CULTURE

The value of librarians who provide access to materials is largely socially defined. The influence of social charter on access services can be seen when various types of ancient libraries are considered. Based on the archeological remains of ancient Egyptian, Sumerian, Assyrian, Babylonian, Greek, and Roman libraries, one historian suggests that there are potentially four predominant ancient library types: "the temple collection; . . . the governmental archive; . . . organized business records; and the collection of family or genealogical papers."[5] It is likely that each type of ancient library had a different set of access rules.

As librarians began to circulate materials, they typically adopted whatever procedures were extant for analogous transactions in their culture. Before circulation was institutionalized as a library procedure, librarians had to determine what level of physical access they would give to various classes of patrons. The sponsoring institution typically determined that access level. Since priests or religiously devoted scribes managed temple libraries, the amount of religious information that was freely accessible was controlled by the dominant religious tradition. In Egypt, a priest's decision to display a text on the exterior or interior of a building was actually an access management determination.

Similarly, the physical access to government archives that was determined by the prevailing political power was an access management decision. In Assyria, it appears the kings were interested enough in building library collections that they directed the selection of library materials.[6] Though documentation of rules governing the access to business and personal libraries is scarce, whatever rules of access that evolved would have been dominated by local political power.

Exactly when library materials began to be regularly circulated is unknown. Most ancient civilizations only allowed circulation of materials within the library, analogous to our modern special collections' reading rooms. By the second century A.D., there are recorded instances where patrons took books home. "Although books in the Roman public libraries did not circulate outside the building as a general rule, it is apparent from several classical references that influential people could on occasion borrow them for home use."[7]

Marcus Aurelius coached a friend through an access method that is still common today. First try to use your influence on the desk clerk; if that does not work, bribe him.[8] This tells us little about the mechanics of Roman circulation systems, but it does illustrate that a substantial part of the circulation transaction, the use of influence and bribery, was borrowed from a social-political context outside of the library. Aurelius' suggested method of circulation underscores how societal practices, such as bribery, laid the foundation for the rules that governed patron access.

ACCESS SHAPED BY COMMERCIAL PRACTICE

The influence of prevailing social attitudes as well as the adoption of commercial practices to library procedure is also documented in the legal deeds that established endowed Ottoman libraries. These deeds often listed conditions imposed by the benefactors on the use of the collection.[9] The conditions included what times the library should be opened and when librarians should guard the collection. The deeds also designated elements of patron classification, restriction of circulation privilege, variance in loan period, and the requirement of security deposits before material could be circulated.[10] Many of these variables changed with contemporary attitudes towards society in general, starting with the trend of libraries lending, followed by a more conservative reaction to book loss as a result of that lending. The Ottoman libraries seemed to have comfortably applied commercial contract concepts to solve their access problems.

The influence of commerce on the circulation system is clearly seen by the wide use of deposits as a method of access control. Implicit within the deposit system is a technology to track how much was paid, by whom, and for what library title. This technology had already been developed in the context of commercial finance that had evolved over centuries. Librarians simply applied available transactional models from outside the library to internal procedures.[11]

CIRCULATION UNDERPINNINGS OF ACCESS SERVICES

The rather abstract review of ancient and early modern library history is intended to make it easier to recognize how librarians have borrowed from their particular milieu to manage the access to their collections. With the creation of the American Library Association in 1876, and the publication of *Library Journal*, the foundation for the modern library was firmly in place.

In the late 19th and early 20th centuries branches were established, women and children were recognized as legitimate clientele for the library, the concept of open stacks was generally accepted, hours of service were greatly increased, and the belief that the library should provide information or reference service to its patrons was widely endorsed.[12]

Academic libraries were the beneficiaries of the standardization of public library procedures. What would ultimately become the dominant circulation method in public libraries had been established by the commencement of the 20th century. The system of using book pockets with descriptive bibliographic cards, which were removed and filed at charge and then returned to the book after discharge and before reshelving, is named the Newark method reportedly after the library where the process originated.[13] Though academic libraries adopted this method in varying degrees,[14] derivations of this method underlie most, and likely all, automated circulation systems.[15]

College libraries dramatically increased in size and scope in the first quarter of the twentieth century. "During most of the nineteenth century, academic libraries were primarily concerned with preservation. The books were considered precious artifacts for a handful of privileged researchers; they were not necessarily for a general education."[16] Academia had been profoundly influenced by what is labeled the German method of higher education.[17] The new emphasis on graduate and undergraduate research meant that both circulation and in-house use of books in college libraries exceeded that of public libraries on a per capita basis.[18]

The depression that followed the economic exuberance of the early twenties forced academic libraries "to pause and reflect on their nature and purpose in the general educational scheme."[19] In a sentence that could describe the late 1980s as well as the late 1920s one author noted, "[t]he need to extend services with strained budgets led to a search for new and more efficient means of providing library services. Various new methods of book charging and circulation were introduced, some being widely adopted and others soon disappearing."[20]

The continued and expanded emphasis on individual research caused significant changes in the conceptualization and provision of library services. The need to service undergraduate borrowers led to the elevation of the status of circulation departments; as two commentators concluded in 1933, "[w]hatever the position of the library in the institution may be, the loan department should be the center of the activities of the library."[21]

But loan librarians turned out to be the victims of their own success. The combination of the shortage of librarians caused by the expansion of academic libraries following World War II and the residual effects of librarians attempting to apply derivations of Frederick Winslow Taylor's concepts of scientific management, led to the debate over the need for professional circulation librarians. The application of commercial clerical practices to improve the efficiency of circulation transactions ultimately led the American Library Associations' Subcommittee on Personnel Administration to conclude that "registration and circulation" were "non-professional in nature," because they were based on "good clerical procedures."[22] Sadly, this conclusion ignores the fact that a librarian had to adapt the commercial clerical practice to a library setting.

The successful adaptation of commercial technology and service models to the service transactions in libraries is still considered suspect. The dramatic differences in approach to the privacy of patron information between public services librarians and e-commerce vendors illustrate this point. Librarians have gone so far as to request that ILS vendors restrict the fields in their databases to prevent the ability to track certain types of personal information,[23] while e-commerce vendors continue to build complex systems that track consumer behavior down to the last mouse click. Suggestions to implement this technology quickly run into traditional "professional" confidentiality concerns.

Regardless of suspicion, commercial practices continue to influence the tools and procedures of access services. Circulation systems have an "obvious resemblance to inventory management" systems because circulation procedures developed within the twentieth century consumer economy.[24] The debate over implementing commercial techniques seems to continue the myopic perspective, persistent at least since 1948, that somehow the task of adapting existing technology to the library environment is not a professional endeavor. It is unclear who, besides a professional librarian, has the appropriate perspective to leverage technology from other disciplines. Historically, the technology transfer, including the transfer of culturally accepted rules for access to information, has been the purview of professional librarians.

THE FUTURE OF ACCESS SERVICES

Access services librarians' willingness to adapt existing social conventions and technology to solve patron access problems sets the stage for future directions. As in the past, librarians continue to adapt to patron demand for access. Currently, ILS vendors have developed a significant ability to track patron information. Though comparisons between library patron management systems and systems of other industries have been prevented by the increasingly competitive nature of the service sector, it is clear that e-commerce vendors are capable of storing a more diverse array of patron data than libraries. Five major ILS vendors present at the ALA Mid-Winter January 2000 meetings demonstrated that they had developed multiple patron statistical categories over the past five years to meet the needs of various libraries. Three of the five vendors had already started to develop the patron database to the extent that it could be used to manage access to remote databases. One of the vendors actually offered the ability to log every patron contact with objects within the database, if a library could afford to implement the module. These developments may offer partial solutions for managed digital access.

Though there is still a surprising lack of support for the proposal to establish a MARC standard for patron records, virtually all ILS vendors offer the ability to load elements of patron records from various external sources. Most academic institutions have scripted methods to load registrar's office or bursar's records with varying degrees of difficulty.

The decentralization of systems administration is also a recent development that will improve user access. Of the five vendors referred to above, all had implemented design metaphors that would allow system administrators to delegate traditional systems responsibilities to access services librarians. Arduous tasks, such as debugging circulation rules and loan periods, typically reserved for late-night-pizza-binging-system-administrator-frenzies, can now be delegated to access services staff who benefit from the control that comes with the new responsibilities. Users benefit from having the department they complain to being able to fix the problem.

ILS development has increased the ability of access services staff to respond to changing service needs. But the scalpel should not be mistaken for the surgeon. With each new innovation in patron service technology, a flood of policy decisions develop. This is largely the burden of access services personnel to coordinate. "[A]ccess services places the user at the center of its activities. Efficient delivery of access services connects users to the material they seek."[25] This transaction-centered definition should be the basis of managing patron access to digital media.

Though ILS vendors have provided new tools and access services librarians have applied the new technology to the patron transactions, several areas lack development. The first area is in the management of patron rights to electronic objects. Many library vendors offer the ability to store patron passwords or personal identification numbers. This affords at least the appearance of security when distributing services to patrons. With passwords in place, patrons can renew their materials online, they can make requests for services online, such as holds, recalls, or ILL requests, and the library has some level of assurance that the requesters are who they claim to be. The method is not perfect; however, it appears to satisfy most confidentiality concerns. It should be noted that this self-service model is borrowed wholesale from the financial services industry; credit card companies, brokerage houses, and banks all saw the advantage of unmediated financial transactions years before the library.

ACCESS SERVICES AND RIGHTS MANAGEMENT

The authentication of patrons is often rolled into the more general concept of rights management. At the Howard W. Hunter Law Library, the Head of Access Services is also the law school copyright compliance officer. We hope this is the beginning of a trend towards including copyright clearance in access services departments.[26] But the additional assignment has demonstrated the second area of needed development.

Housing copyright compliance in the library makes sense from a data management perspective. The library already has a patron database, a list of vendors (the predominant copyright holders), and a list of copyrighted works. Though most catalogers would cringe at the thought of cataloging individual articles, if the ILS has an ILL module, there are already fields that store article-level information that is segregated from the sacrosanct bibliographic database. Whether ILL offices are included in access services departments or not, they have been tracking copyright compliance for years.

From a patron management perspective, access services is the logical place to have patrons seek copyright permission. At the psychological level, patrons are used to learning about collection restrictions from the service desk. At least since the second century A.D., patrons have been documented trying to work within and around existing policies to gain access to materials. In institutions such as mine, where access services also manages the copy center in the law school, procedurally it makes sense to have faculty request permission through the entity that will ultimately make the materials available to them or to their students. Even in libraries without copy center responsibility, this line of reasoning holds true for materials that are being placed on course reserve.

The development work needed to harmonize the existing technologies in a cohesive fashion is really fairly small. The various data units are there: patrons, titles, vendor records, order information, statistical information about use, etc. One missing element is a place to store license information in a systematic way. Once this is developed, then matrixes can be established to allow patrons with certain sets of criteria to access specific digital resources. Since librarians in access services departments are already managing this type of collection access, the format type becomes incidental.

The benefit of providing distributed services to patrons, at least in theory, is that they do not have to come to the service desk to connect with what they need. This reduces the amount of staff time needed to physically complete transactions. Since service organizations preserve their market position through creatively developing their offerings, the saved time can be reinvested in improving, expanding, or repackaging library services.

CONCLUSION

Historically, access services librarians have distinguished themselves with their ability to apply technology within cultural rules of interaction to transactional centered problems. Though primary examples provided here have been devoted to circulation practices, the tendency can be demonstrated in the implementation of reserve collections–including e-reserves, ILL, or in document delivery operations. The most pressing access issue is managing patrons' rights to remote information resources. As these resources become more popular with both faculty and students, neither systems nor reference librarians will have time to manage the patron access database. The responsibility should be placed squarely on the librarians who have been dealing with access problems in all their forms for centuries. It is uncertain that having access services librarians solve yet another administrative challenge will do anything for the discipline's identity crisis. It will, however, leverage these librarians' existing customer service, dispute resolution, and reality therapy skills. Possibly more significantly, having one department focus on managing access to library resources frees another to help patrons appropriately use those resources, traditionally a reference services mission.

NOTES

1. Pat Weaver-Meyers and Virginia Steel, *Access Services: The Development of a Holistic Approach to Convenience Information Services: An Editorial Essay on the Future of Access Services,* 17 Collection Mgmt. 237, 237 (1992).
2. This method of analysis is clearly unscientific and statistically invalid. At best it illustrates the less than universal adoption of the access services label. When more formal survey methods are employed a clearer picture will be developed; however, it is doubtful that even a simple majority of law libraries have adopted the integrated access services approach.
3. Michael Kammen, *Selvages & Biases: The Fabric of History in American Culture* 55 (1987).
4. D. N. Marshall, *History of Libraries Ancient and Mediaeval* 2 (1983).
5. Michael H. Harris, *History of Libraries in the Western World* 7 (4th ed. 1995).
6. *Id.* at 19.
7. Harris *supra* note 5, *id.* at 62.
8. Harris *supra* note 5, *id.* at 63.
9. Ismail E. Erünsal, *Ottoman Libraries: A Brief Survey of Their Development and System of Lending,* 34 Libris 65, 70 (1984).
10. *Id.* at 72. Interestingly enough the deeds varied in prescribed circulation period, but one month, three months, six months, and one year periods were all found in Ottoman documents. *Id.* at 74.
11. In 1889 H. J. Carr noted that "Charges of books are not exactly analogous with ordinary mercantile charges. Nevertheless, methods in vogue for the latter have

governed more or less in determining the practices to be followed by librarians for charging books to borrowers." H. J. Carr, *Report on Charging Systems*, 14 Libr. J. 203, 204 (1889).

12. Harris, *supra* note 5 at 247.

13. Alice P. McDonald, *Circulation Procedures in Law Libraries,* 12 L. Libr. J. 58, 58 (1972). McDonald and others have accepted the Newark attribution for the method; however at the 1896 ALA Cleveland Conference, Frank Hill reported that the credit for the foundation of this system must be given to the Evansville (Ind.) Library. He continues by asserting that "the originality, if any, certainly belongs to Bassett Cadwallader, of Evansville, Ind." Frank Pierce Hill, *Preparing a Book for Issue; and Charging Systems,* 21 Libr. J. 51, 52-53 (1896); *see also,* Jennie M. Flexner, *Circulation Work in Public Libraries* 78-82 (1927).

14. "Partly because of the more detailed control over college libraries, partly because of the individuality of various colleges and universities, there is less uniformity in the methods used in loan departments of different college and university libraries than in similar departments in public libraries." Charles Harvey Brown & H. G. Bousfield, *Circulation Work in College and University Libraries* 9 (1933).

15. The three basic components of automated circulation systems are (1) patron records, (2) bibliographic/item records and (3) date time records. All three of these records are discernable in the Newark system.

16. Deborah Carver, *From Circulation to Access Services: The Shift in Academic Library Organization,* 17 Collection Mgmt. 23, 24-25 (1992).

17. The shift from traditional classical education to what is now representative as higher education in the United States is often framed around two events, the appointment of Charles W. Eliot as president of Harvard in 1869 and the establishment of Johns Hopkins University in 1876. The features associated with German education that were "imported" into the U.S. include "the lecture system, laboratory instruction, the seminar, the clinical method, the PhD. Degree, the elective principle, the semester plan of arranging the academic year, and the methods employed in organizing instruction and research." W. H. Cowley and Don Williams, *International and Historical Roots of American Higher Education* 136 (1991). Charles Eliot's review of "the recent . . . attempt to organize a system of education based chiefly upon the pure and applied sciences, the living European languages, and mathematics, instead of upon Greek, Latin, and mathematics, as in the established college system" illustrates the direction of educational reform as well as the tension inherent in the transformation. Charles W. Eliot, *The New Education*, 23 Atlantic Monthly 203, 204 (1869).

18. Brown & Bousfield *supra* note 13 at 6-7.

19. Harris *supra* note 5 at 254.

20. *Id.*

21. Brown & Bousfield *supra* note 13 at 11.

22. Carver, *supra* note 15 at 29 (quoting American Library Association, Board of Personnel Administration. Subcommittee on Analysis of Library Duties 52 (1948).

23. "A good rule of thumb to follow when deciding what personal information to include in the library's patron database is to limit it to that data which is absolutely essential to the efficient function of the online circulation system–each additional

piece of information provides yet another possibility for security breaches." Kathleen G. Fouty, *Online Patron Records and Privacy: Service vs. Security,* 19 J. Acad. Libr. 289, 290 (1993).

24. William Saffady, *Introduction to Automation for Librarians* 196 (3rd ed 1994).

25. Alberta S. Bailey & Lora L. Lennertz, *The Role of the Access Services Manager in Policy Formation,* 17 Collection Mgmt. 119, 120 (1992).

26. For a brief discussion of the benefits associated with assigning copyright management responsibilities to access services *see* Greg R. Notess, *The Impact of Networked Information on Access Services,* 17 Collection Mgmt. 105, 113 (1992).

Index